I0243701

More Classical Music Insights –

from Mozart to Muhly and More

by Betsy Schwarm

author of the
Classical Music Insights series

Cover by Wayne Rigsby, Gearbox Creative, Inc.

Images, top row, left to right:
    Antonio Vivaldi and Antonín Dvořák

Images, bottom row, left to right:
    Igor Stravinsky and Felix Mendelssohn

Chapter headers by RJ Miller

Author photo by Conor Glesner

Copyright by Betsy Schwarm – 2013
www.classicalmusicinsights.com

Author's permission required for use, other than short excerpts in the context of a review.

ISBN 978-0-9898832-0-7

Table of Contents

Chapter One: What is Classical Music Anyway? 1-13

Chapter Two: Symphonies...14-57

Haydn: Symphony no. 101 in D major, "Clock"..........................16-17
WA Mozart: Symphony no. 36 in C major, K. 425, "Linz"........17-19
Beethoven: Symphony no. 3 in E-flat major, "Eroica".............20-22
Beethoven: Symphony no. 6 in F major, "Pastorale"................22-24
Schubert: Symphony no. 8 in b minor, "Unfinished"...............24-26
Berlioz: *Romeo and Juliet* dramatic symphony, op. 17.............26-27
Mendelssohn: Symphony no. 3 in a minor, "Scottish"..............28-29
Franck: Symphony in d minor..30-31
Brahms: Symphony no. 4 in e minor..31-32
Tchaikovsky: Symphony no. 6 in b minor, "Pathetique"...........32-34
Dvořák: Symphony no. 8 in G major, op. 88..............................34-35
D'Indy: Symphony on a French Mountain Air..........................36-37
Mahler: Symphony no. 1 in D major, "Titan"............................37-38
Sibelius: Symphony no. 2 in D major, op. 43............................38-39
Beach: Gaelic Symphony...40-41
Vaughan Williams: Symphony no. 2, "London".......................42-43
Turina: *Sinfonia Sevillana*..43-44
Prokofiev: Symphony no. 5 in B-flat major..............................44-45
Still: Afro-American Symphony..46-47
Messiaen: *Turangalîla* Symphony..47-48
Barber: Symphony no. 1..49-50
Górecki: Symphony no. 3, op. 36...50-52
Daugherty: Metropolis Symphony..52-53
Marsalis: Swing Symphony..54-55
Greenberg: Symphony no. 5..55-57

Chapter Three: Other Symphonic Works ,.................58-90

Telemann: Tafelmusik...59-60
Beethoven: Leonore Overture no. 3...60-62
Berlioz: Roman Carnival Overture...62-63
Mendelssohn: *Calm Sea and Prosperous Voyage*..................63-64
Saint-Saëns: Carnival of the Animals..64-65
Tchaikovsky: *Capriccio Italien*, op. 45..66
Dvořák: Carnival Overture, op. 92..67-68
Rimsky Korsakov: *Russian Easter Overture*..........................68-69
Elgar: *In the South*, op. 50...69-70
R. Strauss: *Also sprach Zarathustra*, op. 30..........................70-72
Dukas: *The Sorcerer's Apprentice*...72-73
Vaughan Williams: *Fantasia on a Theme of Tallis*................74-75
Ravel: *Le Tombeau de Couperin*..75-76
Respighi: *Trittico Botticelliano*..77
Enesco: *Rumanian Rhapsodies*...78

Varèse: *Amériques*..79-80
Webern: *Im Sommerwind*..80-81
Honegger: *Pastorale d'ete*..81-82
Grofé: *Grand Canyon Suite*..82-83
Gershwin: *An American in Paris*..83-84
Ellington: *Black, Brown and Beige*..85-86
Shostakovich: Jazz Suites..86-87
Jenkins: *Palladio*..87-88
Torke: *Javelin*..88-89
Puts: *River's Rush*..90

Chapter Four: Concerti...91-127

Vivaldi: Four-Violin Concerto in b minor..................................93-94
JS Bach: Double Concerto in d minor, BWV 1043...................94-96
WA Mozart: Piano Concerto no. 17 in G major........................96-97
Beethoven: Triple Concerto in C major, op. 46........................97-99
Donizetti: English Horn Concertino..99-100
Chopin: Piano Concerto no. 1 in e minor..............................100-101
R. Schumann: Concert Piece for four horns...............................102
Brahms: Double Concerto in a minor..................................102-103
Bruch: *Scottish Fantasia*..104-105
Tchaikovsky: Violin Concerto in D major............................105-106
Grieg: Piano Concerto in a minor, op. 16............................107-108
R. Strauss: Duett-Concertino..108-109
Ravel: Piano Concerto for the Left Hand.............................109-111
Bartók: Concerto for Orchestra..111-112
Ibert: Flute Concerto..113-114
Castelnuovo-Tedesco: Guitar Concerto no. 1......................114-115
Korngold: Violin Concerto...115-116
Gershwin: Piano Concerto in F..117-118
Shostakovich: Piano Concerto no. 1, op. 35........................118-119
Barber: Violin Concerto...120-121
Bernstein: *Prelude, Fugue and Riffs*..................................121-122
Rautavaara: Violin Concerto..122-123
Williams: Escapades for saxophone and orchestra..............124-125
Zwilich: Trombone Concerto...125-127
MacMillan: *Veni veni emanuel*..127-128

Chapter Five: Chamber Music........................... 128-163

Corelli: Trio Sonatas, op. 1, 3, & 4......................................130-131
Marais: *La sonnerie du Ste. Genevieve du Mont du Paris*..........132
JS Bach: Partita no. 2 in d, BWV 1004 – Chaconne............133-134
Haydn: String Quartet in D major, op. 64, no. 5, "Lark".....134-135
JC Bach: Six Sonatas for keyboard with violin, op. 10.......136-137
WA Mozart: Clarinet Quintet in A major, K. 620................137-138
WA Mozart: Serenade in D major, K. 250, "Haffner"........139--140
Beethoven: String Quartets, op. 59, "Razumovsky".............140-142

Schubert: String Quintet in C major..................................142-143
Verdi: String Quartet in e minor..143-145
Brahms: Horn Trio in E-flat major......................................145-146
Saint-Saëns: woodwind sonatas..146-147
Dvořák: Piano Trio in e minor, "Dumky"..............................148-149
Ysaÿe: solo sonatas 149-150
Debussy: Sonata for flute, viola, and harp.........................150-152
Bartók: Contrasts for clarinet, violin, and piano 152-153
Tailleferre: String Quartet..153-154
Hindemith: sonatas..154-155
Ullmann: String Quartet no. 3...156-157
Shostakovich: Piano Quintet in g minor.............................157-158
Takemitsu: *Toward the Sea*..158-159
Glass: String Quartet no. 2, "Company"..................................160
Golijov: Dreams and Prayers of Isaac the Blind................161-162
M. Newman: *Pennipotenti*...162-163
Frank: *Leyendas – An Andean walkabout*.........................163-164

Chapter Six: Keyboard and Guitar Works 165-191

Couperin : Pieces de clavecin, Book 2................................167-168
JS Bach: Goldberg Variations, BWV 988..........................168-169
WA Mozart: Piano Sonata in a minor, "Alla Turca".............169-170
Beethoven: Sonata no. 14 in c-sharp minor, "Moonlight"......171-172
Schubert: Wanderer Fantasy in C major............................172-173
Mendelssohn: Songs without Words..................................174-175
R. Schumann: Carneval, op. 9..175-176
Liszt: Piano Sonata in b minor..177-178
Gottschalk: *The Union* 178-179
Tárrega: *Recuerdos de la Alhambra*..................................179-180
Chaminade: Etudes de concert, op. 35..............................180-181
MacDowell: *Woodland Sketches*, op. 51............................181-182
Debussy: Preludes..183
Granados: *Goyescas*...184-185
Rachmaninoff: Preludes...185-186
Villa-Lobos: Preludes and Etudes for Guitar.....................186-187
Shostakovich: Preludes and Fugues...................................187-188
Messiaen: *Vingt Regards sur l'enfant Jésus*......................188-189
Brouwer: *El Decameron Negro* 189-190
Adams: *Hallelujah Junction*..190-191

Chapter Seven: Lieder and Art Songs 192-218

Schubert: *Der Winterreise*, D. 911 193-195
Schubert: *Der Hirt auf den Felsen*, D. 965 196-197
Berlioz: *Les Nuits d'ete* 197-198
Robert and Clara Schumann:
    12 Songs from "Liebesfrühling" 199-200
Brahms: Five Songs, op. 49 200-201
Dvořák: Gypsy Melodies op. 55 201-202
Grieg: *Heart's Melodies*, op. 5 202-203
Tosti: songs 203-204
Chausson: *Chanson perpétuelle* 204-206
Mahler: *Lieder eines fahrenden Gesellen* 206-207
R. Strauss: Six Songs, op. 27 207-208
Ravel: *Sheherazade* 208-209
Falla: Seven Popular Spanish Songs 210
Butterworth: *A Shropshire Lad* 211
Copland: Twelve Songs of Emily Dickinson 212-213
Barber: *Knoxville, Summer of 1915* 213-214
Britten: *Winter Words*, op. 52 215-216
Bolcom: *Cabaret Songs* 216-217
Laitman: Four Dickinson Songs 217-218
Muhly: *Far Away Songs* 218-219

Chapter Eight: Opera and Operetta 220-257

WA Mozart: *La Clemenza di Tito* 222-224
Rossini: *William Tell* 225-226
Bellini: *I Capuletti e Montecchi* 227-229
Berlioz: *Les Troyens* 229-230
Balfe: *The Bohemian Girl* 231-232
Wagner: *Parsifal* 232-234
Verdi: *Macbeth* 234-236
J. Strauss Jr.: *The Gypsy Baron* 236-237
Tchaikovsky: *The Queen of Spades* 237-239
Sullivan: *The Mikado* 239-240
Massenet: *Cendrillon* 241-242
Puccini: *La Fanciulla del West* 242-244
R. Strauss: *Ariadne auf Naxos* 245-246
Wolf-Ferrari: *The Secret of Susanna* 247-248
Weill: *Street Scene* 248-249
Copland: *The Tender Land* 250-251
Menotti: *The Saint of Bleecker Street* 251-253
Previn: *A Streetcar Named Desire* 254-255
Catán: *Il Postino* 255-256
Portman: *The Little Prince* 256-257

Chapter Nine: Stage and Screen.......................258-286

Purcell: *The Fairy Queen*..260-261
Beethoven: *Egmont*...261-263
Schubert: *Rosamunde*...263-264
R. Schumann: *Manfred.*,..264-265
Delibes: *Le roi s'amuse* 265-266
Sullivan: Shakespearean scores 266-267
Nielsen: *Aladdin.*..267-268
Vaughan Williams: *Scott of the Antarctic*.....................268-270
Stravinsky: *The Soldier's Tale*......................................270-272
Prokofiev: *Lt. Kije*..272-273
Copland: *Music from Movies* 273-274
Bernstein: *On the Town*...275-276
Jarre: *Lawrence of Arabia*...276-277
Goldsmith: *Patton*...278-279
Williams: *Lincoln*..279-280
Barry: *Dances with Wolves*...281-282
Glass: *The Hours*...282-283
Silvestri: *The Polar Express*...283-284
Horner: *Titanic*..284-285
Zimmer: *Pirates of the Caribbean*...............................285-286

Chapter Ten: Dance Inspirations.......................287-316

Lanner: *Die Mozartisten*, op. 196.......................................288-290
J. Strauss Jr.: *Roses of the South*....................................... 290-291
Borodin: *Polovtsian Dances*..292-293
Saint-Saëns: *Danse macabre*, op. 40.................................293
Tchaikovsky: *Swan Lake*, op. 20...294-295
Dvořák: *Prague Waltzes*...296
R. Strauss: *Dance of the Seven Veils*..................................297-298
Glazunov: *The Seasons* 298-299
Ravel: *La Valse*..299-300
Gliere: *The Red Poppy* 301-302
Falla: *The Three-Cornered Hat*..302-303
Bartók: *Rumanian Dances*..303-304
Kodaly: *Dances of Galanta*..304-305
Stravinsky: *Petrushka* 306-308
Prokofiev: *Cinderella*..308-309
Milhaud: *Creation du monde*..309-311
Copland: *Billy the Kid*...311-312
Khachaturian: *Gayane*..313-314
Stucky: *DreamWaltzes*..314-315
Feeney: *The Hunchback of Notre Dame*............................315-316

Chapter Eleven: Choral Music............................317-347

Desprez: Ave Maria..319-320
JS Bach: Cantata no 80, "Ein Feste Burg"..........................320-322
Handel: *Zadok the Priest*...322-323
Pergolesi: Stabat Mater..323-324
Haydn: Mass no. 9 in C, *"Mass in Time of War"*..................324-325
WA Mozart: Solemn Vespers of a Confessor.......................326-327
Beethoven: *Christ on the Mount of Olives*...................... 327-328
Berlioz: Requiem...329-330
Mendelssohn: part songs..331
Brahms: *Schicksalslied*, op. 54...................................332-333
Vaughan Williams: Serenade to Music..............................333-335
Rachmaninoff: *The Bells*, op. 35.................................335-337
Stravinsky: Symphony of Psalms....................................337-338
Poulenc: *Quatre motets pour le temps de Noël*..................339-340
R. Thompson: *Frostiana*..340
Britten: *War Requiem*...341-342
Argento: *Walden Pond*...343-344
Rutter: *When Icicles Hang*...344-345
MacMillan: *Strathclyde Motets*....................................345-346
Whitacre: *Cloudburst*..347-348

Chapter Twelve: Coda..349-354

Appendices

   I. Glossary..355-363
   II. Pronunciation Guide... 364-366
   III. Sources 367-372
   IV. Previous Books..373-381
   V. Acknowledgements...382
   VI. Author Biographical Notes.....................................382

Index...383-400

Note: Chapter One contains a
chronological listing of all featured composers,
together with their first names and dates.

Author's Note

This book is a follow-up to my two previous books: *Classical Music Insights* and *Operatic Insights*.

If you were so kind as to read one of my previous books, this one will be entirely new to you – not only the compositions that I've chosen to profile, but also the introductory material.

If you have not had the chance to encounter one of my earlier books, that fact will not handicap your appreciation of this one. They are all inter-related in subject matter, but are not dependent upon one another.

No music degree is necessary here, nor is a reading knowledge of printed music. All one needs is ready ears, an open mind for new information, and an active interest in understanding the music of the great composers – both of the past and of today.

Happy listening!

Betsy

Chapter One:
What is Classical Music Anyway?

Let those notes above be played – or loudly sung – rather than just lying silently on the page, and nearly everyone could put a name to the music. However, that name might not be the title that the composer himself gave it. According to Richard Strauss (1864 – 1949), it's the introduction to his tone poem *Also sprach Zarathustra* (featured in Chapter Three). Since Strauss died fully twenty years before his music came to be attached to Stanley Kubrick's film *2001: A Space Odyssey*, he could not have anticipated that many millions of persons would think of it as the obelisk music from that film. The fact that this music has acquired such wide-spread recognition proves that classical music possesses an immense audience, and far greater familiarity than some would imagine.

That fact is part of why I've decided to write a third book about classical music. Indeed, I hope to help those who already have an interest in classical music to better understand how this incredibly varied music came to be what it is, and what the composers were hoping to achieve in the creation of it. Additionally, I want to share insider stories about the persons who crafted this music, bringing them out of the ivory tower so that listeners can see them as real people. Those who already know some – or even much – classical music well will likely find here some new options to consider. Whether it's Ludwig van Beethoven (1770 – 1827) or Jay Greenberg (b. 1991), it is music that expresses something in its creator's heart, something that the creator intends to share with listeners.

Purists will insist that what many think of as "classical music" is better called "art music," that is, music composed according to the artistic standards of its day. Such a definition sets it apart from folk music and pop music, and helps to make clear that those artistic standards will vary from time to time. So, the purists say, we shouldn't just call it "classical" as it has far more variety than that single term would imply; moreover, they've reserved "classical" for the time of Mozart and Beethoven, not for all time.

Technically, those purists are right. However, if society as a whole wishes to call all this range of expression "classical music," it seems petty to quibble. Moreover, quibbling only reinforces ideas of elitism, and classical music is not something reserved for the elite. Anyone with ears and a brain can enjoy it. So, although our subject matter for this collection is broadly speaking "art music," it is the word "classical" that appears in the title.

Great music of artistic value was composed even in the Middle Ages and the Renaissance. From those time periods, the vast majority of what has survived is sacred music. Since it was the church that largely controlled education, and since without education, one would be quite unlikely to learn how to notate music, it was church music that was preserved. By the Renaissance, powerful monarchs began to arise and sought musical diversion, though even this music might imitate the styles of church music. Often, music was composed for singers with no instrumental accompaniment, a technique known as "a cappella."

Around 1600, in what is termed the Baroque Era, secular (non-religious) music starts to become more prevalent than strictly sacred music. One also begins to find music intended for instrumental performance – with no singers whatsoever. The increasing power of the royal courts and the gradual appearance of something resembling a middle class, with both the royalty and the middle class seeking musical diversion, triggered the first of those innovations. As to instrumental music, technological improvements in instrument construction, particularly for string instruments, made it ever more practical and desirable to showcase instruments, rather than singers.

With or without singers, Baroque music tended to be light in character, with faster passages possessed of a great many notes. Preferred instruments were strings, usually with harpsichord: a delicately-voiced predecessor of the piano. Woodwind instruments were occasionally used, brass instruments rarely, and percussion instruments hardly at all.

All that changes after about 1750, when one reaches that which is termed the Classical Era. One can think of it as "Classical" not only because of the way that its music tends to be carefully balanced, like an ancient Greek façade, but also in terms of a newer sense of a "classic" being an oldie but goodie. This is not to imply that the Baroque composers – amongst them the unsurpassed Johann Sebastian Bach (1685 – 1750) – were never used as role models. However, as the Classical Era contains both Wolfgang Mozart (1756 – 1791) and Ludwig van Beethoven (1770 – 1827), along with others of the Viennese greats, it is, indeed, a time rife with oldies but goodies.

Classical composers liked their music more varied than Baroque music tended to be, and, having tired of the harpsichord, replaced it with early modern pianos. They also made sure that a healthy contingent of woodwinds, brass, and even a bit of percussion would be mixed into any an ensemble that, in the Baroque Era, might have been limited to strings.

By the early 1800s, and thanks in part to Beethoven's influence, one begins to find styles moving toward what will be called "Romantic." To that generation, "romantic" did not imply hearts and flowers, but instead, stronger emotional expression. So compositions of this time may be powerfully expressive, and if the emotions expressed can be the composer's own, so much the better – according to thoughts of the day. If composers weren't putting their own lives into their music, they might choose instead to turn to literature, or natural beauty, or perhaps evocations of one's ethnic culture. None of those ideas were unknown to previous generations of composers, but it's after 1820 or so that such ideas become frequent, rather than deviations from the rule.

As the 19th century progressed, society began to look for new ways to use music. The old ideas were still practiced by some composers; Johannes Brahms (1833 – 1897) was a prominent and popular example. However, others were actively turning away from past practices. Earlier, the Baroque composers all possessed – and, to varying degrees, used – the same rule book, and the Classical composers liked the same general outlines, even if details were approached in different ways. By contrast, Romantic Era composers tend to prefer to do things their own way. Just because two composers are contemporaries does not mean their music will be similar in style.

That trend only intensified as the 20th century approached. The Hungarian Béla Bartók (1881 – 1945), the Russian Igor Stravinsky (1882 – 1971), the Spaniard Joaquin Turina (1882 – 1949), and the Austrian Anton Webern (1883 – 1945) were all near contemporaries. One could easily have invited all four men to the same dinner party, though if their varied musical styles can serve as any indication, it might not have resulted in a convivial evening. If one is seeking something different around every musical corner, the early 20th century is a fine place to look.

Step even a few decades into the 20th century, and one finds more and more divergent influences upon composers. Formerly, composers needed to please their immediate audience. Before the Baroque Era, this was generally the church. During the Baroque Era, it was probably the king, then during the Classical Era, aristocrats as well as the new middle class. Romantic Era composers had as their audience a broad range of all available society. Moreover, with the new technologies of the early 20th century, "all available society" meant anyone within reach of a phonograph or a radio. Stravinsky had little good to say about radio, stating in his autobiography that he thought it made audiences lazy; however, that it was influential, even he could not deny.

By the late 20th century, phonographs and radio were becoming rather old-school, and new media – particularly the internet – allow composers to reach out to an even wider range of potential listeners. That wider range means that they are likely to design their music to interest a range of listeners that is wider yet. Moreover, they become influenced by a vast array of cultures and technologies that were in every way unimaginable even to Stravinsky, let alone Mozart or Bach. Classical music – call it "art music" if one must – is not just a European/North American interest. It is popular everywhere, and some examples of it show influence from cultures and ideas found almost anywhere imaginable on the globe. For that matter some composers have found inspiration in sounds from radio telescopes, which, after all, have little to do with this particular globe, other than by bringing astonishingly distant sounds to human ears.

Of the composers featured in this collection, who fits where? The 220 articles in this collection cover works by 138 composers, and here they are, in chronological order:

Renaissance:
    Josquin Desprez (c. 1440 – 1521)

Baroque:
    Arcangelo Corelli (1653 – 1713)
    Marin Marais (1656 – 1728)
    Henry Purcell (1659 – 1695)
    François Couperin (1668 – 1733)
    Antonio Vivaldi (1678 – 1741)

More Classical Insights

    Georg Philipp Telemann (1681 – 1767)
    Johann Sebastian Bach (1685 – 1750)
    George Frideric Handel (1685 – 1759)
    Giovanni Pergolesi (1710 – 1736)

Classical:
    Franz Joseph Haydn (1732 – 1809)
    Johann Christian Bach (1735 – 1782)
    Wolfgang Amadeus Mozart (1756 – 1791)
    Ludwig van Beethoven (1770 – 1827)

Early Romantic:
    Gioacchino Rossini (1792 – 1868)
    Franz Schubert (1797 – 1828)
    Gaetano Donizetti (1797 – 1848)
    Vincenzo Bellini (1801 – 1835)
    Joseph Lanner (1801 – 1843)
    Hector Berlioz (1803 – 1869)
    Michael Balfe (1808 – 1870)
    Felix Mendelssohn (1809 – 1847)
    Frederic Chopin (1810 – 1849)
    Robert Schumann (1810 – 1856)
    Franz Liszt (1811 – 1886)

Mid Romantic:
    Richard Wagner (1813 – 1883)
    Giuseppe Verdi (1813 – 1901)
    Clara Wieck Schumann (1819 – 1896)
    Cesar Franck (1822 – 1890)
    Johann Strauss Jr. (1825 – 1899)
    Louis Moreau Gottschalk (1829 – 1869)
    Alexander Borodin (1833 – 1887)
    Johannes Brahms (1833 – 1897)
    Camille Saint-Saëns (1835 – 1921)

Leo Delibes (1836 – 1891)
Max Bruch (1838 – 1920)
Peter Tchaikovsky (1840 – 1893)
Antonín Dvořák (1841 – 1904)
Jules Massenet (1842 – 1912)
Sir Arthur Sullivan (1842 – 1900)
Edvard Grieg (1843 – 1907)
Nicolai Rimsky-Korsakov (1844 – 1908)
Paolo Tosti (1846 – 1916)

Late Romantic:
Vincent d'Indy (1851 – 1931)
Francisco Tárrega (1854 – 1909)
Ernest Chausson (1855 – 1899)
Sir Edward Elgar (1857 – 1934)
Cecile Chaminade (1857 – 1944)
Giacomo Puccini (1858 – 1924)
Eugene Ysaÿe (1858 – 1931)
Gustav Mahler (1860 – 1911)
Edward MacDowell (1862 – 1908)
Claude Debussy (1862 – 1918)
Richard Strauss (1864 – 1949)
Paul Dukas (1865 – 1935)
Jean Sibelius (1865 – 1957)
Carl Nielsen (1865 – 1931)
Alexander Glazunov (1865 – 1936)
Amy Marcy Cheney Beach (1867 – 1944)
Enrique Granados (1867 – 1916)
Ralph Vaughan Williams (1872 – 1958)

Early 20th Century:
Sergei Rachmaninoff (1873 – 1943)
Arnold Schoenberg (1874 – 1951)
Maurice Ravel (1875 – 1937)

More Classical Insights

Reinhold Gliere (1875 – 1956)
Manuel de Falla (1876 – 1946)
Ermanno Wolf-Ferrari (1876 – 1948):
Ottorino Respighi (1879 – 1936)
Béla Bartók (1881 – 1945)
Georges Enesco (1881 – 1955)
Zoltan Kodaly (1882 – 1967)
Igor Stravinsky (1882 – 1971)
Joaquin Turina (1882 – 1949)
Edgard Varèse (1883 – 1965)
Anton Webern (1883 – 1945)
George Butterworth (1885 – 1916)
Heitor Villa Lobos (1887 – 1959)

Mid 20th Century:
Jacques Ibert (1890 – 1962)
Sergei Prokofiev (1891 – 1953)
Germaine Tailleferre (1892 – 1983)
Arthur Honegger (1892 – 1955)
Darius Milhaud (1892 – 1974)
Ferdé Grofé (1892 – 1972)
Paul Hindemith (1895 – 1963)
William Grant Still (1895 – 1978)
Mario Castelnuovo-Tedesco (1895 – 1968)
Erich Korngold (1897 – 1957)
George Gershwin (1898 – 1937)
Victor Ullmann (1898 – 1944)
Francis Poulenc (1899 – 1963)
"Duke" Ellington (1899 – 1974)
Randall Thompson (1899 – 1984)
Kurt Weill (1900 – 1950)
Aaron Copland (1900 – 1990)
Aram Khachaturian (1903 – 1978)
Dmitri Shostakovich (1906 – 1975)

Olivier Messiaen (1908 – 1992)
Samuel Barber (1910 – 1981)
Benjamin Britten (1913 – 1976)
Leonard Bernstein (1918 – 1990)

Current and Recent Names:
Gian Carlo Menotti (1911 – 2007)
Maurice Jarre (1924 – 2009)
Dominic Argento (b. 1927)
Einojuhani Rautavaara (b. 1928)
Andre Previn (b. 1929)
Jerry Goldsmith (1929 – 2004)
Toru Takemitsu (1930 – 1996)
John Williams (b. 1932)
Henryk Górecki (1933 - 2010)
John Barry (1933 – 2011)
Philip Glass (b. 1937)
William Bolcom (b. 1938)
Ellen Taaffe Zwilich (b. 1939)
Leo Brouwer (b. 1939)
Karl Jenkins (b. 1944)
John Rutter (b. 1945)
John Adams (b. 1947)
Steven Stucky (b. 1949)
Daniel Catán (1949 – 2011)
Alan Silvestri (b. 1950)
James Horner (b. 1953)
Michael Daughtery (b. 1954)
Philip Feeney (b. 1954)
Lori Laitman (b. 1955)
Hans Zimmer (b. 1957)
James MacMillan (b. 1959)
Osvaldo Golijov (b. 1960)
Rachel Portman (b. 1960)

More Classical Insights

Michael Torke (b. 1961)
Wynton Marsalis (b. 1961)
Maria Newman (b. 1962)
Eric Whitacre (b. 1970)
Gabriela Lena Frank (b. 1972)
Kevin Puts (b. 1972)
Nico Muhly (b. 1981)
Jay Greenberg (b. 1991)

Please note that, though nearly all of the greatest names of the past are here – as many as would fit in a collection of moderate size – there are also many current and recent composers, as well as women composers and representatives of various ethnic backgrounds. It was my wish to make clear that classical music is not something nostalgic. Although there is much fabulous music from the earlier generations – one can hardly argue against Beethoven's genius – there are yet plenty of interesting and worthwhile composers around today.

The central chapters of this collection – Two through Eleven – are organized by type of music, so that works of similar genre appear in the same chapter. Individual articles in these chapters appear chronologically, not by premiere date, but by composer birth year.

At times, you'll see that the title of a composition is followed by a number indicating "opus" (op.), or some similar designation. These derive from the order in which a composer's work was published. Since a new work might sit on the shelf for some time before finding a publisher, these numbers may or may not represent a strict order of composition.

Some composers, for various reasons, didn't always publish their works with opus numbers, or didn't publish their works at all. For the most prominent of these composers, later music historians have compiled catalogs to organize that person's works, catalogs which carry their own designations. With Johann Sebastian Bach, the most highly regarded catalog is the "Bach Werke Verzeichnis" (Catalog of Bach's Works), routinely abbreviated as BWV. For Wolfgang Amadeus Mozart, it's the Köchel catalog, the work of one Ludwig Köchel, and abbreviated as K. For Franz Schubert, it's the Deutsch catalog, compiled by Otto Deutsch, and abbreviated as D. For Antonio Vivaldi, it's the Ryom catalog, abbreviated as RV.

These numbers indicate the approximate order in which a composer's works came into being. The exception with the BWV catalog and Ryom catalogs is that, as specific data on chronology is limited, they do not pretend to specify dates, and instead organize works by type. However, anyone who is not a professional in the world of classical music has no pressing need to memorize these numbers. Even some professionals don't bother to memorize them, so please don't let them intimidate you.

Musically knowledgeable readers may find themselves looking over this selection of works and puzzling about my choices. Why is Beethoven's Symphony no. 6 here, but not no. 5? Why Verdi's *Macbeth*, but not *La traviata*? In these two specific cases and in many others, the works that aren't here are in one of my earlier books. My first book, *Classical Music Insights*, contained 220 articles about great music of all varied genres; the 220 articles in this collection are an entirely different selection. There is also my *Operatic Insights*, which includes 101 operas, none of which appear here in *More Classical Insights*. In case you would be curious to know which works are featured in those two books, I have included that information in one of the appendices of this collection.

How many of the composers and compositions in this collection will still earn attention in the long range of history is impossible to determine. Many have already stood the test of time; others are too new on the scene to be sure how history will receive them. However, perhaps by seeking out their works, we can place ourselves in a mindset to be still seeking out their music in future years. Classical music is a timeless art, and will outlive all of us, a fact that would please Mozart, Beethoven, and all the others.

Chapter Two: Symphonies

It is a graceful, somewhat wistful theme by Franz Schubert (1797 – 1828). The melody above is not the very first melody in his Symphony no. 8, but this, the second prominent theme, is, in fact, more famous than that which precedes it. As Schubert never completed the symphony, the work has come to be known as his Unfinished Symphony. That fact has led generations of music students to set words to this melody: "This is the symphony that Schubert wrote but never finished." It's a mnemonic trick to help them recognize the music, and serves well for non-music majors, too.

In this chapter, we'll hear about the background of this famous work – unfinished, but not forgotten. We'll also learn about many other symphonies, some frequently appearing in concert performance, others more recent additions to the field.

A "symphony" can mean a large group of instrumental players, as in the San Francisco Symphony. However, it can also refer to a type of music, and that's the sort of symphony with which this chapter is concerned. This sort of symphony is a large scale composition in several movements written for a large number of instrumental performers, though without any featured soloist. If it had a featured soloist, it would be a concerto, examples of which are featured in Chapter Four.

How large is "large" and how many is "several" depends on the time in history. In Mozart's time in the late 18th century, a "large" number of performers was about forty, and "several" movements was generally three or four. That number of movements remained relatively constant, but the number of performers was ever increasing. Within even a single generation after Mozart, symphonies were played by fifty to sixty players; after another eighty years, closer to 100 players would be required.

What's a "movement" of a composition? A movement in a larger scale composition is comparable to a chapter in a book: a mostly self-contained portion of a greater whole. Chapter One is not the entire book, nor is Chapter Ten, or Chapter Whatever. However, all those different chapters taken together tell the entire story. The same is true with movements of a composition. Some composers might repeat bits of melodies from one movement in another movement, to ensure that all the parts sound like an organic whole. Others preferred contrast to continuity. In either case, the movements need to feel and sound as if they belong as different parts of a coherent set.

This chapter is the longest single chapter in this book. This is in part because, since it's the first chapter where we meet most of the composers, it has a larger amount of background biography than any of the later chapters. However, there is also the fact that symphonies tend to be large and ambitious works with much to be said about them. The great Austrian symphony composer Gustav Mahler (1860 – 1911) said that, in his opinion, a symphony was an entire world. From a musical perspective, that is very much the case. So, a world awaits.

♪♪♪♪

Haydn: Symphony no. 101 in D, "Clock"

Franz Joseph Haydn (1732 – 1809) spent nearly thirty years working for the aristocratic Esterhazy family. It was a secure life, but Haydn was so isolated from the world that he little realized how far his fame had spread. All he knew was that the Esterhazys so appreciated his music that everything he wrote they were eager to hear. He was nearly sixty before he had an opportunity to discover his fame for himself.

Haydn's chance for freedom came in 1790 with the death of his long-time employer, Prince Nikolaus Esterhazy. Nikolaus had been devoted to music, especially to Haydn's, but his successor, Prince Anton, had little interest in the arts. Anton valued Haydn only for the prestige which he brought to the Esterhazy court. The music itself held no attraction for him, and he never gave Haydn any real duties, so, when the composer asked for permission to visit London, Prince Anton easily agreed. Haydn was gone for a year and a half. A second London tour would follow in 1794-95.

Haydn's London visits were spurred by an invitation from Johann Peter Salomon, a German-born violinist and impresario, who presented six months of concerts in London each season. Salomon was well aware how popular Haydn's music, especially his symphonies, had become. He imagined that the master himself would be an even bigger attraction, if only he could get Haydn to London.

Londoners turned out by the thousands to watch Haydn conduct performances of his works. Critics and audiences alike were generous with their praise, which must have been a gratifying experience for someone who had labored so long as a servant. Among the new works heard at these concerts over the course of the two tours were twelve new symphonies, the last symphonies Haydn ever wrote.

One of the most popular of the collection, the Symphony no. 101, premiered in London March 3, 1794. The work acquired its nickname, the "Clock," for a prominent tick-tock rhythm first heard in the low strings in its slow second movement. Its other movements follow the general symphonic plan with which Haydn had had great success over the years: a spirited first movement with slower introduction to seize the attention of the listener; a dance-like third movement; and a vibrant finale. So popular had Haydn's approach to symphonies become that even his most gifted colleagues – Mozart and Beethoven amongst them – felt it was a model worth imitating.

♫♫♫♫

Mozart: Symphony no. 36 in C, K. 425, *"Linz"*

On August 4, 1782, in St. Stephen's Cathedral in Vienna, Wolfgang Amadeus Mozart (1756 – 1791) married Constanze Weber. None of the composer's family members were able to attend the wedding, and it was not until late the next year that he and his wife were able to travel to his native Salzburg so the family could meet her. In the interim, their first son had been born and named for his paternal grandfather. When the couple departed for Salzburg mid-summer, they left the infant Raimund Leopold in the care of a wet nurse.

On their way home to Vienna in October, Wolfgang and Constanze stopped off in the city of Linz in southern Austria to visit Johann Joseph Anton, the Count Thun, who had been a friend of Mozart's family since the composer was a boy. An enthusiastic supporter of his young friend, the count immediately announced a concert of Mozart's music. This ought to have been delightful news for Mozart, for concerts are always desirable when one is a composer. However, the situation was awkward. Mozart had amongst his luggage no music they could play, and the concert was only four days away. What's a composer to do? The answer lies in a quick note that Mozart sent to his father: "As I have not a single symphony with me, I am writing a new one at breakneck speed." Against all odds, the work was finished in time for its premiere November 4, 1783, and was duly named for the city in which it had been composed.

Was this piece truly written in only four frantic days? That such a fabulous symphony could be completed so swiftly seems astonishing. Merely scribbling down the notes of this expansive work could require that much time, so surely the process of imagining them would take far longer. Yet salvation may have come from one rare feature of Mozart's prodigious talent. This master composer was accustomed to creating his music essentially in his head, mentally assembling an entire work down to the details of its orchestration long before physically writing a single note. Thus, though he had no symphonies with him on paper for immediate distribution to the players, he may well have had one in his head, a complete symphony that was only awaiting transcription from his memory, with minor instrumental adjustments to suit the particular members of Count Thun's orchestra, which apparently had neither flutes nor clarinets, but did include trumpets, as that is how the work is scored.

The story of the *Linz* Symphony does not end with its premiere. Early in 1784, after a prosperous season of winter concerts, Mozart sent a copy of the piece to his father, who was still employed with the court orchestra in Salzburg. Leopold conducted the piece in concert September 17, 1784. Informing his son of the occasion, he strongly complimented the new work, pronouncing it to be "excellent." That same month, Wolfgang and Constanze welcomed their second child. Sadly, little Carl Thomas had no siblings to welcome him. His predecessor had died as an infant, during his parent's Salzburg sojourn.

Mozart's Linz Symphony blends oboes, bassoon, trumpets, horns, and timpani with strings. Throughout the work, one finds driving passages as well as poignant ones, often in close order. All sections of the orchestra have melodic material of interest, which often contrasts to melodies for the other sections that precede or follow. So the music never maintains a single idea past the limits of interest. It makes for delightful variety in tone color, and a work that, overall, has something new to offer on every page. Recall that this symphony had been carried around in its creator's imagination, much as other men might have carried it about in a briefcase. Mozart was, indeed, a talent apart from the everyday world.

♪♪♪♪

Beethoven: Symphony no. 3 in E-flat,
   op. 55, *"Eroica"*

When Ludwig van Beethoven (1770 – 1827) composed his Symphony no. 3, he broke many of the existing rules of how a symphony should be composed. He had known the rules, and more-or-less followed them with his first two symphonies, but here he chose a new path. The work was most of an hour in length, half again longer than any of Haydn's, and brought out stronger and more determined emotions than any composer had dared to express in music to that time. The work stunned the public, the press, and even the performers, all of whom had been accustomed to music being intended essentially for entertainment. Here, however, was a new idea: that a symphony could present its creator's image of the world, or at least his impression of how he thought the world ought to be.

It is fitting that this piece had such a powerful impact on the musical world, for it was inspired by one of the most powerful of men of the day. Beethoven had been a great admirer of Napoleon Bonaparte, whose vanquishing of royalty the composer viewed as heroic. Furthermore, with a concert tour to Paris in the works, the composer may have been considering how to smooth his reception with notoriously capricious Parisian audiences. Whatever the initial inspiration, in 1803 Beethoven complied with a suggestion from the French ambassador to Vienna that he begin a symphony honoring the so-called First Consul. He described the piece as his "Bonaparte Symphony," and might have published it under that title, had not events taken a different turn.

More Classical Insights

In 1804, Napoleon crowned himself Emperor of France, and Beethoven, in a tremendous fury, ripped the title page from the score. According to his student Ferdinand Ries, he stormed that now even his hero had become a tyrant, and that he would not dedicate a symphony to such a person. The symphony's new sub-title, "Eroica," implied more of a general heroism than specific deeds, and its inscription, "composed to celebrate the memory of a great man," seems to refer to the earlier Napoleon, the idealistic young hero who now lived only in memory.

When the work was published in 1806, it was dedicated not to Bonaparte, but to Prince Franz Joseph von Lobkowitz, one of Beethoven's most loyal patrons. That Lobkowitz had offered to pay handsomely for the privilege even before Beethoven became disenchanted with Napoleon may well have precipitated the composer's action. Moreover, the planned Parisian concert tour had been cancelled, so there was nothing to be gained on that front.

The *Eroica Symphony* premiered in Vienna April 7, 1805. Four years later, by then profoundly deaf, Beethoven himself conducted the work at a charity concert at the Theater-an-der-Wien. By the time of the latter performance, France and Austria had fallen into war. The French had occupied Vienna, and French troops filled the streets. Napoleon had been amongst them, but apparently did not attend the concert. Whether the diminutive ruler ever knew of the work's former connection to himself is uncertain.

With his Eroica Symphony, Beethoven starts things off with a bang, in fact, two of them: a pair of forceful chords that flings open the gate. It is a gate that generally remains wide open, for this "Eroica" symphony is indeed heroic in nearly every bar of the music. Particularly notable, however, is the second movement, which the composer himself labeled a funeral march. It is the only thoroughly dark portion of the symphony, and, as it happens, the longest individual movement. Perhaps Beethoven, knowing that the rest of the work would tend toward brilliance and glory, felt that he needed to make the most of this one opportunity for shadows.

♪♪♪♪♪

Beethoven: Symphony no. 6 in F, op. 68, *"Pastoral"*

One often hears of Beethoven as a misfit iconoclast, boorishly dressed, with no regard for established conventions, a man famed for bellowing at princes who paid insufficient attention to his music. To say that he had limited social skills would be understating the case. He simply didn't get along with people, but perhaps those people never saw him at his best, for the composer himself preferred to be away from people and pavement. Beethoven was always most at ease when vacationing in the countryside, where he could take long solitary walks through the fields and the woods. Although this love of nature is heard in several Beethoven works, no piece is more clearly in that spirit than the Symphony no. 6.

Although early sketches for this symphony date from 1802, its actual composition waited until the summers of 1807 and 1808. Beethoven spent these months in the town of Heiligenstadt. Today, Heiligenstadt is just another suburb of Vienna, but, back then, it was a rural retreat, a green escape from the heat of the city, and a perfect place for the reclusive Beethoven. In Heiligenstadt, his mind at rest, he was able to compose not only this symphony, but also the Symphony no. 5, the Cello Sonata in A major, and the two op. 70 Piano Trios. Beethoven produced so much music during this period that he was uncertain which symphony was finished first. He initially cataloged the *Pastoral Symphony* as number five and the now-famed Symphony in c minor as number six. The numbering was only reversed at publication.

On returning to Vienna in the fall of 1808, Beethoven organized a gala concert to premiere the two symphonies, together with other new works. The concert took place at the Theater-an-der-Wien on December 22. Here's the program: first, the Symphony no. 6, followed, in order, by the concert aria, *"Ah, perfido"*, two movements from the Mass in C major, the Piano Concerto no. 4, the Symphony no. 5, and, last but not least, the *Choral Fantasy*. It was four hours of music, new music to their ears. The theater was unheated, the orchestra was under-rehearsed, and the soprano soloist had a bad case of stage-fright. The whole experience led one listener to comment later that "one can have too much of a good thing --- and still more of a loud".

Each of the Pastoral Symphony's five movements has a sub-title to let listeners – and performers – know what ideas the composer had in mind. So in the first movement, one hears bright and sunny melodies evocative of Beethoven's feelings upon finding himself again in the countryside. In the second movement, he is relaxing by the side of a brook, a brook apparently frequented by quails, cuckoos, and nightingales, whose voices are evoked by the woodwinds. The third movement turns to human activity with a merry gathering of villagers, here, it seems, occupied with folk dances. Their merry-making comes to an abrupt end with the arrival of a thunderstorm, its tumult and fury raging away throughout the orchestra. With the fifth movement, the storm has passed and, as Beethoven declares in his subtitle, the shepherds are singing and all are "happy and thankful after the storm." Perhaps dusk has fallen in Heiligenstadt, and Beethoven, enjoying a rare bit of peace of mind, is resting from his labors.

♫♫♫♫

Schubert: Symphony no. 8 in b, D. 759, "Unfinished"

The Symphony no. 8 of Franz Schubert (1797 – 1828) is called his "Unfinished" Symphony, yet the same could be said of at least five of his other larger works. Operas, string quartets and other compositions also remain in abbreviated form, for Schubert, intensely prolific though not always well focused, left many partial manuscripts behind when he died all too young. Yet of all those embryonic compositions, this one exquisite symphony is the best known, and, in some ways, the most enigmatic, for death did not cause its fragmentation. Rather, Schubert abandoned the piece in mid-stream in October 1822, and, in the six years that remained to him, never picked up the work again.

This situation has puzzled historians for generations. Given the beauty of the two existing movements, filled as they are with lyric themes and lush orchestrations, it seems unimaginable that the composer would not have recognized the symphony's value, yet there is no solid evidence to explain Schubert's neglect of the work. Nonetheless, scholars have remained eager to offer their own theories. Some claim it that Schubert intended to write only two movements, as Beethoven had done with two of his late piano sonatas. Indeed, Schubert revered Beethoven and often turned to him for inspiration, but in this case, the connection is a tenuous one, for there exists the fully-orchestrated opening of a third movement scherzo. If Schubert had planned to stop at two movements, why did he begin a third? The presence of that fragmentary scherzo dismisses this theory, and also undermines the idea that Schubert did complete the piece, but lost its remaining movements.

What seems most likely is that the composer, having just become ill with syphilis, did not feel up to the task of completing an ambitious work that, based upon the length of its two existing movements, would have far exceeded his earlier symphonies in scope. Instead, he set aside the score and turned to a far more manageable task: the composition of his *Wanderer Fantasy,* a solo piano composition that was published promptly and earned for the composer an income he never would have gained from a symphony. That work appears in Chapter Six.

What is certain is that the piece did not remain long in its composer's possession. In 1822, when he was at work on the symphony, Schubert gave the work-in-progress to a musical friend, Anselm Hüttenbrenner. In 1853 – three decades later and 25 years after Schubert's death – Hüttenbrenner arranged the two existing movements for piano duet, and performed them in concert with his brother Josef, but the original score remained concealed. Then, in 1865, the original version of the symphony came into the hands of a Viennese conductor who offered its highly-belated premiere December 17, 1865. At that point, the work was enthusiastically received by the public and the press. It was far too late for Schubert, but late attention is better than none at all.

♪♪♪♪

Berlioz: *Romeo and Juliet*, op. 17

In 1827, Hector Berlioz (1803 – 1869) was only 24 and knew no English. Yet an English theater company had come to Paris to offer a season of Shakespeare, and the young Frenchman determined to give it a try. Having read the plays in French translation, he thought he should experience them in their native language, whether or not he could make much of the text itself. There, with John Kemble's company at the Odéon Theatre on September 11, the impressionable young man experienced what in his memoirs he called "the grand drama of my life:" falling in love twice over, with Irish actress Harriet Smithson, appearing as Ophelia, and with the Bard himself.

Harriet he would pursue determinedly until five years later, she consented to become his wife; their marriage would not be a success. Shakespeare lasted longer in Berlioz's life and more positively. To borrow a sentence from those memoirs, "This sudden and unexpected revelation of Shakespeare overwhelmed me," leading to the composition of a handful of compositions, including one based on the familiar tale of *Romeo and Juliet*.

Berlioz's *Romeo and Juliet* is neither entirely an opera nor exactly a symphony, for an opera would have more singing but a symphony rather less. It is also not quite Shakespeare, as the French text was not strictly translated but rather reworked by Emile Deschamps. However, Berlioz was never really a man for rules, so it was thoroughly in character for him to create something truly new that he termed a "dramatic symphony." That he was able to undertake such a radical work at all was in large part thanks to the Italian violinist Nicolo Paganini (1782 – 1840), who having become acquainted with the Frenchman's music, had paid a grand sum for a viola concerto, which itself would become *Harold in Italy*, op. 16. With those funds in his bank account, Berlioz had the opportunity to undertake something after his own heart, this story of star-crossed lovers. The composer himself conducted the work's premiere November 24, 1839, at the Paris Conservatoire.

A grand score about an hour and a half in length, Berlioz's *Romeo and Juliet* is written for an orchestra and chorus, together with contralto, tenor, and bass soloists. Most of the singing is concentrated near the beginning and near the end of the work. For those who lamented the lack of singers in the love scenes, Berlioz defended himself in the preface to the score, noting "duets of this kind have been treated vocally so often, and by the greatest masters, that it seemed both interesting and prudent to try a different form of expression," that is, purely instrumental. Also notable is the Queen Mab Scherzo of Part IV, derived from Mercutio discoursing to Romeo upon the enchanting power of dreams. Berlioz's vision of that unreal state of mind is lively and quirky, making excellent use of his mostly self-taught flair for orchestration. As a whole, the work is an inspired overview of the composer's approach to giving musical color to dramatic action.

Mendelssohn: Symphony no. 3 in a, op. 56, *"Scottish"*

Elder son of a wealthy, music-loving family, Felix Mendelssohn (1809 – 1847) grew up with many advantages. He was only twenty and already an important name in music as well as an experienced traveler when he first came to Britain in the summer of 1829. He began with piano recitals in London – Mendelssohn was a gifted pianist – before making his way off to Scotland. The Scots were not standing in line for him to appear in the concert hall; rather, the young composer, fascinated by what he had read about Scotland, was eager to see it for himself.

Accompanied by a friend, Mendelssohn roved amongst the lakes and moors of the Highlands, sending home exuberant letters about his adventures. He exulted in the storms ("weather that made the trees and rocks crash") and the emptiness of the countryside ("we wandered ten days without meeting a single traveler"). Here was a place quite alien to his native Berlin. Mendelssohn responded viscerally to the highlands and closely observed the music there.

Nonetheless, it was an Edinburgh experience that proved to be the most affecting. After a visit to the ancient Palace of Holyroodhouse, Mendelssohn wrote home to his family, "In the evening twilight, we went to the palace where Queen Mary lived and loved, into a little room with a winding staircase leading up to it ... It is roofless now. Grass and ivy grow there, and, at a broken altar, Mary was crowned Queen of Scotland. I believe I found in that old chapel the beginning of my *Scottish* Symphony."

Although the work's soul was born at that memorable moment, the actual process of composition was long delayed, for young Mendelssohn was a busy man. It was not until 1842, at the request of the London Philharmonic, that he ultimately took up the idea again and brought it to completion. The premiere of the *Scottish* Symphony was given January 20, 1842 in Berlin. Six weeks later, Mendelssohn conducted the piece again with the Leipzig Gewandhaus Orchestra, and in June he brought it to London. The symphony is dedicated to Queen Victoria, a Mendelssohn devotee who often invited him to the royal residence to accompany her at the piano as she sang his songs.

Rather than quoting actual Scottish melodies, the *Scottish* Symphony recalls that blend of vitality and melancholy peculiar to Scotland. Of particular note is the first movement's reverent opening theme (to which the composer refers in his letter), building to surging melodies that seem to speak of a coastal storm. The second movement scherzo is buoyed by dotted rhythms and airy staccato passages that capture the light-footed spirit of Highland dancing. A reflective third movement gives way to masculine might in the fourth, as the powerful drive of the closing pages seems to call up images of a Scottish army striding toward victory. For a man who grew up in urban environs, Mendelssohn did a fine job of capturing the atmosphere of a very different place.

♪♪♪♪♪

Franck: Symphony in d minor

Permit no one to tell you that Cesar Franck (1822 – 1890) was French. Indeed, he did spend much of his career in Paris, but in his youth, he was refused admission to the Paris Conservatoire because, born in Liège, he was Belgian. Only when he was thirteen did his family relocate to Paris and begin the process of becoming naturalized, so the boy could gain admission belatedly to the Conservatoire. He would be fifty years old before his residency was well enough documented to allow him to earn a professorship at the school. Franck's style and character were firmly established long before he came to Paris, and music-loving Belgians take pride in their native son.

Franck's only symphony, written in 1888 and premiered the following year, enjoys great popularity, especially amongst English horn players who treasure the lovely solo passages he gives them. Incidentally, that instrument, a lower-pitched cousin of the oboe, has no relationship at all to the French horn, which is a brass instrument.

Written in three movements, rather than the more usual four, the work combines into its middle movement the gentle moods usually heard in a second movement with the dance-like spirits of a typical third movement. The first and last movements of the symphony are its grandest, with broad orchestral phrases that hint at a middle-ground between the conservative Brahms and the radical Wagner.

Indeed, in Franck's time, writing a symphony of any type was still rather unusual in France. It was more often a German or Austrian endeavor, for the French seemed to prefer music for the dramatic stage. When a Parisian composer turned his mind to composing a grand orchestral work, he would have done so with expansive Germanic melodies singing in his ears.

♫♫♫♫

Brahms: Symphony no. 4 in e minor, op. 98

The last of four symphonies by Johannes Brahms (1833 – 1897) was begun in the summer of 1884 while the composer was vacationing in the Austrian lakeside mountain resort of Mürzzuschlag in southern Styria. It was a productive period for Brahms, who had completed his Symphony no. 3 only one year earlier and several dozen songs in the intervening months. Since then, in recognition of the composer's fondness for the region, Mürzzuschlag has opened a fine Brahms museum.

Although Brahms often spent years slaving over the manuscripts of his larger works, this new symphony progressed rather quickly, and was completed during the following summer's holiday. Brahms himself conducted its premiere October 25, 1885, in Meiningen, home of one of Germany's finest orchestras. That debut was well received, but its later Viennese reception was more mixed. Critics of the day, even those usually receptive to Brahms' music, found it dark and intense, with its spacious last movement utterly occupied with a set of variations on a short fragment of melody. However, one observer, the influential critic Eduard Hanslick, finally declared "it is like a dark well; the longer we look into it, the more brightly the stars shine back." The composer himself, dryly noting the work's prominent dance rhythms, labeled it the "Waltz and

Polka Affair." Any score offering an abundance of dance rhythms was likely to win over the Viennese in time.

The symphony would ultimately serve as the Viennese people's farewell to Brahms. In the spring of 1897, it was included on a well-attended concert program, and Brahms himself managed to be there. He was too weak to handle conducting duties, as he was already fatally ill with liver cancer; however, he managed to acknowledge the magnificent ovation with which the symphony was received. Within a month, he was in his grave. His own Symphony no. 4 was the last symphony he ever heard.

♪♪♪♪

Tchaikovsky: Symphony no. 6 in b minor, op. 74, "Pathetique"

The Symphony no. 6 of Peter Tchaikovsky (1840 – 1893) is forever associated with the tragedy of his sudden death. Early in the last year of his life, he began work on a new symphony, but progress was slow. Concert tours to France and England and the awarding of a doctorate of music from Cambridge cut into the time available for composition. Thus, though Tchaikovsky could compose quickly when the muse was with him, it was not until the end of August that he was able to complete the Symphony no. 6.

Its premiere, with the composer himself on the podium, was given in St. Petersburg two months later, on October 28. The work seemed unusually somber, particularly in its finale that, both in tempo and dynamics, fades into nothingness. Tchaikovsky's brother Modest suggested at the time that the work ought to be called by the French word "pathetique," [the Russian equivalent is "pateticheskoy"] meaning melancholy, and Tchaikovsky supposedly agreed. However, if Modest or anyone else bothered to ask the reason behind the symphony's gloomy mood, Tchaikovsky's answer is lost to time. His only remembered comment about the new piece is, "Without exaggeration, I have put my whole soul into this work."

Nine days later, on November 6, the composer was dead. His family blamed cholera, but physician's statements were contradictory and friends were skeptical. Cholera, they insisted, was a poor man's disease, almost unheard of amongst the upper classes. Surely Tchaikovsky would have known how to prevent exposure. In addition, as the composer's friend and colleague Nicolai Rimsky-Korsakov (1844 – 1908) commented in his own memoirs, the highly-contagious nature of cholera would have precluded the open-casket ceremony that actually occurred. Why, Rimsky asks, were mourners allowed to kiss the departed goodbye? On that question, Tchaikovsky's family remained determinedly silent.

At the time, the mystery remained unresolved. However, evidence that came to light in 1978 suggests that Tchaikovsky spent his last months distraught over a barely concealed scandal in his personal life. The homosexuality that he had fought to conceal throughout adulthood was about to become public knowledge. Did he commit suicide in the hope that ending his life would also silence the rumors? It is entirely possible, for deep depressions were common to him, and he had attempted suicide at least once before. Perhaps this was another attempt that was also meant to fail, but instead tragically succeeded.

Musicologists with psychological leanings have tried to associate the possibility of suicide with the fact of the somber symphony. They see parallels between the composer's increasing despair and the symphony's fading conclusion. Certainly, other composers have written symphonies in minor keys without taking their own lives, but the usual expectation was that a symphony, even one in a minor key, would end with energy, if not with optimism. Yet Tchaikovsky's final symphonic statement slowly dissipates into ever-deepening gloom. It is, some suggest, the musical voice of suicidal depression.

Such an analysis ignores an historical fact. Tchaikovsky began work on the piece nearly a year before its premiere, long before the rumors started. At that time, he wrote to his nephew that the new symphony would conclude with what he called "an adagio of considerable dimensions," which is certainly the manner in which the work ultimately draws to a close. If this composition is evidence of a troubled mind, then that mood had persisted for many months. What is more likely is that the symphony was simply the ultimate expression of Tchaikovsky's life-long obsession with dark emotions.

♪♪♪♪

Dvořák: Symphony no. 8 in G major, op. 88

Begun in August, 1889, the Symphony no. 8 by Antonín Dvořák (1841 – 1904) was finished in November of that year. The Czech composer, not yet fifty, had risen from unpromising peasant roots to gain acceptance as a composer of world renown who had made five triumphant concert tours to England. Despite this reputation, his publisher, the

German firm Simrock, still treated Dvořák as an unknown quantity, insisting upon short works for quick sale, and offering only paltry prices for symphonies. With this newest symphony, Dvořák put his foot down, declaring that he preferred to write long works, and, if the publisher didn't like it, the composer would go elsewhere, which he did. Thus, the Symphony no. 8 was released with great success in 1892 by a British publisher, who capitalized on the composer's popularity in England. Simrock learned his lesson. From then on, he published all of Dvořák's music and the composer earned the fees he demanded.

Although it was first published in England, there is nothing English about the substance of the Symphony no. 8, its melodies, rhythms, and harmonies being purely Bohemian at heart. It wasn't even premiered in England. Dvořák conducted its first performance in Prague February 2, 1890, and its second performance two months later in London. In 1891, Dvořák conducted it again, together with his *Stabat Mater*, at a Cambridge ceremony where he was awarded an honorary Doctorate of Music. As a self-described "country fiddler," one imagines that he found the Cambridge ceremony to be an astonishing affair.

Incidentally, even the English publisher first labeled this work the composer's Symphony no. 4. The confusion arose because as of this time – indeed, until well into the 20th century – Dvořák's first four symphonies had not yet appeared in print. Even the famed Symphony "From the New World," which followed this one by four years, was long numbered incorrectly as the fifth, rather than the ninth. Old record sets and old printed copies of his symphonies still bear the evidence of this situation.

♪♪♪♪♪

D'Indy: *Symphony on a French Mountain Air*

Parisian-born Vincent D'Indy (1851 – 1931) was not literally a one-hit wonder; he produced many dozens of works in all genres of the day, from opera to military band. Yet of all his compositions, one has attracted far and away the most attention. He might have regretted the relative lack of notice granted to the others, but it is better to have one acclaimed masterwork to one's name than none.

His single most popular work is the deserving *Symphony on a French Mountain Air*, completed late in 1886, and premiered in Paris March 20, 1887. Its central theme is borrowed from a song the composer heard sung by a distant shepherd in the Cévennes region of France. The melody is introduced within moments of the first movement's beginning as gentle and flowing theme for the English horn, then reappears here and there in the orchestra, changing in mood as it moves about. By the final movement, the music has taken on a bright and dance-like spirit, and it seems to end in sunshine.

One unusual feature of the work is the presence in the ensemble of a piano. That fact would often make of the piece a piano concerto, but not here. D'Indy uses the piano as one more instrument within the orchestral ensemble, with the piano no more prominent than anyone else. His countryman Camille Saint-Saëns (1835 – 1921) had done the same thing with his own Symphony no. 3, which also brings an organ into the performing forces. Neither man felt he needed to restrain himself to the standard orchestral complement.

♪♪♪♪♪

Mahler: Symphony no. 1, "Titan"

Gustav Mahler (1860 – 1911) was Bohemian born, with a sickly mother and an abusive father. He saw numerous siblings die in childhood, and then in adulthood struggled for acceptance in a world in which those of Mahler's Jewish background faced numerous roadblocks to success. So tragedy was familiar to him long before a heart disorder ended his life too soon. However, his Symphony no. 1 is not all darkness and sorrow. Here, not quite thirty and first trying his hand at composing something ambitious, he set about the task with bold and heroic images in mind.

When the piece premiered in Budapest on November 20, 1889, it bore the title "Titan: a symphonic poem in the form of a symphony." The allusion was to Jean Paul's popular novel, *Titan*, in which the protagonist has only his inner strength as a defense against a world of evil. According to Mahler's written program for the work, the first half of the symphony portrays "The Days of Youth, Flowers, and Thorns," whereas the second half is a human comedy, like Dante's divine comedy, in which the dark side of the world is exposed.

The work was not a success. Apparently, it seemed long and serious to be the work of a man so early in his career. Even extensive revisions failed to win a supportive audience for this monumental work during its composer's life, but enlightened listeners found much in it to admire. It has come to be regarded as a herald for the future, in which Mahler would become acclaimed as the master of grand and spacious orchestral statements.

The first movement has all the uplift of a mountain climb on a beautiful day. With the second movement, bright folk-dance rhythms appear. With the third movement, a mood of dark humor arrives with a minor-key resetting of *Frére Jacques*; Mahler himself attested that he had been inspired by a print portraying forest animals escorting a great hunter to his grave. For the final movement, Mahler opts for stormy and dramatic themes with much variety of emotions, ultimately resolving all into a mood of general optimism.

♪♪♪♪

Sibelius: Symphony no. 2 in D major, op. 43

When a composer has written a work named *Finlandia*, it is easy to remember that he is Finnish by birth. Yet Jean Sibelius (1865 – 1957) was not merely a native of that northern land. He was also a devoted patriot who used his compositional skills to speak out on behalf of Finnish pride and independence, for throughout his long life, Finland was ever under the control of some foreign power. First it was Sweden, then Russia, but never Finland itself under its own rule. Much of Sibelius' music draws upon Finnish folk culture, but he also turned his attention to grander, more abstract forms of composition, which could still be viewed as emblematic of Finnish pride.

Sibelius spent February, 1901, with his wife Aino and young daughters in Rapallo, Italy, where together with a holiday apartment, Sibelius also rented a working studio where he could tend to his music without the distractions of toddlers. Perhaps it was the Italian setting that caused the composer, as he later admitted, to imagine a scene direct from Mozart's opera *Don Giovanni*: that of the infamous lover confronting in his last moments the avenging statue brought to life. With this dramatic scene in mind, Sibelius sketched a dark theme that would eventually gain a central position in the symphony's second movement. Yet darkness is not the dominant mood of the symphony; there is also grandeur and glory and the spacious air of the Finnish countryside, an air that the Finns inhaled enthusiastically.

The composer's countrymen interpreted the symphony's dark moments as symbolic of their oppressors, at this time in their troubled history, the powerful Russian Empire. The symphony's many bright passages – culminating in a blazingly heroic finale – were interpreted as foreshadowing their eventual freedom and triumph. The changeable tempos may be seen as indicative of how the tide of events can change unexpectedly, that there may be set-backs, but one must persevere, keeping in mind the bright sun on the horizon, and in this case, the glorious brass that will usher it into clearer view.

When Sibelius conducted the symphony's premiere in Helsinki March 8, 1902, the sold-out house rose for a frenzied ovation. Three more performances were given in the next eight days; all three were also sold-out. The Symphony no. 2 was one of the greatest triumphs of Sibelius' career. He had shown through music that even someone who was neither a military leader nor sports figure could yet stand as hero to his people.

♪♪♪♪

Beach: Symphony in e minor, op. 32, *"Gaelic"*

There had been women in music before Amy Cheney Beach (1867 – 1944). However, few had risen to the level of fame accorded to such major figures as Beethoven, and women who acquired a strong reputation more often did so as performers than as composers. In the US, the situation was even more marked. Girls were encouraged to study music as a social skill, but not as a career. When young Amy Cheney debuted as pianist with the Boston Symphony at age 17, her family saw it as charming, but did not imagine that she might find a profession in the field.

Within months of that debut, she married a Boston physician, Dr. HHA Beach, and abruptly retired from the concert stage. That loss to 19th century audiences has, in the long run, benefited music lovers, for having surrendered her place on the stage, Amy Cheney, now calling herself Mrs. HHA Beach, turned instead to composition. In her 25 years of marriage (ended only by her husband's death), she completed far more works than she could have written if she had also been performing. She is noted today as one of her generation's leading American composers of either gender.

It is usually said that Beach's *Gaelic Symphony* was the first symphony written by an American woman. This is true, but the statement is misleading, for the piece is neither particularly American, nor notably feminine. It is, rather, Beach's response to Dvořák's call for Americans to explore their musical roots.

The Bohemian composer, known for writing works in his own nationalist style, had come to the United States in 1892 to lead the National Conservatory of Music in New York City. He was surprised to see how little attention American composers paid to the folk music of their nation, for it was his opinion that, from these roots, an American musical voice must develop. Although himself an outsider, Dvořák urged composers to more fully examine their musical heritage, and numerous composers responded to that call by using spirituals and hymns in their symphonic works.

Beach turned instead to Irish melodies, a logical choice for a composer who, living in Boston, was well aware of the Irish influence in this nation. By her own account, she was attracted to the melodies by what she described as "their simple, rugged, and unpretentious beauty." Those same adjectives could be applied to the symphony as a whole, which premiered October 30, 1896, in Boston.

Her symphony's first movement, with much energy to seize the listeners' attention, borrows a melody from one of Beach's own art songs. The lively second movement has a graceful theme that reappears in varied form in the movement's middle pages. For the third movement, Beach sets two melancholy Irish themes in counterpoint, so that they are heard simultaneously. With the final movement, she returns to the same melody tht she'd used in the first movement, her own art song "Dark is the Night," though here given even more dramatic expression. American composers of either gender had not been known for writing symphonies, but Beach proved that the old European standards could also be mastered west of the Atlantic.

♪♪♪♪

Vaughan Williams: Symphony no. 2, "London"

Born to a family of eminent English barristers and judges, Ralph Vaughan Williams (1872 – 1958) seems an unlikely candidate for the career of composer. In fact, when he set out to the Royal College of Music, his parents persuaded him that composition would be more genteel than performance, and so he directed his musical energies there. By the early 20th century, he had become one of the leading English composers of his generation, and he continued to be held in high regard to end of his long life.

One most often encounters his shorter instrumental pieces, such as *The Lark Ascending* and the *Fantasia on a Theme of Thomas Tallis*. The earlier of those was profiled in my book *Classical Music Insights*; the latter you'll find in Chapter Three of this collection. However, Vaughan Williams composed much else, including nine symphonies, and the most famed of these was the second of the series.

Vaughan Williams' so-called London Symphony premiered in London very early in World War I, on March 27, 1914, to critical acclaim. During the war years themselves, the composer would serve first as a medical orderly and then as an artillery officer. Only after the armistice did the military see fit to place him in charge of music for the army, organizing concerts for the soldiers' diversion. However, in the years immediately after the war, he would revise much of what he had written in the symphony. Despite the dark days in which it was conceived, it is a symphony of optimism with some passages of lyrical beauty and others of determined energy, as if the composer was intent upon portraying a better side of mankind. The revised version premiered in 1920.

The nickname "London" dates from the beginning and has led some prominent observers to imagine specific London scenes, from Big Ben to the Thames itself, as the inspiration of various musical passages. Vaughan Williams himself strongly discouraged such suggestions, writing once, "The work must succeed or fail as music and in no other way." If one imagines that one hears the famed chimes of Westminster, it is only what the composer described as "a coincidence." In his imagination, the work was more "A Symphony by a Londoner," where he had lived since 1897, than a symphony specifically about London itself.

♪♪♪♪

Turina: *Sinfonia Sevillana*, op. 23

Joaquin Turina (1882 – 1949) was Spain's answer to Claude Debussy (1962 – 1918), and like the Frenchman, received his advanced musical training at the Paris Conservatoire. Turina's own music features a blend of influences: the gently evocative shading of Impressionism, the robust harmonies of neo-Romanticism, and the energetic rhythms of Spanish folk music. All those characteristics appear in his *Sinfonia Sevillana*, which premiered September 11, 1920.

The symphony is structured in three movements, each with a descriptive subtitle referring to some scene specific to Seville. Of the work, Turina observed that he meant it to be more programmatic than symphonic. That is, the intended scenes are more his focus than any adherence to strict symphonic structures à la Brahms. So Brahms might not have regarded as a symphony. However, of Turina's instrumental works, it is the grandest in scope, and so the only one to which he gave the name "symphony."

The first movement "Panorama" offers an overall view of the city, perhaps in the morning, as the building energy and hastening tempos seem to speak of the residents waking up and setting about their daily activities. The second movement "Por el rio Guadalquivir" concerns itself with riverside scenes, and also offers changeable moods. In both these movements, the varied voices of woodwinds are called upon to provide a tapestry of colors, though in the second movement, there is also a prominent and lyrical part for solo violin. The third movement "Fiesta en San Juan Azalfarache" brings the symphony to a close with consistently buoyant melodic ideas, buoyed along with vibrant dance-like rhythms. As a whole, the work proves that Turina, often a specialist in chamber music, still had much to say with orchestral forces.

♫♫♫♫

Prokofiev: Symphony no. 5 in B-flat major, op. 100

The Symphony no. 5 of Sergei Prokofiev (1891 – 1953) dates from the years of World War II, when he and many other notable artistic figures of the Soviet Union were living together in seclusion away from the war for their own protection. He began the piece in 1944 at the Ivanovo estate some eighty kilometers west of Moscow, where he devoted his mornings to tennis and volleyball, his evenings to musical discussions with friends, and his afternoons to composing. When he completed a new work, he would commandeer the community piano and play through the new creation for his colleagues, who recalled that he had no sympathy for those who made less diligent use of their time. Prokofiev finished his new symphony that summer, though its premiere had to wait until it was safe to go back to Moscow.

The Symphony no. 5 premiered in Moscow January 13, 1945, with Prokofiev himself leading the orchestra. By this time, the approaching defeat of the Nazis was becoming ever more certain. Indeed, on the very day of the symphony's premiere, Moscow received notice of a great Soviet victory on the banks of the Vistula. Thus, the subdued first notes of the new work were heard against a background of artillery salutes celebrating the news, and the composer's friends recalled that, when he first stepped up to the podium, he had delayed giving the downbeat, waiting for a quieter moment. With that scenario in mind, Prokofiev's music – by turn triumphant and reflective, romantic and heroic, serene and angry – seems especially appropriate to the day. It is as if, in his labors of the previous summer, he had anticipated the joys that would come with winter.

This would be Prokofiev's last concert appearance. Not long afterward, he suffered a serious fall and concussion, from which he never fully recovered. The resultant decrease of strength and energy caused him to cut back on public appearances, though he was still able to compose. Prokofiev died in 1953. Ironically, the Soviet leader Joseph Stalin died on the very same day, and all the nation's newspapers were more concerned with Stalin's passing than with Prokofiev's.

♪♪♪♪

Still: *Afro-American Symphony*

Growing up in Little Rock, Arkansas, William Grant Still (1895 – 1978) learned to love classical music through his stepfather's record collection. However, reasoning that a black man such as himself had little hope of a career in classical music at the time, he chose instead to enter the world of jazz. While living in New York City, he invested his spare time in composition lessons with George Whitefield Chadwick (1854 – 1931), one of the leading American classical composers of the day. Chadwick encouraged Still to try his hand at something ambitious, and soon the young man was at work on a symphony. Years later, Still joked that, had it not been for the Great Depression forcing the closure of some of New York City's jazz clubs, he might not have found the time to finish the work. It premiered in 1930 with the Rochester Philharmonic; the event marked the first time that a professional orchestra had performed a symphony by an African-American composer.

Rather than designating it his Symphony no. 1, Still chose a descriptive title reflective of his heritage. It is a parallel that carries over into the musical style, with bluesy harmonies and jazzy rhythms. Structurally, it accomplishes much of what a classical symphony was supposed to do. Still opens with a stately movement that spends its central pages developing and varying its thematic material. A gentle, rather reflective second movement offers distinct contrast, as does the bright and bouncy third movement, dancing as it does with what seems like celebration. The final movement, grandest of all, brings the entire symphony to a proud conclusion.

Along the way, Still further reinforces the jazzy atmosphere with his instrumental choices. Bass clarinet stands in for tenor saxophone, and the percussion section includes marimba and banjo. Admittedly, banjos were not often found in Harlem jazz. However, Still had grown up in the South, and it was New Orleans jazz that first came to his attention. Here is a symphony that only William Grant Still could have written

♪♪♪♪

Messiaen: *Turangalîla Symphony*

The musical legacy of Frenchman Olivier Messiaen (1908 – 1992) lies in four particular areas. He served for sixty years as organist at the La Trinité church in Paris, and so wrote a significant amount of organ music. He often incorporated bird songs into his compositions, thereby keeping nature close at hand. His *Quartet for the End of Time*, which premiered in 1941 at a German prison-of-war camp where Messiaen had been held since being captured at the Battle of Verdun, stands as one of the most ambitious of chamber works, tasking four players with conveying the power of the Bible's Book of Revelations. Lastly, and grander yet in scale, his *Turangalîla Symphony* is one of the most eerie and unexpected works of the 20th century.

Though far from his final work, *Turangalîla* can yet be viewed as the ultimate summation of Messaien's musical vision. Over an hour in length and spanning ten distinct movements, it is also unusually scored, with the standard orchestra supplemented by piano, glockenspiel, celesta, vibraphone, and the electronic *ondes martenot,* predecessor of modern-day synthesizers. With these forces, Messaien was able to evoke an exotic, bell-like effect from time to time, and, with the oscillating tones of the *ondes martinot,* haunting moods that make some listeners think of abstract science fiction films. The varied ways in which an *ondes martinot* can color and bend its notes are matched by no other instrument of its time.

The work was commissioned by conductor Serge Koussevitzky for the Boston Symphony, where he had long championed new music. It was premiered by that ensemble with Leonard Bernstein conducting December 2, 1949. The title is a word of the composer's own invention, combining the Sanskrit words for the flow of time and for play or love. Messiaen saw it as a kind of Tristan story of forbidden love, though here a tale borrowed from mythology of India, not Celtic lands.

A soft love theme, gradually evolving, ties together the even-numbered movements. Odd-numbered movements tend toward more grim and brutal moods. Taken as a whole, it shows what a symphony can be in the hands of a composer whose gaze is directed far beyond the framework of what Beethoven or Brahms would have called a 'symphony.' If the first critics were a bit puzzled by the work, their predecessors were also startled by what many of the greatest names in music tried in groundbreaking scores. *Turangalîla* is a new way of imagining sound, and those with open minds will find here much wonder.

More Classical Insights

♪♪♪♪

Barber: Symphony no. 1, op. 9

Only 26 when he composed it in 1936, Samuel Barber (1910 – 1981) called this work his Symphony no. 1, but it would have no successor. Although he would produce many more orchestral scores in the four and a half decades that remained to him, for those pieces he would choose instead other, less specific vocabulary, particularly "essay." After all, an orchestral "essay" can be whatever a composer wishes it to be, whereas the word "symphony" carries with it certain expectations of scope and organization. Barber was enough of a conservative to be aware of those expectations, and having flouted them in this one early score, chose not to flout them again. The symphony premiered in Rome December 13, 1936, for at the time, the young American was living in Europe.

What would those symphonic expectations have been? In addition to being a work for large orchestra, a symphony was generally planned in several broad movements or chapters, each cohesive in itself though combining adequately with the others. It was presumed that each movement would offer several varied melodies and that the composer would show how he could re-imagine bits of those melodies in new guises.

In this one symphony, Barber does most of those things, though in a single broad, interconnected movement some twenty minutes in length. Tempo changes imply breaks between movements, but having a single continuous musical vision, the composer does not break the action into movements per se. Rather, he opts for a flow of emotional energy; moreover, connecting the work helps the listener to perceive that early melodic fragments reappear in varied form as the work continues. Listeners who know Barber only from his deeply melancholy *Adagio for Strings*, which followed soon on the heels of this symphony, may be startled to find how much overt drama he could build into his music.

♪♪♪♪

Górecki: Symphony no. 3,
   "Symphony of Sorrowful Songs"

It is not unknown for a symphony, normally an instrumental work, to include parts for singers. Gustav Mahler (1860 – 1911) did so in several of his symphonies, Jean Sibelius (1865 – 1957) and Ralph Vaughan Williams (1872 – 1958) did so occasionally. Most famously, Ludwig van Beethoven (1770 – 1827) brought into his Symphony no. 9 not only a vocal quartet, but also a full choir. Each of them understood how in the broad canvas of a symphony, the addition of human voices can be just the touch needed to achieve perfect expression.

Like his great predecessors, Polish composer Henryk Górecki (1933 – 2010) also appreciated the value of adding a singer to what is otherwise a symphonic work. The singer in this case is a solo soprano in lyric range: neither exceptionally high nor exceptionally low in pitch, and nuanced, but not heavily dramatic. She is not heard on every page of the symphony, but has the challenging task of managing the Polish phonetics and the rapt moods of what the symphony's subtitle aptly describes as "sorrowful songs."

Written in 1976 and dedicated to the composer's wife, Górecki's Symphony no. 3 uses melodies drawn in part from 15th century Polish prayers. It is to the strings that those melodies are usually entrusted through string writing that is rich and complex, indulging in unusual harmonies that catch the ear, but unlikely to offend it. Flowing lines build with the gentle drama of a sunrise. Nothing happens suddenly, though one gradually comes to realize that the music is markedly more passionate than it was before. After a spacious orchestral introduction, the soloist joins with a haunting 15th century lament in which a mother mourns her son's passing.

The second movement gives to the soprano a prayer written by an eighteen-year-old Polish girl imprisoned by the Nazis during World War Two. "Do not weep, Mother," she pleads, for the Virgin Mary will support her; the words become all the more poignant when one realizes that they were etched into the wall of a Gestapo prison in Poland in 1944, and signed with the girl's name. Throughout this section of the symphony, Górecki's score is quietly radiant, like the serene confidence of a believer.

The composer carries this reflective mood through the remainder of the symphony. In the third and final movement, the text comes from a Polish folk song of a mother whose son has been lost in battle.

At no time is Górecki's symphony cheerful, but it is strongly meditative and extraordinarily lovely, as the lasting fascination that the public feels for the piece might indicate.

When the work's first major recording, with soprano Dawn Upshaw and the London Sinfonietta, came out in the 1990s, it spent weeks near the top of the Billboard charts both in Britain and the US: not the charts for classical recordings, but those for all recordings of all types. The American conductor David Zinman, who led the Upshaw recording, says of the piece, "It's like listening to the angels."

♪♪♪♪

Daugherty: *Metropolis Symphony*

Iowa native Michael Daughtery (b. 1954) has a reputation for dramatic and colorful orchestral scores that are often inspired by quintessential elements of the American experience. His catalog includes such titles as *Route 66*, the opera *Jackie O*, *Niagara Falls*, and the *Motor City Triptych*. His is music that speaks close to the hearts of American audiences, yet its high energy and richly varied timbres makes it exciting for audiences of all descriptions.

Of his *Metropolis Symphony*, Daugherty says it "evokes an American mythology" and further describes it as "a compositional metaphor." From that standpoint, the piece might be an American parallel to Wagner's *Ring Cycle* operas, for the German, too, was presenting his own musical interpretation of familiar characters from his nation's folklore. His Siegfried might not quite be every man's Siegfried, but even Wagner rarely saw music as universal truth. So though a particular listener might imagine the Man of Steel, Lois Lane, and Lex Luthor differently, here is one possible musical interpretation, and knowing what ideas attach to which movement can help the listener to perceive Daugherty's vision.

The first movement focuses upon Lex Luthor, the arch-villain of the original comic book series, his diabolical character captured with frantically intricate solo violin lines, punctuated at intervals by shrill referee whistles. For the second movement, Krypton, the scene is Superman's home planet as it faces imminent destruction. Here, the music is rife with ominous harmonies, dark moods, and alarm bells. The third movement's subtitle – Mxyzptlk – is not a random selection of letters. Rather, it is the name of a trouble-making inter-dimensional spirit in the original saga. His unpredictable nature is rendered in the mercurial and restless scherzo.

Lois Lane appears in the fourth movement, not evoked by music of gentle romance, as one might expect, but rather with tense, perpetual motion themes, as if evocative of her hectic, often dangerous career. The final movement, "Red Cape Tango," blends the sensuous pulse of the dance with a dark theme – first heard in the bassoon – derived from the ancient Dies Irae (Day of Wrath) chant. Daugherty attests that he was imagining the Man of Steel's frequent dances with death, and it is with that image that the symphony sweeps to its close.

Daugherty's *Metropolis Symphony* premiered in 1994 with the Baltimore Symphony Orchestra and conductor David Zinman. The work is dedicated both to the ensemble and to the maestro.

♪♪♪♪

Marsalis: *Swing Symphony*

Being born into a musical family is no guarantee of musical gifts, but it surely can't hurt. Johann Sebastian Bach (1685 – 1750), Wolfgang Amadeus Mozart (1756 – 1791), and countless others have shown that family understanding and support are crucial to the nurturing of musical leanings. Consider, then, the case of the Marsalis family of New Orleans. Father Ellis already had deep roots in the city's jazz scene before his six sons came of age. Most of the boys would follow their father into musical professions, particularly the eldest two: saxophonist Branford and trumpeter Wynton.

Anyone paying attention to music since the early 1980s cannot have failed to notice the achievements of Wynton Marsalis (b. 1961). Barely into his twenties, he won Grammy awards for recordings both in the jazz category and in the classical category in the same year – an unprecedented achievement that he managed twice, in two consecutive years: 1983 and again in 1984. Along the way, he began bridging his two worlds, bringing the rhythms and timbres of jazz into the broader structures of classical music. The result has been dance pieces, chamber music, and – so far – three symphonies. It is the most recent of these three that concerns us at this time.

Marsalis' third symphony, bearing the title *Swing Symphony*, was written on a joint commission from the Berlin Philharmonic, the New York Philharmonic, the Los Angeles Philharmonic, and the Barbican Centre of London. Marsalis describes it as a "symphonic meditation" on the evolution of classic jazz, from its roots in ragtime to more contemporary developments. The scoring sets a jazz ensemble against a standard symphony orchestra. However, that orchestra becomes far from "standard" when one studies the percussion section, which amongst more familiar choices, also includes congas, bongo, cowbells, police whistle and siren, washboard, and various ethnic drums.

It is a mix that ensures the *Swing Symphony* has the energy to truly swing and to convey the largely urban atmosphere in which jazz evolved, an atmosphere upon which Marsalis reflects in each of the symphony's movements. Throughout, the orchestra picks up on the energy and spirit of the varied jazz influences, sometimes echoing what the jazz ensemble is doing, rather as Bach managed his forces in the Brandenburg Concertos nearly three centuries earlier. A good idea never goes out of date.

The *Swing Symphony* premiered in Berlin June 9, 2010, with Marsalis importing soloists from Jazz at Lincoln Center in New York City to manage the jazz ensemble parts. Since then, the work has gone on to each of the other commissioning organizations and stands as an ambition example of how jazz and classical can co-exist in the 21st century and beyond.

♫♫♫♫

Greenberg: Symphony no. 5

Many startlingly young composers have been compared to Mozart; few have lived up to the comparison. It's one thing to write music before reaching the age of ten, as Mozart did. However, it's entirely another to be that young and be writing music that is likely to stand the test of time. In that august company, place Jay Greenberg (b. 1991).

The native of New Haven, Connecticut, was taking private composition lessons at the age of six, and, by the account of his instructor, showing such intensity of focus that it was the instructor, not the child, who needed breaks. At ten, Greenberg moved on to Juilliard on scholarship, and twice was profiled on *Sixty Minutes*. Not yet old enough to vote, he already had a recording contract with Sony Classical. Such are the sort of achievements that Mozart would have managed at the same ages, had the technology existed at the time; Jay Greenberg has the advantage of being a 21st century musical genius.

Greenberg's Symphony no. 5 was completed in 2005, when he was fourteen, and soon recorded by the London Symphony Orchestra. With four movements spanning half an hour, the piece is no less ambitious than anything Mozart wrote at that age, and is more adventurously conceived than many works by some adult composers.

Of the piece, Greenberg himself observes that it combines "a typically Romantic melodic sweep with Classical counterpoint and the methodical thinking of the 20th century's serialists." That is, there are broadly spacious melodic structures, along with complicated layering of simultaneous musical lines. Moreover, one finds connections to the avant garde of the 1920s, when the detailed structures of music were considered more important than whether or not the resulting piece was a crowd-pleaser. Greenberg has managed to satisfy his audiences without ignoring his own musical impulses.

More Classical Insights

Jaunty moods, bold ones, and lyrical ones appear in turn, coming together to make a symphony of impressive mastery, were the composer of any age, let alone only fourteen when he finished it. The musical future bodes well for Jay Greenberg, and that fact bodes well for classical music as a whole. It is, indeed, still an active art form even into a new century.

Chapter Three:
Other Symphonic Works

Frenchman Paul Dukas (1865 – 1935) was so self-critical of his creations that little of his music survives; he simply destroyed more of it than is left to us today. Here, however, is a bit of one of those works of which he approved. It is a theme he wrote to convey the atmosphere of magical brooms on the march. Although the composer himself, dying five years before the original Disney *Fantasia* film, would not have imagined Mickey Mouse contending with those brooms, that is surely how most current listeners imagine it.

It isn't from a symphony, but it certainly makes use of a symphony orchestra. In this chapter, I have placed articles on 25 works performed by large instrumental ensembles but not termed by their creators to be "symphonies." Sometimes, this term was avoided because the work in question is simply too short to really be a "symphony," perhaps comprising only a single movement, as is the case with Dukas' *The Sorcerer's Apprentice.* At other times,

More Classical Insights

the composer didn't want to call it a "symphony," lest insiders expect it to align with certain rules and plans for structure (and ambition) that the composer was intending to ignore.

As time goes on, following one's own ideas became increasingly preferable to following instructions. Thus, the majority of works featured in this chapter originated in the past 150 years, and many within the past fifty years. Working outside the box has become ever more popular.

♪♪♪♪

Telemann: *Tafelmusik (Banquet Music)*

Georg Philipp Telemann (1681 – 1767) is now less famous than Johann Sebastian Bach (1685 – 1750). In and of itself, that fact is not startling, for the same could be said of the vast majority of composers. Yet during their own time, Telemann was the bigger name, and, in fact, far more productive as a composer. Telemann's catalog contains over one thousand sacred cantatas, over 100 concertos, several hundred works of chamber music: the list goes on. By the end of it, it is clear that Telemann was the most prolific composer who ever lived, creating twice as many works as Bach, who was himself no laggard at composition. Of course, no one would assert that quantity is proof of quality. However, Telemann was the most influential composer of his day, and Bach clearly admired him, for he asked Telemann to serve as godfather to his son Carl Philipp Emanuel Bach (1714 – 1788).

Telemann's *Tafelmusik (Banquet Music)* was published in 1733 in Hamburg, where he would spend nearly fifty years as the city's director of music. The position required composing for the local aristocrats, but also for the general public. Consisting of three collections of orchestral and chamber works, the *Banquet Music* apparently had been completed months earlier, since late in 1732 advertisements for its forthcoming publication appeared, announcing that subscribers to the first edition – that is, those paying in advance for the privilege of reserving a copy – would have their names listed on the cover page. Telemann's popularity is proven by the fact that over 200 persons accepted the offer, including various noblemen, diplomats, churchmen, wealthy bourgeois, and professional colleagues, amongst them Georg Frideric Handel (1685 – 1759).

The various shorter compositions which together make up *Tafelmusik* serve as a fine primer on Baroque musical ideals as epitomized by Telemann. The music alternates between lively and gracious moods with the main string ensemble supplemented by various winds for the sake of variety. Often, ballroom dance rhythms dominate the various movements. Were it actually used as music for a banquet, it would make for an expansive evening; taken all together, the collected works total over four hours of diversion.

♪♪♪♪

Beethoven: *Leonore* Overture no. 3, op. 72b

The only opera of Ludwig van Beethoven (1770 – 1827) is a tale of a woman's struggle to rescue her husband from unjust political imprisonment. In its first version, premiered at Vienna's Theater-an-der-Wien in 1805, it was called *Leonore*. However, the presence of Napoleon's army at the city gates caused that production to close promptly. By the time a second premiere took place the following spring, Beethoven had made revisions to the opera, including to its overture. Even without the threat of war, the opera was less than a triumph.

Only in 1814, when Vienna's Kärntnertor-Theater expressed an interest in presenting the work, did the composer begin to revise the opera anew, providing new dialog, new arias for the principal singers, and a new setting for the finale. At this time, the opera took its final title: *Fidelio,* derived from the masculine disguise worn for most of the opera by the wife character, Leonore. The premiere, May 23, 1814, was a critical and popular success, yet it was not until the second performance three days later that Beethoven managed to complete the newest and final version of the overture. Each time he revised the score, the composer wrote a new overture; the earlier ones, all bearing the opera's original name of *Leonore,* have survived as concert pieces, and are hardly ever attached to the opera itself.

The third of the Leonore overtures was particularly ill-suited to dramatic use, largely because it was rather overly dramatic. A quarter hour in length, it not only caused a long delay before the curtain could rise, but also stole much of the thunder of the opera to follow. Overtures should be appetizers, tempting listeners to continue with the next course; Beethoven, by contrast, provided most of a meal. So many musical morsels are offered that one has little reason to stick around for the rest of the show.

The very qualities that led to this overture's eviction from its own opera make it ideal for concert performance, for here is the opera in a nutshell, without requiring singers. Here one finds in musical terms Leonore's despair at her husband's imprisonment, then joyous rushing string phrases as she imagines his freedom. A dark passage with grim brass chords evokes setback, thanks to the villain. Then a stormy rising string theme drives magnificently into a trumpet fanfare, signaling reprieve for the poor prisoners. A hymn-like woodwind theme suggests their emergence into daylight. Fanfare and hymn alternate, before giving way to a light-hearted theme that swells into a glorious happy ending, complete with a dose of syncopation and the grandest of grand finales. Beethoven may have overdone it, but he did so in the most magnificent of terms.

♪♪♪♪

Berlioz: *Roman Carnival* Overture

From his earliest days as a composer, Hector Berlioz (1803 – 1869) dreamt of writing operas, of giving musical life to a theatrical work. At this goal, he never entirely succeeded. Of his five attempted operas, one was never completed; another was completed but never performed. A third opera, his epic *Les Troyens* (see Chapter Eight), only earned partial performances during its composer's lifetime, and the remaining two operas, despite reaching the stage, failed dismally. With such a track record, one cannot blame Berlioz for recycling old opera melodies into works for concert performance. It was the only way that he could assure that the music would be heard.

Prominent in his list of Berlioz' operatic failures is his 1838 opera *Benvenuto Cellini,* inspired by the colorful and charismatic Italian sculptor and goldsmith of the 16th century. Cellini's adventures, as related in his autobiography, make for amusing reading, but the opera apparently lacked the zest of Cellini himself. After four performances, *Benvenuto Cellini* was pulled from the stage at the Paris Opéra. Even Berlioz conceded that his score was flawed, yet did not utterly abandon the work. Six years later, in 1844, he resurrected portions of the opera in a free-standing concert overture titled *Roman Carnival*, a lively and scintillating piece that enjoyed far more popularity than the opera that inspired it. Buoyed by its sparkling energy, Berlioz' *Roman Carnival Overture* has become one of his most popular works.

♪♪♪♪

Mendelssohn: *Calm Sea and Prosperous Voyage* Overture

Thanks to his parents – wealthy patrons of the arts in Berlin – Felix Mendelssohn (1809 – 1847) grew up with the major names of the arts and literature on the opposite side of the table at Sunday dinner. One particularly frequent visitor was the great German writer and statesman, Johann Wolfgang von Goethe (1749 – 1832). Although Goethe was of Felix's grandfather's generation, he admired the young prodigy's skills. Young Mendelssohn came to know of Goethe's voluminous writings, and though he would never tackle the man's masterpiece, *Faust*, many of his shorter works found musical expression in Mendelssohn's care.

Calm Sea and Prosperous Voyage draws inspiration from a pair of related Goethe poems. In the first, sailors becalmed on a windless sea express their fears; for a sailing ship, "calm" is not a positive experience, for there may be no timely escape. In the second, a strong breeze has brought life to the sails and the sailors joyfully make their way into the harbor.

Combining the two into a single instrumental piece, Mendelssohn shows himself more interested in the joyful scenes. Indeed, he begins with quiet tension, but soon the breeze wafts in on the flute and before long, the ship is in buoyant motion again. The work premiered in Berlin September 8, 1828, a few months before the young composer's twentieth birthday.

♪♪♪♪

Saint-Saëns: *Carnival of the Animals*

French composer Camille Saint-Saëns (1835 – 1921) was one of history's greatest musical talents. By the age of eleven, the young pianist had memorized all of Beethoven's 32 piano sonatas. As an adult, he wrote over 300 compositions, while also studying archaeology, astronomy, botany, geology, and philosophy. Somehow, he found time for it all, through a rich and varied career that spanned over eight decades, from the height of Mendelssohn to the early days of Stravinsky. In musical style, he never entirely admitted that the 20th century had arrived; perhaps in part because of that fact, he never lacked for popularity.

One of Saint-Saëns' most beloved compositions is one that he refused to allow to reach the public during his life, fearing that it would undermine his serious reputation. That work is the *Carnival of the Animals*, dating from 1886. Scored for orchestra with the addition of a pair of pianists, the piece takes a light-hearted musical journey through a gallery of diverse animals, including pianists pounding their way through scales and fossils whose clacking bones are memorably depicted by xylophones in variations on the old French folk song "Ah vous dirai-je, Maman," known to English listeners as "Twinkle Twinkle Little Star."

Private jokes, intended for the composer's professional friends, include the elephants tramping along to a vastly slowed version of the *Dance of the Sylphs* by Hector Berlioz (1803 – 1869) and the tortoises grinding through a similarly plodding can-can from *Orpheus in the Underworld* by Jacques Offenbach (1819 – 1880). Both men were personally known to Saint-Saëns.

Other jokes are more generally obvious, as lions roar, hens cluck, cuckoos call out their own name, and kangaroos bounce buoyantly. The music for "Persons with Long Ears" could only be meant to portray donkeys, as their hee-haws come through loud and clear. Most frequently extracted of all the various movements is the next-to-the-last scene for "The Swan," adapted for ballet performance by no less than Anna Pavlova.

Sometimes, one encounters performances or recordings of *Carnival of the Animals* complete with a narrator who presents brief humorous verses about the various creatures. These are not part of the composer's original creation. Rather, they are an addition by the American poet Ogden Nash (1901 – 1971), whose twisted rhymes and quirky wit might have amused Saint-Saëns, had he only had the chance to hear them.

♪♪♪♪

Tchaikovsky: *Capriccio Italien, op. 45*

Few regions seem more dissimilar than Russia and Italy. The long winter nights of the former have little in common with the latter's sunny street scenes, and whereas Russian music is often imagined as morose à la Dostoyevsky, in Italy, the image is one of *la dolce vita*. Those Russians who visited Italy in the 1800s could have only viewed it as incredibly exotic. Certainly, that was the reaction of Peter Tchaikovsky (1840 – 1893) when he wintered in Rome in 1879/80. The Mediterranean sojourn inspired him to compose an effervescent musical tribute to that southern region.

The *Capriccio Italien* was begun during that visit and completed in May of 1880. Its premiere was given in Moscow in December of that same year. As Tchaikovsky explained to his friend and patron, Nadezhda von Meck, the melodies used in the caprice were in some cases borrowed from published collections. Others were songs the composer had heard in the streets of Rome, and the brass fanfare that begins the caprice was played every evening at the army barracks across the street from his hotel. Throughout, there are ever-changing musical moods, as if one were paging through a photo album compiled from a busy vacation. Usually, Tchaikovsky was sharply critical of his own works, but of this piece he approved, saying, "Its success was incontestable." The *Capriccio Italien* is resolutely high-spirited, and one of the most ebullient of the composer's works.

♪♪♪♪

More Classical Insights

Dvořák: *Carnival Overture, op. 92*

Just before his 50th birthday, Czech composer Antonin Dvořák (1841 – 1904) was invited to come to New York City to direct a new academic institution, the National Conservatory of Music. At first, he was disinclined to go, as his children were young and he himself had an aversion to large cities. However, the money was too good to refuse, and soon he was presenting a series of farewell concerts in Europe, particularly in his home base of Prague.

Amongst the newly composed works heard on these concerts was a set of three orchestral pieces, based on the same musical themes. At first, Dvořák envisioned the compositions as a three-part suite to be called *Nature, Life and Love*; however, those rather generic titles were finally rejected, as was the idea of a unified work. Instead, he published the works as separate compositions, and gave them the more specific titles of *In Nature's Realm, Carnival,* and *Othello*. Dvořák himself conducted the premieres on April 28, 1892, in a farewell concert given in Prague just before his departure for the United States. Six months later, in New York, he led a performance with the Metropolitan Opera Orchestra at Carnegie Hall.

Most frequently performed of the three, *Carnival Overture* is the one originally intended to portray life. If that seems too large a topic for ten minutes of music, remember that Dvořák was a country boy who reached beyond humble village roots to achieve international success in the arts. The boisterous spirit of the piece may reflect the pastoral celebrations he recalled from childhood, with much exuberant folk dancing on display. It may also be representative of another tradition: the spring "Carnival" festival known in some lands as Mardi Gras. In either case, it would be the high-spirits of life that are spotlighted, and this convivial music achieves that task perfectly.

♪♪♪♪

Rimsky-Korsakov: *Russian Easter Overture,* op. 36

The catalog of Russian composer Nicolai Rimsky-Korsakov (1844 – 1908) shows him to be rather a composer with a one-track mind. In various periods of his life, he tended to concentrate on particular genres, producing multiple works of a single type, as if he were determined to get it exactly right before attempting anything new. In 1887 and 1888, orchestra music stood high on his personal radar, leading to the creation in rapid succession of three of his most widely beloved works: *Scheherazade,* op. 34; *Capriccio Espagnol,* op. 35; and the *Russian Easter Overture, op. 36.*

The last of the three chronologically is the *Russian Easter Overture,* based firmly in the music of the Eastern Orthodox Church. After searching through a collection of church canticles, Rimsky-Korsakov selected several favorite melodies and wove them into a descriptive overture evoking the jubilant traditions of the Russian Easter.

According to the composer himself, the first two tunes, "Let God Arise" and "An Angel Wailed," suggested to him Isaiah's prophecy concerning the resurrection of Christ. In these passages, the composer offsets a shadowed mood with glittering harp scales and a rising clarinet solo. The bulk of the piece, a triumphant allegro strongly seasoned with brass, draws upon the melody, "Let Them That Also Hate Him Flee

Before Him." Here Rimsky-Korsakov includes the joyous pealing of bells, so central to the Russian religious tradition.

The resulting scene is not merely a religious celebration, but also a more earthy springtime festival, and for the composer, both were equally critical. As he asserted in his autobiography, "this legendary and heathen side of the holiday, this transition from the gloomy and mysterious evening of Passion Saturday to the unbridled pagan-religious merry-making on the morn of Easter Sunday, is what I was eager to reproduce in my Overture."

♪♪♪♪

Elgar: *In the South, op. 50*

When a composer is English, as was Sir Edward Elgar (1857 – 1934), he might mean many things by the phrase 'in the south." It could simply mean the coast of the English Channel. Alternatively, it could refer to anything south of the English Channel, which would be the bulk of Europe and much of the rest of the world. Elgar himself, son of a church organist in the English cathedral town of Worcester, attested that what he had in mind was Italy.

Elgar first visited Italy in the winter of 1903-4. Although he was already past forty years of age, he had only recently found much success in his musical career, with the premiere in 1899 of his grand orchestral work called the *Enigma Variations*. Then, in 1901, came the first and most famous of his five *Pomp and Circumstance* Marches. The time seemed ripe for a winter in Italy.

Elgar later declared that the trigger event that set him working on his musical souvenir of the trip was witnessing a shepherd playing his pipe in the shadow of an ancient Roman ruin. The juxtaposition of the peasant with the grand memories of the Caesars set Elgar to thinking and a musical work began to form in his mind. "The rest," he eventually observed, "was merely writing it down."

Musically, listeners are presented with both the shepherd's pipe and the forceful spirit of ancient Rome, contrasted with a joyous melody that may represent the Englishman himself on this first Southern excursion.

At the time he began the work, he would not have known that he would be knighted by King Edward VII during the following summer. 1905 was, indeed, a good year for Elgar.

♪♪♪♪

Richard Strauss: *Also Sprach Zarathustra, op. 30*

It seems a simple idea: compose an instrumental composition that is intended to evoke a particular mental image. Program music, it's called, and it was a particular favorite of the 19th century Romantic Era composers. They loved nothing more than an imaginative story to express in their music, particularly one that they could mine from literature.

Richard Strauss (1864 – 1949) was one of the most devoted composers of program music of his time, with roughly a dozen such works in his catalog. Some depict straightforward images, as in his *An Alpine Symphony*, which takes one up and down a mountain, with all the sights along the trail. More complicated is the intellectually dense material to be found in *Also sprach Zarathustra*, inspired by the Friedrich Nietzsche (1844 – 1900) work of the same name. Very broadly speaking, it deals with how mankind might evolve to a higher existence, and as such, it ideally suited to the setting in which its introduction became most familiar: Stanley Kubrick's 1969 film *2001: A Space Odyssey*.

After the final rehearsal for the work's Frankfurt premiere, the composer wrote gleefully to his wife Pauline, "Zarathustra is glorious --- by far the most important of all my pieces, the most perfect in form, the richest in content and the most individual in character... The Passion theme is overwhelming, the Fugue spine-chilling, the Dance Song simply delightful. I'm enormously happy and very sorry that you can't hear it... In short, I'm a fine fellow, after all, and feel just a little pleased with myself." He conducted the work's premiere November 27, 1896, and within days took it to Berlin. In the years to follow, *Zarathustra* continued to remain before the public, benefiting from Strauss' thriving career as a guest conductor.

Zarathustra is written in eight continuous sections, each with a subtitle borrowed from Nietzsche. It begins with a sunrise scene that, thanks to Stanley Kubrick, is two of the most famous minutes in all of classical music. This bold fanfare, ever increasing in pitch and dynamics, will reappear throughout *Zarathustra* as a Nature motif, and is the musical motto that appears at the head of Chapter One of this collection.

The turbulent Passion theme, that had so pleased Strauss in rehearsal, appears in the fourth movement, "Of Joys and Passions." His fugue appears in movement six, "Of Science," and, given the complicated interactions of melodies in a fugue, relating one to science seems particularly apt. The Dance Song, which Strauss himself called "delightful," is a joyous waltz that appears in the next to last movement of the full suite.

Strauss concludes his musical vision not as Nietzsche had – in troubled darkness – but rather with gentle ambiguity. He offers no more answers than Nietzsche did, yet manages to hold out hope. The difference in their interpretations may be further reflected in the fact that, of the two men, it was Nietzsche, not Strauss, who spent his last years in emotional disarray.

♪♪♪♪

Dukas: *The Sorcerer's Apprentice*

Although Paul Dukas (1865 – 1935) was a classmate of Claude Debussy (1862 – 1918) at the Paris Conservatoire, their musical styles are quite different. Debussy, featured elsewhere in this collection, came to be identified with the gentle textures of Impressionism. Dukas, by contrast, preferred his music stronger, more assertive, and at times influenced by German styles. Despite being longer lived, Dukas was the less prolific composer, largely because he was highly self-critical and allowed little of his music to survive. One of the rare works of which he approved was one that would ultimately accompany Mickey Mouse on a magical adventure. Its brisk, wry marching theme for brooms appeared at the head of this chapter.

More Classical Insights

Dukas' most enduring work, *The Sorcerer's Apprentice*, premiered May 18, 1897. Its direct inspiration was a ballad by Johann Wolfgang von Goethe (1749 – 1832), though the tale may have originated in ancient Greece. In vivid musical phrases, Dukas tells of the misadventures of a presumptuous apprentice, a young man – or mouse, as Disney tells it in *Fantasia* – who wishes to assume for himself the magical powers of his master. In the absence of his superior, the apprentice dons the magic hat and uses its powers to command a broom to carry water. All seems well, until the broom performs its task too well, leaving the room awash in water. Chopping the broom up into bits is no help, as each splinter becomes a new and equally determined broom. At last, only the timely return of the sorcerer can solve the problem and save the apprentice.

Each moment of the story is gloriously illustrated in Dukas' score, from the shimmering descending line of the opening bars that seems to sing of magic, to the march of the broom in the bassoon, the dreams of power, the apprentice's frantic calls for help, and the dramatic hatchet work. Ominous woodwind phrases hint of the splinters coming back to life; then the bassoon march resumes, soon seized by formidable brass as if to hint of the greater numbers now at work. Water surges through the scene in flowing string lines, and one only feels that the apprentice is safe again when the magical descending lines of the opening return, bringing with them rescue at the hands of the sorcerer. A few brassy chords bring the piece to its determined conclusion, in what Disney interpreted as a slap, though no such action appears in Goethe's original poem. Dukas' music is imaginative, exciting, and to nearly any ears, a marvelous amount of fun.

Betsy Schwarm

♫♫♫♫

Vaughan Williams: *Fantasia on a Theme of Thomas Tallis*

Thomas Tallis (c. 1505 – 1585) was an Elizabethan composer especially known for his choral music. His later countryman Ralph Vaughan Williams (1872 – 1958) was a devotee of earlier English music traditions, which he was determined to rescue from the nation's move to modernity. Sometimes, this determination sent him out to English villages to collect folk songs and dances, so as to bring them into publication. At other times, his attention turned to old English church music, and there stood Thomas Tallis.

When England's Three Choirs Festival (still in business in the 21st century) asked Vaughan Williams to write something for its 1910 event, he decided to craft a work based upon Tallis' hymn "Why Do the Heathens Rage?". Knowing that the new piece would premiere amidst the resonance of Gloucester Cathedral, Vaughan Williams sought to make the most of that spacious atmosphere. He divided his players into three contrasting groups: a string orchestra, a smaller string ensemble, and a solo string quartet. In the resulting composition, he focused on the interplay between these forces, often highlighting one group for a short time, then subtly shifting to another, creating a marvelous contrast of textures.

It works best in a live performance, when one can watch how the different strands of music emerge from different parts of the ensemble. However, even in a recording, one cannot help but be impressed by how much variety Vaughan

Williams finds in what might otherwise seem to be a homogeneous set of players.

♫♫♫♫

Ravel: *Le Tombeau de Couperin*

Born in the foothills of the Pyrenees to parents of Swiss and Basque roots, Maurice Ravel (1875 – 1937) was raised in Paris, where he developed interests in diverse cultures. Anything from ancient Greece to Edgar Allen Poe might find its way into his music. However, he was not immune to French culture, and his *Le Tombeau de Couperin* is a product of that side of his interests.

The title translates as "The Tomb of Couperin," though the music is not at all as grim as that image might seem to imply. It is less a mausoleum for than a remembrance of the French Baroque composer François Couperin (1668 – 1733), who shall appear in Chapter Six. Here, rather than offering variations upon Couperin's own melodies, Ravel crafts his own in honor of the sparkling style of Couperin's harpsichord pieces. He originally completed the work in 1917 as a six-movement solo piano suite; then in 1920, he orchestrated four of the movements, those he felt best suited to elaboration with a larger variety of instrumental timbres. In either version, one finds prominent presence of Baroque-style dance rhythms, and the old Baroque idea of a "suite" being a collection of such dances.

That *Tombeau* is sunny and high-spirited not only belies the title, but also the circumstances under which it was written. After all, in the years just prior to 1917, France was embroiled in war, and Ravel had chosen to enlist. Nearly 40 years old, world famous, and short of stature, he could have been exempted. However, he was determined to serve, and spent much of the war serving as a medic and a military truck driver. His health – both physical and emotional – was badly undermined. When Ravel came home, he had become, as his friends attested, a sad and cynical man, though none of that darkness found its way into this particular composition.

The various movements of *Tombeau* were dedicated to friends who had perished in the war. The effervescence of the music suggests that it was more their spirits Ravel was remembering than their deaths.

♫♫♫♫

Respighi: *Trittico Botticelliano (Three Botticelli Pictures)*

Think of it as an Italian *Pictures at an Exhibition*, in this case music of an Italian composer who had studied in Russia, homeland of that more famous artistically inspired work by Modest Mussorgsky (1839 – 1881). *Three Botticelli Pictures*, composed in 1927 by Ottorino Respighi (1879 – 1936) similarly attempts to capture the spirit of visual art in the aural medium of music. Respighi found inspiration in Florence's Uffuzi Gallery collection of paintings by the Renaissance master Sandro Botticelli. Rather than seeking to capture exact scenes, it is the atmosphere of these paintings that inspired him, with the general moods suffusing his music. That Respighi happened to be a scholar of Renaissance music may have further influenced his choice of inspirations.

More Classical Insights

Respighi begins the orchestral suite with "Primavera" (Springtime), in which Botticelli shows a gathering of scantily clad forest nymphs dancing around the goddess of springtime in a forest glade. The painting also depicts a darker spirit, for the north wind intrudes from the right, frightening one of the dancers. However, Respighi's music is concerned primarily with springtime frolics, as the dance rhythms of the music make clear.

The second painting is Botticelli's Christmas themed "The Adoration of the Magi," in which a throng of people, many in Renaissance dress, gather around Mary and the Christ child at the manger. Respighi evokes an appropriately reverent mood, even adding a specifically Christmas element with phrases from the ancient hymn "O Come, O Come Emanuel."

For the last movement, Respighi returns to mythological imagery as portrayed in Botticelli's most famous work, "The Birth of Venus." Here, the goddess of youth and beauty arises from the sea standing naked on a scallop shell, her long hair waving in the wind as spirits gather near to worship and clothe her. Here, Respighi opts for an up tempo mood with flowing string phrases that seem to speak of the waves wafting Venus and the shell to shore.

Taken as a whole, it is a rare example of an Italian composer who, unlike most of his countrymen, rarely bothered with opera but instead found his delight in orchestral color, colors as vivid as those in Botticelli's original paintings. The work is dedicated to the American arts patron Elizabeth Sprague Coolidge, who founded the Berkshire Festival of Chamber Music in 1918.

♪♪♪♪

Enesco: *Rumanian Rhapsodies*

Born in Romania when it was still in the Austrian Empire, Georges Enesco (1881 – 1955) received most of his music education in Paris. There, he altered the spelling of his name into the form in which it is now almost universally given and made contact with some of the leading figures in classical music. He also managed to establish for himself an international reputation. With the post-World War I death of the Austrian Empire in the near future, the change of home base might have saved his career.

Despite his foreign base of operation, Enesco did not forget his homeland, and evoked its spirit in several of his compositions. Most famed of these are the two Rumanian Rhapsodies, both composed in 1901. In his memoirs, Enesco much later claimed that he didn't care for the Rhapsodies, but admitted that this fact was partially due to their excessive popularity. Certainly, they helped his name to gain much familiarity with the music-loving public, due to their exciting variety, with intensely vibrant rhythms giving way to passages of lovely lyricism.

The first of the Rhapsodies is the more effusive of the two, as it virtually begs the audience to indulge in dancing; the second Rhapsody is more lamenting in mood, drawing on the somber side of Rumanian folk songs. Although Enesco would also write five symphonies, three orchestral suites, an opera, and dozens of chamber works, of all his works, the Rhapsodies have held the strongest place in the public attention.

More Classical Insights

♪♪♪♪

Varèse: *Amériques*

Given that the title is spelled *Amériques*, it will likely come as no surprise that the composer was Parisian-born. One might consider it as a French mirror image of Gershwin's *An American in Paris* though without the jazz influence. *Amériques* is the work of Edgard Varèse (1883 – 1965), his first large piece after he moved to the US in 1917. Although it dates from 1921, *Amériques* would not premiere for another few years, when Leopold Stokowski conducted with the Philadelphia Orchestra April 9, 1926. That initial version was a massive undertaking, less for its length (rather less than half an hour) than for its performing forces: well over 120, including fifteen percussionists using everything from timpani to police sirens. For its European premiere, Varèse trimmed the numbers back somewhat, though the orchestra still remained larger and more varied than usual. Few other scores dare to ask for eight horns, two contrabassoons, and a heckelphone (cousin of the oboe). The percussion complement alone guarantees a powerful visual and aural experience.

Later in his career, Varèse would become one of the most prominent names in electronic music. Here, all the instruments are acoustic, but so used as to create a rich tapestry of sounds, often urban in inspiration. At times, it is gentle, as if evoking the recently-departed Debussy. At other times, it is all demonic frenzy, making even the biggest moments of Stravinsky's *The Rite of Spring*, which predates *Amériques* by less than a decade, seem moderate by comparison. It is, apparently, less a Frenchman's impressions of America itself than a Frenchman reacting to the diversified artistic climate of New York City. In a community where "anything goes," one must go far to make an impact, and Varèse managed to go far indeed, taking his listeners along on the journey.

♪♪♪♪♪

Webern: *Im Sommerwind (In the Summer Wind)*

Anton Webern (1883 – 1945) was one of the most progressive of early 20th century composers, using all the cutting edge techniques of the day and even inventing some of his own. One would never know that from *Im Sommerwind*, a lush and rapturous tone poem for orchestra completed in 1904. At the time, Webern was a young Viennese of no particular fame, and *Im Sommerwind* is more an attempt to master existing styles than a step out on his own. As such, it is a fine opportunity to explore Webern's music without needing to have an understanding of pointillism or Twelve-tone techniques, both of which dominate his later music but not this work.

The title of *Im Sommerwind* derives from the work of the German writer Bruno Wille, Webern's elder contemporary. Webern composed it on a summer holiday at his family's vacation home in Austria's Carinthia; imagine placid lakes and forested hills, and one has the idea of the surroundings. The music is marvelously evocative of such a setting, its serene lines and languid moods ideal for lounging in a pretty place with a view. Although strings are dominant, there are also woodwinds, brass, and percussion, adding up to the largest orchestra that Webern ever used in a composition. Rich, rapturous passages arise from time to time, but the most frequent mood is one of a restful idyll. Musically, it is more of a summer breeze than a summer wind.

About a quarter hour in length, *Im Sommerwind* is yet the longest single movement Webern ever composed. He would eventually develop a reputation as a miniaturist: saying a great deal in very short fragments of music. *Im Sommerwind* was sufficiently different from the direction in which Webern's style developed that he never published it; the work only came to print in the 1960s, well after its composer's death.

♪♪♪♪

Honegger: *Pastorale d'ete (Summer Pastorale)*

Whether he was Swiss or French is rather a matter of interpretation, but the official nationality of Arthur Honegger (1892 – 1955) was Swiss, a fact he never troubled himself to alter. His parents were Swiss, but he was born in Le Havre, France, where his father was working as a coffee importer. Formal piano studies would begin back in Zurich, though for composition training, he came to Paris. By the time he was in his 30s, Honegger had gained international fame, and in 1931, when the Boston Symphony was commissioning works in honor of its 50th anniversary, his name was on their list.

Honegger composed in all genres, including film scores, but one of his most popular pieces is the tone *Pastorale d'ete,* from 1920. There are no specific summer incidents to relate, or at least, Honegger never identified them. However, one does find a general sense of an occasion. Honegger's chosen title implies the scene, and the music adds the further thought that this might be a morning scene. He seems disinterested in summer storms or even oppressive heat; rather, Honegger has composed music for a breakfast in the garden, with someone else to do the washing up. It is a sleepy, rhapsodic score filled with long, lyrical string lines, bird-like woodwind phrases and French horns as if from very far away. For Honegger, summer seems to be a very pleasant thing, indeed.

♪♪♪♪

Grofé: *Grand Canyon Suite*

Born in New York City, Ferde Grofé (1892 – 1972) yet came to embody the American Southwest for many a music lover, as it is he who composed the *Grand Canyon Suite*. It came about when the young man was playing in the viola section of the Los Angeles Symphony Orchestra and spent some spare time travelling in the West. Sights and sounds inspired him, and though the work took years to come to fruition, it is Grofé's best-known composition.

By the 1930s, Grofé had come to be associated with the band leader Paul Whiteman (1890-1967) as staff arranger. Having completed a preliminary form of the *Grand Canyon Suite*, he persuaded his boss to premiere it with the band. Yet in his heart, Grofé knew that only an entire orchestra could do justice to the canyon's grandeur. In 1933, he had his chance, when he was appointed conductor of the Capitol Theater Orchestra on Broadway. He revised the suite for this ensemble, and at last audiences could hear the *Grand Canyon Suite* as it had always resounded in its creator's imagination.

The suite is in five movements, each linked by Grofé's use of a musical theme that represents the canyon itself. The first movement is "Sunrise," the second "The Painted Desert," the third the familiar "On the Trail" with its clip-clopping burro hoof beats in the percussion and evocative hee-haw effects. Fourth comes "Sunset" and the fifth is "Cloudburst," though the storm clears in time for the music to end calmly. It is a pattern that might remind some listeners of Beethoven's "Pastorale" Symphony no. 6, and certainly the works have something in common, for both represent their composers' reactions to natural beauty.

The *Grand Canyon Suite* is not Grofé's only important appearance in the history of music. During Grofé's time with Paul Whiteman, the conductor had invited George Gershwin to write a piano concerto that the band could premiere with Gershwin as soloist. The resulting work, *Rhapsody in Blue*, had been written in a great hurry, and Gershwin ran out of time before the band's individual parts could be prepared. Grofé managed this for him, readying the piece for its premiere February 12, 1924. So even before his *Grand Canyon Suite* came to be, Grofé had made his mark in music.

♪♪♪♪

Gershwin: *An American in Paris*

In the first third of the 20th century, many American composers traveled to Paris. Some were merely visitors. Others came to study, but all were attracted by the vibrant ambiance of this most cosmopolitan city. One such traveler was George Gershwin (1898 – 1937), who arrived in Paris in 1928. Gershwin already had a strong reputation for his popular and jazz music. With the recent success of the semi-classical *Rhapsody in Blue*, Gershwin now had his eye on the classical scene. He wanted to study composition with the best-known pedagogues in Paris, but, fearful of being charged with ruining Gershwin's natural skills, no one would touch him.

Although his plans of study were unfulfilled, Gershwin's visit was not completely unproductive. When he boarded the ship for his return to New York, Gershwin had already begun work on what would become *An American in Paris*. The tone poem premiered at Carnegie Hall December 13, 1928. Also on that New York Philharmonic program were the Franck Symphonie in d minor (see Chapter Two) and Wagner's *Magic Fire Music* from his opera *The Valkyrie*.

Gershwin's score offers a kaleidoscope of musical impressions, opening with a light-hearted strolling melody soon interrupted by the honking of taxi horns. A busy street scene ensues, then melancholy bluesy melodies, brought to quick close by the return of Gershwin's dominant lively mood. Throughout, the work displays how effectively this star of the jazz world had internalized the sound of the orchestra. He may have been turned down for advanced studies with the big names in the field, but he had kept his ears engaged and learned what he needed to know to make the most of orchestral color.

Incidentally, the Gene Kelly film that shares its name with Gershwin's composition does, indeed, use its music. However, the film appeared years after the composer's passing, and though inspired by the composition, cannot be said to portray exactly what Gershwin had in mind.

More Classical Insights

♪♪♪♪

Ellington: *Black, Brown and Beige*

If Edward "Duke" Ellington (1899 – 1974) were only the composer of "Satin Doll," he would not be in this collection. However, this unsurpassed master of big band swing also had a vision of broader horizons. One might write many hundreds of three-minute tunes – Ellington himself was not sure how many he'd composed – but eventually, a great artist has something bigger to express. So Duke spread his wings into the classical realm, producing a pair of ballets and a handful of orchestral tone poems.

One of the latter is *Black, Brown, and Beige*, which premiered at Carnegie Hall early in 1943. Ellington attested that it was meant as a tribute to African-American culture. By his account, the opening "Black" movement is a tribute to traditions of prayer and work. The second "Brown" movement remembers the sacrifice of African-American soldiers in the Civil War and later conflicts. For the finale, "Beige," Ellington turns to the Harlem Renaissance, with an evocation of the jazz clubs where he had first built his reputation.

Musically, the first and third movements are strong with the drive of big band swing rhythms; melodic fragments recur in other sections of the ensemble for the sake of melodic unity. The more elegiac middle movement offers relaxed moods. Even Vivaldi would have structured a work in much the same fashion – though with less syncopation – so the jazz master had learned from long-standing classical traditions.

♪♪♪♪

Shostakovich: *Jazz Suites* 1 and 2

Given the imposing tone of much of the music by Dmitri Shostakovich (1906 – 1975), one would likely be surprised to find amidst his catalog anything with the unlikely title of *Jazz Suite,* let alone two of them. Moreover, why would a dyed-in-the-wool Russian – so very Russian that he tolerated the Soviet system rather than abandon his homeland – be writing jazz, and how jazzy would the resulting score be? The answer to the latter question is "not very." Gershwin and Ellington wouldn't have called it jazz, as there is no improvisation and little syncopation. Rather, Shostakovich's *Jazz Suites* are more like café music: light background music for an ensemble the size of a big band, though with more strings than the jazz greats used.

The first of the suites dates from 1934, and was composed for a competition in the composer's native Leningrad that sought to raise the standard for what passed for Soviet jazz. The second suite followed in 1938 at the request of the State Orchestra for Jazz. Given the times, the Soviets were determined to prove that they could match Western achievements, and as long as the question centered on musical achievements, Shostakovich was content to cooperate. Although neither suite is quite jazz in the purest sense, both are enjoyable diversions with light, danceable themes. They serve as valuable evidence of the diverse musical ideas that could come from a single masterful imagination.

More Classical Insights

♪♪♪♪

Jenkins: *Palladio*

The name of Welsh composer Karl Jenkins (b. 1944) is less familiar in the US than in his native Britain, where his albums have been regular top sellers. There, he frequently appears high on favorite classics lists, his patrons include Prince Charles, and his honors include an Order of the British Empire (OBE) presented by Queen Elizabeth II. Yet even in the US, the sound of his music is familiar to many of those who don't know his name, as he composed the lyrical string theme used for the long-running DeBeers diamond television advertisements. Those who fondly recall those ads will delight in his *Palladio*, completed in 1996, for the advertisement theme appears prominently in the first of the work's three movements.

As for the non-diamond related title of this three movement suite, Andrea Palladio (1508 – 1580) was an esteemed architect of the Italian Renaissance whose designs have been widely copied, and whose book on architectural style and technique is still in print five centuries after his birth. To envision Palladio's ideas, consider Jefferson's Monticello, closely based upon the architect's approach to similar country estates in Italy. Jenkins' composition offers comparably graceful lines and balanced proportions, as it recalls the classic ideal of a work in three movements (the first and third calling for fast tempi, the second slower for contrast) devoted to the rich voices of strings.

Each of the three movements is somewhat more expansive than the one that precedes it, and each features recurring rhythmic elements that span the course of the movement. Often, these rhythms are almost minimalist in nature, underlain by a steady pulse and much driving energy. Although the second movement is more tentative in mood, it, too, features a steady background pulsation. The last movement, longest of the three, expands midway into an urgent galloping spirit, which, despite the utter absence of brass and percussion, yet manages to evoke determined motion. Throughout the score, though particularly in the last movement, Jenkins plays with shifting colors and keys for the sake of contrast. One might not have imagined that a simple string ensemble could provide such marked variety, but Jenkins proves the case.

♪♪♪♪

Torke: *Javelin*

The music of American composer Michael Torke (b. 1961) tends to be vividly colored, making the most of instrumental forces – often grand ones – to convey varied and diverse images. Here, after all, is a composer whose catalog includes works called *Ecstatic Orange* and *Bright Blue Music*.

Torke is not a man likely to name a new composition anything descriptive but mundane, such as Symphony no. 4 in C major. In Torke's view, a title should not just say how the work is structured, but instead should communicate something about its inner personality. Upon writing a work inspired in part by the Atlanta Summer Olympics of 1996 and athletically naming it *Javelin*, Torke admitted the title might also relate to the American muscle car of the same name.

Javelin was, indeed, associated with the Summer Olympics of 1996. However, having also intended to produce something for the Atlanta Symphony's 50th anniversary season of 1994/95, Torke completed the score over a year before the Olympics, in time for it to premiere in Atlanta September 8, 1994. Of the piece, the composer observes that he "wanted to use the orchestra as a virtuosic instrument," so that no single section would dominate. Rather, nearly every section gets its opportunity to shine, and the most is made of the contrasting voices of one section against another.

Given the selection of instruments that Torke requires, there is much opportunity for contrast. In addition to the usual suspects, one also finds piccolo, English horn, E-flat clarinet, bass clarinet, harp, and a vast assortment of percussion: timpani, glockenspiel, vibraphone, tambourine, triangle, claves, snare drum, bass drum, wood block, and suspended cymbals. Each time a melodic fragment moves to a new place in the ensemble, it takes on distinctive new shading.

In all, Torke says "What came out (somewhat unexpectedly) was a sense of valor among short flashes and sweeps." As the composer suggests, listeners will find "flashes" and "sweeps" galore, with much sparkle and color. Whether one is thinking of the Olympics or of a classic American car, or even of a fine orchestra reaching a landmark in its history, all those adjectives seem to apply, connecting Torke's electrifying composition to multiple images. In the two centuries since the passing of Mozart, orchestral music had taken on an impressive degree of vibrancy.

Puts: *River's Rush*

In the days before motorized transportation, a powerful river was often the most efficient means of getting from one place to another. Give a city two such rivers and it becomes a transportation hub. Such is the heritage of St. Louis, Missouri, and it was for that city's main orchestra that Kevin Puts (b. 1972 in Michigan) composed his *River's Rush* in 2004. Although the most prominent ensembles to perform his music in concert are from the Northeast – including the Boston Pops and the National Symphony Orchestra of Washington, DC – here he crafted a work specifically with his own native Midwest in mind.

The work is replete with propulsive energy as rising and falling arpeggios gradually develop into melodic material. Often, Puts sets one melody simultaneously against another, as if evoking how the Mississippi and Missouri Rivers come together at St. Louis, but for a while flow side by side, rather than immediately mixing their waters. With strings matched by harp, piano, a full complement of woodwinds and brass, and four percussionists, Puts has a varied palette of instrumental colors at his disposal. It is music for an epic adventure, like those that early explorers would have experienced on either of the region's great rivers.

Chapter Four: Concertos

These are not the very first notes from this work by Edvard Grieg (1843 – 1907); those belonged to the orchestra. However, immediately after the orchestra seizes the attention of the audience, the pianist storms in with this bold melodic fragment, leaving listeners in no doubt that this work is mostly about the pianist. Indeed, when Grieg's only Piano Concerto is being performed, the vast majority of eyes and ears will be focused on the soloist.

That's what a concerto is: a work that is mostly about the soloist, and how he or she is balanced against the orchestra. Ideally, that balance should be resolved more or less amicably, with everyone satisfied with the amount of spotlight he or she receives. All concerned must have an equally vested interest in the overall effect of the music. This can be a challenge when the orchestra and its conductor have a strong sense of self, or when there is more than one soloist, as is the case with some of the works in this chapter. However, if the composer knows his or her business – and all those chosen for this chapter do – then musical fisticuffs can be avoided.

Sometimes, one will encounter the word "concerti" as the plural of a single concerto. There's nothing technically wrong with that word; it's the Italianate form of what

English-speakers would call "concertos," and it's been in use for centuries. Mozart used it, and he wasn't even Italian. However, since one of the goals of this collection is to demystify the art form, I've chosen to use instead the more customary English plural. So Antonio Vivaldi (1678 – 1741) composed several hundred violin concertos; Peter Tchaikovsky (1840 – 1893) composed exactly one.

Seven of the 25 concertos in this chapter have more than one soloist, one of those seven having an entire orchestra worth of solo parts. Another concerto has just one person acting as soloist, but myriad solo instruments: such is the nature of works that feature percussion instruments, for percussionists like to demonstrate the impressive variety of tools at their disposal. The other works all have one soloist each, more often than not, wielding either a violin or a piano. This is not due to my personal preference; rather, the vast majority of concertos were conceived as showcases for one or the other of those instruments, often because that is the instrument of which the composer himself was master.

A determined effort has been made to include some less likely suspects in the solo role, especially as works from the 20th and 21st centuries were reached. So this chapter also contains concertos for most of the woodwind section, including saxophone, as well as French horns, trombone, and even guitar. Given a composer with imagination, and, perhaps, inspiration provided by some particular soloist, any instrument can be deserving of a turn in the spotlight.

♪♪♪♪

More Classical Insights

Vivaldi: Four-Violin Concerto in b minor,
    RV 580, op. 3, no. 10

Antonio Vivaldi (1678 – 1741) was known as the "Red Priest" for his hair and his occupation. The hair may have stayed red, but the role of priest was purely temporary. Vivaldi gave up saying mass almost immediately after his ordination in 1703, claiming that respiratory problems prevented him from taking part in the service. However, even at the time, skeptics suggested that Padre Vivaldi simply preferred music to sermons. Before long, he had been named violin instructor at the Ospedale della Pieta, an orphan girl's school in Venice. He would later rise to be director of all the school's music programs, though he was more often on the concert circuit with his own violin than in his office tending to school business.

Vivaldi's affiliation with the Ospedale and the lasting support of his numerous other patrons allowed him to produce a vast amount of music. The actual figures are still under debate. However, evidence suggests that he crafted about 500 concertos, most of them for violin, as well as a great quantity of other works. Much of his music was not published until long after his death, when there was a revival of interest in his music in the early 20th century. However, his concert appearances led to demand for many of the concertos, and a quantity of these came to print in the composer's own time. One of these is the concerto that concerns us at the moment.

Vivaldi's Four-Violin Concerto in b minor was one of a set of twelve concertos published together as his opus 3 with a dedication to the Grand Prince of Tuscany, and bearing the overall title "L'estro armonico" (The Inspiration of

Harmony). The set was published in Amsterdam in 1711, as the first of Vivaldi's works to come to print outside of Italy. Each of the twelve concertos features the violin, sometimes just one soloist, sometimes two, sometimes four, as in the case of the b minor concerto. Thanks to the wider distribution that came with a foreign publisher, the set of concertos came to wider attention than his earlier published works.

The b minor one came into the hands of Johann Sebastian Bach (1685 – 1750), at the time a little-known court musician and composer in central Germany. Bach was so intrigued by Vivaldi's work and how the Italian kept each of his soloists equally occupied in turn, that he made a transcription of this concerto, altering the four violins into four harpsichords and changing the key to a minor so as to better suit the changed soloists. In this form, and in Bach's catalog, rather than Vivaldi's, it is designated BWV 1065. It is unlikely that Bach would have bothered to create this transcription had Vivaldi's original score not impressed him, which makes it particularly rewarding to go back and rediscover the original piece.

♫♫♫♫

JS Bach: Concerto in d minor for two violins, BWV 1043, "Double Concerto"

Johann Sebastian Bach (1685 – 1750) was and is most strongly identified with the harpsichord and the organ. However, he was also a fine violinist. In the violin works he produced, one finds clear evidence of his close familiarity with what the instrument can do.

This is nowhere clearer than in the concerto widely known as his Double Concerto. Some of his harpsichord concertos also have two soloists; however, the one called the "Double" is for two violins, with the harpsichord present only as "basso continuo" support for the orchestral ensemble.

The concerto's surviving manuscript bears no date, but evidence suggests that it was written during his years with the small royal court in Cőthen, Germany. This was a happy time in his career, when according to his letters to relatives, he felt his music was particularly appreciated. It is unlikely that he wrote the concerto after that time, as his subsequent move to Leipzig in 1722 shifted his attention more toward sacred music with little time left for instrumental pieces.

Throughout the concerto, there is much echoing of themes from one soloist to the other, with occasional passages in which the orchestra briefly takes the lead, as if to give the soloists a break. Often, Bach draws upon techniques of fugues, in which several layers of carefully structured melodies are heard simultaneously, with each melody moving from one set of instruments to another. It was a technique he would soon bring to its highest form in the organ works of Leipzig, but here he shows that an orchestra and soloists, too, can manage complicated interwoven themes.

Later, this master of transcription – in fact, master of nearly all things musical – reworked the Double so that the two violins were replaced by two harpsichords. The change allowed Bach to make the solo parts even more complicated, as a violin can manage no more than two notes at a time, but a keyboard instrument can manage many more. In the process of transcribing it, Bach transposed it as well, slightly lowering the key to c minor. The BWV catalog gives this rather new work a different number, making it BWV 1062.

♪♪♪♪

Mozart: Piano Concerto no. 17 in G major, K. 453

Music historians have long blessed Wolfgang Amadeus Mozart (1756 – 1791) for his habit of writing completion dates at the ends of his manuscripts. Since he did so for nearly everything he wrote in the last decade of his life, we can be reasonably certain that his Piano Concerto no. 17 was completed April 12, 1784, the last of four piano concertos that he had written in a two month period. Spring was usually busy for Mozart, as the sacred time of Lent caused dramatic theaters – but not concert halls – to close. Lacking competition from theaters, concert attendance soared, and the showman in Mozart's heart was not about to miss a good opportunity. As a gifted pianist, he would want some new music to perform on these concerts, hence the series of concertos.

With such a busy schedule of concert appearances, Mozart certainly played his new Concerto no. 17 himself. However, the specific person for whom it was first intended was his piano student, Barbara von Ployer. The young lady was clearly a talented musician, for this concerto demands grace and fluidity from the soloist with little use of routine techniques. On the occasion of the concerto's premiere June 13, 1784, Fraulein von Ployer took the solo part, then joined with her teacher in a performance of his Two-Piano Sonata, K. 448. Mozart had invited the influential composer Giovanni Paisiello (1740 – 1816) to witness both the student and the music. Although his letters reveal that

Mozart preferred composing over teaching, he must have been gratified to count such a talented young artist amongst his protégés.

Fraulein von Ployer was not the only creature of Mozart's acquaintance to carry this concerto in her repertoire. His pet starling also knew the work, for Mozart had devoted some idle moments to teaching the bird the principal theme of the last movement, a theme that is, admittedly, rather chirpy and bird-like in nature. Yet the starling was an imperfect student. One note it sang wrong every time and, according to a remark the composer made in a letter to family, another note was consistently held too long. It seems that even the example of the concerto's creator was insufficient to convince Mozart's starling to sing the piece exactly as written. Perhaps the starling had listened closely enough to the set of variations that Mozart builds upon that melody that it decided to try a variation of its own.

♫♫♫♫

Beethoven: Triple Concerto in C major, op. 56

In the length of his career, Ludwig van Beethoven (1770 – 1827) composed exactly seven full concertos. Five of them were for solo piano, the instrument he personally played, and most of those were premiered by Beethoven himself. Another concerto was for solo violin, and was intended for a colleague of the composer's. The only other multi-movement concerto that he composed, standing exactly midway in the run of seven concertos, is the so-called "Triple Concerto" for piano, violin, cello, and orchestra.

The three solo instruments are often found in the realm of chamber music as what was called a "piano trio." Beethoven's first published work, his opus 1, had been a set of three piano trios and more would follow. Moreover, he was himself considered one of the most astonishing pianists in Vienna, and had plenty of colleagues on whom he could draw to fill the other two solo parts. He knew enough about the workings of a piano trio, about what each of those three instruments did particularly well, so as to be well equipped to balance the solo parts.

Never a quick composer, Beethoven began work on the Triple Concerto in 1804 and at least a year passed before it reached completion. Its premiere would not be given until the spring of 1808. These were years in which the composer was struggling with encroaching deafness. His letters reveal that he was frequently gutted by anguish – quite reasonable anguish in a man whose life was music. Had this concerto, or any of the works completed in these years, emerged wracked with audible turmoil, no one could have faulted the composer. However, Beethoven sometimes managed to set aside his misery, and such is the case with the Triple Concerto.

According to the composer's sometime friend, Anton Schindler, the piano part was kept simple so as to suit the abilities of the composer's piano student, the Archduke Rudolf, younger brother of the Austrian emperor. However, the piano part is not, in fact, a particularly easy one, and it has always seemed unlikely that the young nobleman would have been able to wrap his fingers around it. Moreover, recent research has indicated that Beethoven and the Archduke may have not become associated in time to make such an intention possible. Since Schindler has been shown in other instances to possess a somewhat creative memory, and since no documentary evidence, such as a program from the premiere, has survived, the story must be regarded as an interesting possibility that cannot be validated.

The concerto was dedicated to Prince Franz Joseph von Lobkowitz, to whom Beethoven would also dedicate his Symphony no. 3, op. 55 (see Chapter Two). The prince was not Beethoven's specific employer; the composer's temperament would not have recommended him to regular aristocratic service. However, the prince was a devoted music lover who often hosted musical soirées in his ballroom. Beethoven was occasionally the chief beneficiary of these high-profile events, and was content to reward his supporter with a dedication.

♪♪♪♪

Donizetti: English Horn Concertino

With over five dozen operas to his name, amongst them the tragic *Lucia di Lammermoor* and the comic *Elixir of Love*, Gaetano Donizetti (1797 – 1848) would seem to be a specialist of the operatic stage. Indeed, even his earliest biographers, setting to work shortly after his death, promoted that interpretation. However, Donizetti's catalog of works is much more varied than that of most other operatic masters. He also composed a great deal of sacred music, many secular songs, and even orchestral pieces, chamber music, and solo piano works. His countrymen Gioacchino Rossini (1792 – 1868) and Giuseppe Verdi (1813 – 1901) together did not produce so many non-operatic scores, and Donizetti's, far from being just curiosities, are well worthy of attention.

Donizetti's Concertino for English Horn and Orchestra premiered in his native Bergamo June 19, 1817, when the composer was not yet twenty. He had already begun to write operas, though these had not yet been performed. For a young unknown to arrange the staging of a full-scale opera was difficult. A short, smaller-scale instrumental piece, such as this concertino, was more readily accommodated.

Less than a quarter hour in length, the Concertino is a set of variations upon a theme, which is first stated by the orchestra and then gradually developed by the soloist. The work begins serenely but then builds in energy, with ever more nimble passagework for the soloist. The final pages are vibrant and effervescent. It is a charming work, all the more valuable in that the English horn (alto cousin of the oboe) has regrettably little solo music in its repertoire. English horn players who have tired of transposing oboe music can thank Donizetti for awarding them this delightful little showpiece.

♪♪♪♪

Chopin: Piano Concerto no. 1 in e minor, op. 11

Only twice did Frederic Chopin (1810 – 1849) produce large-scale compositions, both concertos for piano and orchestra. In 1829, not yet 20 years old, the young pianist wrote a concerto in f minor, which he premiered in his native Poland March 17, 1830. It was so successful that he immediately began work on a second concerto, this time using the differently-shaded key of e minor.

The concerto features some of the most expansive orchestral writing that Chopin would ever produce. However, when the pianist steps in, it is with bold authority, demanding a great variety of skills from the player, who is then rarely out of the spotlight. The gentler second movement, half the length of the first, seems to anticipate the composer's twilight-flavored nocturnes, and the final movement is perky and buoyant, more in the spirit of his waltzes, though the meter is not that of a proper waltz. One could not waltz to it, but one could surely dance and spin. In this one early concerto, Chopin seems to try out the ideas that will flavor the bulk of his compositions for years to come.

At the concerto's premiere in Warsaw October 11, 1830, the piece and its composer were both warmly greeted by an enthusiastic audience. It would be his final concert in Warsaw. Soon after, he would be on the road to Vienna, and then a series of concert performances in the major cities of Europe. Within the year, he would be in Paris, which would be his home base for the rest of his life.

Although the Concerto in e minor was the second concerto that Chopin composed, it was the first to be published. It appeared in print in 1833, three years after its creation, and three years before its companion came to print. Thus, despite its marginally later origin, the Concerto in e minor is known as the Concerto no. 1.

♪♪♪♪♪

Robert Schumann: Concert Piece for four horns
and orchestra, op. 86

Robert Schumann (1810 – 1856) did not play French horn. He was himself an influential music journalist, a composer of moderate reputation, and husband of Clara Wieck Schumann (1819 – 1896), one of the greatest pianists of the age. However in 1849, they were living in Dresden, a city possessed of a magnificent orchestra with an unusually strong horn section. That fact moved Schumann to write a concerto for four horns which stands alone in his or any catalog. No other composer ever felt confident of having four superior horn players at his disposal at the same time. By turns brilliantly vibrant and expressively lyrical, it gets as much out of its solo instruments as anyone could wish.

The work's premiere was given not in Dresden but up the road in Leipzig, February 25, 1850. There in Leipzig, where Robert and Clara had met and married, the orchestra had been long directed by their great friend, Felix Mendelssohn (1809 – 1847). Mendelssohn was now in his grave, but the Schumanns retained affection for the city and its orchestra. Returning there with such a vibrant and triumphant work must have been gratifying, especially as Clara's father had predicted that his new son-in-law would never find success.

♪♪♪♪

Brahms: Double Concerto in a minor, op. 102

Dating from 1887, the Double Concerto by Johannes Brahms (1833 – 1897) was the last work he completed using the orchestra. Here, in having two soloists, Brahms may have hoped to kill two birds with one stone. He had long ago promised his friend, the cellist Robert Hausmann, a solo concerto, but had never gotten around to writing it. Also, Brahms had recently had a falling-out with his long-time colleague, the violinist Joseph Joachim, who felt that Brahms had sided with Joachim's ex-wife during their recent divorce proceedings. Through the balm of one composition, Brahms hoped to soothe all three of their souls. The new concerto premiered in Cologne October 18, 1887, with Brahms conducting and Joachim and Hausmann as the soloists.

Each of the three movements opens with a phrase that becomes the major melodic material for that movement, ever reappearing in varied bits and pieces. Often, fragments of melodies begin with one soloist before moving to the other, until finally both are playing at once with orchestral support. That the cello is usually the soloist to go first may not reflect favoritism on Brahms' part; rather, the darker, weightier tone of the cello may have better served a wish of starting each new idea with authority.

As a change from the assertive storms of the first movement, the second movement is a gentle romance in mood, its phrases rising and falling like sweet sighs. For the finale, Brahms opens with a lively, dance-able melody of alternating quarter and eighth notes that prances effusively along. More flowing themes appear for contrast, though that opening dance theme continues as the main idea. The Double Concerto may have begun in a minor key, but Brahms is clearly determined that it will end in high spirits, as a concerto to combine the efforts of three long-time friends perhaps ought to do.

Betsy Schwarm

♪♪♪♪

Bruch: *Scottish Fantasy, op. 46*

Not one drop of Scottish blood flowed in the veins of Max Bruch (1838 – 1920). Born in Cologne, he was as German as the Rhineland in which he was raised. Yet he managed to compose as charming and evocative a fantasy on Scottish themes as any composer of Celtic origin ever had or ever would. Consider that surprising fact, and another – that though himself Christian, Bruch nonetheless produced a *Kol Nidrei* setting that is radiant with the Jewish spirit – and it becomes clear that this utterly German composer harbored diverse interests and inspirations.

Bruch completed his *Scottish Fantasy* – a folk-flavored violin concerto free in form – in 1880, during the first weeks of his English residency as director of the Liverpool Philharmonic. With that city already in the north of England, the composer found inspiration in an even more northerly locale, thanks to the novels of Sir Walter Scott. Moved by those passionate tales of love and vengeance, Bruch began researching Scotland's traditional tunes, finally selecting four, the most famous of these being the old war song "Scots Wha Hae," on which to base his new work.

The work's exact title when it was published in Berlin late that year was "Fantasie unter freier Benutzung schottischer Volksmelodien," that is, "Fantasy with Free Usage of Scottish Folk Melodies." As a title, it is rather unwieldy, hence the usual contraction to the simpler *Scottish Fantasy*. However, that original title serves to make clear that the melodies are not always quoted in a straight-forward manner. Rather, they are freely reworked according to the composer's imagination. So whether or not a particular listener knows the words to each of the songs becomes less the issue than the fact of their Scottish character – sometimes nimble, sometimes moody – that Bruch manages to preserve, despite his own German origins.

Regardless of its Highland origins, the *Scottish Fantasy*'s premiere was given in Hamburg late in 1880. The virtuoso Spanish violinist, Pablo de Sarasate (1844 – 1908), to whom the piece was dedicated, did the honors as soloist. It is a work that Bruch came to prefer to his more popular Violin Concerto in g minor (1866), a work of which he had sufficiently tired that he begged violinists to please play the *Scottish Fantasy* instead. No one would be more delighted than he to know that it is the less famous, though no less delightful, *Scottish Fantasy* that stands in the spotlight at this moment.

♪♪♪♪

Tchaikovsky: Violin Concerto in D major, op. 35

Few great masterworks have had a more difficult path to success than the only violin concerto by Peter Tchaikovsky (1840 – 1893). He wrote it for a young violinist in whom he had an interest. However, as that fellow, Yosif Kotek, was too little known to premiere the work, Tchaikovsky invited a bigger star, Leopold Auer, to undertake it. Not only did Auer refuse, but he also belittled the piece as being ill-suited to the instrument, and the premiere date that Tchaikovsky had scheduled was cancelled for lack of a soloist. Several other violinists also rejected the opportunity to give the concerto its first performance. At last Tchaikovsky settled for Adolph Brodsky, who premiered the concerto in Vienna December 4, 1881.

At that point, Tchaikovsky might have thought the worst trials were behind him. However, Eduard Hanslick, the most influential of Viennese critics, came to witness the performance and was not impressed. His infamous review reads, in part, as follows:

> "The violin is no longer played; it is beaten black and blue.... Tchaikovsky's Violin Concerto gives us for the first time the hideous notion that there can be music that stinks to the ear."

In Hanslick's defense, he would later have far kinder things to say about Tchaikovsky's Symphony no. 6, but that concession would be after the composer's death. For now, a deeply wounded Tchaikovsky had to face the failure of a major composition. Refusing to blame Brodsky for the debacle, he thanked his colleague for championing the piece, changed the Concerto's dedication from Auer to Brodsky, and chalked it all up to experience.

Years later, Leopold Auer came to praise Tchaikovsky, confessing in the final year of the composer's life that he had misjudged the Concerto and belatedly adding it to his repertoire. Indeed, it is a work with many delights to offer, both to listeners and to performers. Its first movement has a dance-like spirit, its second sings, and its third bustles with action, bringing the concerto to a close with pyrotechnic drama. Tchaikovsky didn't play the violin himself, but he certainly understood what one could do with the instrument.

♪♪♪♪

Grieg: Piano Concerto in a minor, op. 16

Norwegian composer Edvard Grieg (1843 – 1907) was a skillful pianist, but not a strong one. Most of his solo piano music is short and graceful, rather than electrifying, better suiting it to his personal lack of strength. His only Piano Concerto – in fact, his only concerto for any instrument – was premiered by another pianist, a man with greater power and drama at the keyboard. Grieg understood the work required such resources. Its pounding opening lines, quoted at the beginning of this chapter, were simply more than he could manage himself.

The concerto dates from the summer of 1868 when the composer, his wife Nina, and their infant daughter were enjoying a Danish vacation. They had come south from their own native Norway in search of more clement weather, for the 25 year-old composer was suffering from the after-effects of a lung ailment contracted in Leipzig. Denmark's air proved to be at least somewhat curative, and Grieg found the energy to begin and finish this concerto in only a few months. It premiered in Copenhagen to a thunderstorm of acclaim. The soloist for the evening, Edmund Neupert, wrote to Grieg delightedly of the reception it had received.

From that declamatory opening phrase, Grieg proceeded to share fine melodic material between the piano soloist and sections of the orchestra. The serene second movement provided a bit of respite for all, before the charging energy of the finale arrives, tinged with spirited Norwegian folk-dance rhythms. As a whole, it is a work of vibrant colors.

The concerto so impressed the superstar pianist Franz Liszt (1811 – 1886) that in 1869, he invited Grieg to his home in Rome to talk about music and play through the concerto. It inspired the elder composer to declare to Grieg, "You have the right stuff! [Sie haben das Zeug dazu!]" Since that landmark day, generations of pianists and audiences have shown that Liszt's enthusiasm was well-placed. Although Grieg never composed another concerto, this one work does indeed have "the right stuff."

♪♪♪♪

Richard Strauss: Duett-Concertino in F major

Son of the principal hornist at the Munich Court Orchestra, Richard Strauss (1864 – 1949) was exposed to music from his earliest years. He began studying piano at the age of four, started composing at six, and soon was permitted to sit in on his father's rehearsals and performances, provided that music of the dreaded radical Wagner was not on the program. Throughout his long life, Strauss would always adore the works of the man he called "the immortal Mozart." He would eventually become one of the founders of the Salzburg Festival, launched with the particular purpose of bringing greater glory to Mozart's birthplace.

Strauss' own compositions generally feature more Romantic grandeur than Mozartean delicacy, and yet within his lengthy catalog lie significant works that share in Mozart's elegance and serenity. The most obvious example is his opera *Der Rosenkavalier,* which is even set in Mozart's day. Less familiar, but equally Neo-Classical in mood, is the Duett-Concertino, scored for solo bassoon, solo clarinet, strings, and harp.

Dating from the years just after World War II, the Duett-Concertino came into being at the request of Hugo Burghauser, former principal bassoonist of the Vienna Philharmonic, an ensemble that Strauss had conducted on numerous occasions. Although Burghauser had immigrated to the United States in 1938, he had not forgotten his old colleague, and the fact that the term "old" was sadly apropos – Strauss was 82 – did not prove to be a handicap. Strauss completed the piece with months to spare before its premiere April 4, 1948 in Lugano, Switzerland.

Burghauser was not able to attend, but Strauss dedicated the work to him and, in writing to his friend of the piece, he observed, "My father always used to say it was Mozart who wrote most beautifully for the bassoon." In this graceful score, Strauss shows himself worthy of comparison with the master whom he admired above all others.

Imaginative minds hear it as a Beauty-and-the-Beast tale in music, with the two woodwind soloists as the protagonists. Whether or not one finds a fairy tale with it, the Duett-Concertino has plenty of charm and spirit.

♫♫♫♫

Ravel: Piano Concerto for the Left Hand

Privileged son of a wealthy intellectual family, Viennese-born Paul Wittgenstein (1887 – 1961) had envisioned for himself a life as a concert pianist. Then World War I intervened. In 1914, Wittgenstein was critically injured in combat, losing his right arm, then was confined to a prisoner-of-war camp in Siberia. Not until 1916 would he gain release. Home at last, but lacking an arm: a career at the keyboard should have seemed impossible. Yet Wittgenstein would not be denied. Drawing upon his family's financial resources, he began contacting the great composers of the day, asking if they would write for him piano pieces requiring only the left hand. Of the many who agreed, five are featured in this collection: Richard Strauss, Erich Korngold, Benjamin Britten, Sergei Prokofiev, and Maurice Ravel.

At the time that Wittgenstein premiered Ravel's Concerto for the Left Hand in Vienna November 27, 1931, left-hand piano works were not unknown. The Russian composer/pianist Alexander Scriabin (1872 – 1915) had written several such pieces upon straining his right hand through over-practice, and Johannes Brahms (1833 – 1897) produced one for his colleague Clara Schumann (1819 – 1896) under similar circumstances. Those, however, were temporary indispositions. Wittgenstein, by contrast, was attempting to play despite permanent disability. Could it be done? Wouldn't the music fall short with half a pianist in the spotlight? As the works written for him show – and Ravel's is the best known of the collection – such fears were groundless. Although the textures of the pianist's part are of necessity thinner than they would otherwise be, the resulting transparency has an appeal of its own in the clarity of musical line. Moreover, rather than sulking in the lower ranges that are usually the left hand's province, Ravel's solo part ranges across the keyboard, mixing as well with light-hearted woodwinds as it does with the grumbles of timpani.

Many interpreters read war imagery into the Concerto's darker moments. Angry brass, ominous snare drums, and a distant marching beat are seen as evocations of Wittgenstein's experience. Indeed, there may be a connection, yet it is worth remembering that Ravel had his own wartime memories, thanks to a stint as medic and driver near the front. Although he came home physically intact, the emotional blows were real, and Ravel would not have been the first composer to get something off of his chest and into his music. His *Le Tombeau de Couperin* (see Chapter Three) had gently memorialized friends lost to war. If here he returned to the idea in somewhat darker mien, yet he never stays long in melancholy. For every dark theme, there is one of triumph or passion. Although this concerto sorrows, still it sings more than it weeps.

♪♪♪♪

Bartók: Concerto for Orchestra

During the years of World War II, Hungarian composer/pianist Béla Bartók (1881 – 1945) was a political exile, driven from his homeland, living in New York, his music little known, and dying of leukemia. Had he become bitter, no one could have faulted him. Yet Bartók benefited from the attentions of two good friends: the violinist Joseph Szigeti (1892 – 1973) and the conductor Fritz Reiner (1888 – 1963). They, too, were exiled Hungarians, and ensured that Bartók's medical bills were covered. In addition, determining that their ailing friend might benefit from occupational therapy, they convinced conductor Serge Koussevitzky (1874 – 1951) to commission something from

Bartók. Koussevitzky personally delivered the first installment of the fee to the composer's hospital room.

At first, Bartók protested that he was far too weak to begin something new. His weight had fallen below ninety pounds, and he had no expectation of living much longer. Yet Koussevitzky would not be denied. Finally accepting the commission, Bartók found work to be the best possible tonic. Despite his illness, he gained enough strength to leave the hospital and spend the summer of 1943 in the Adirondacks, where, between August 15 and October 8, he completed the Concerto for Orchestra. This sudden burst of activity led to more compositions: a violin sonata for Yehudi Menuhin (1916 – 1999), a third piano concerto for Bartók's wife, and the beginnings of a viola concerto. It was an impressive output for even a healthy man, yet Bartók was far from well. Although he managed to attend the concerto's premiere December 1, 1944, as Koussevitzky conducted the Boston Symphony, Bartók would not survive another year.

Although he rarely bothered to explain his music, Bartók did write program notes for this composition. He clarified the use of the term "concerto" by pointing out that, although there is no single soloist, different instruments and groups of instruments are occasionally treated in a soloistic fashion, a compositional technique popular in the Baroque era. He also described the overall spirit of the piece in this way: "The general mood of the work represents, apart from the jesting second movement, a gradual transition from the sternness of the first movement and the lugubrious death-song of the third, to the life assertion of the last." It is not possible to read that sentence without recalling the composer's own situation. If the concerto ends with "life assertion," it may be that Bartók himself, in his final months, found some measure of contentment.

♪♪♪♪♪

Ibert: Flute Concerto

Born in Paris, Jacques Ibert (1890 – 1962) studied at the Paris Conservatoire until the outbreak of World War I, when naval service interrupted his education. He came home safely and soon was composing the spirited and varied works on which his musical reputation would rest. A second term of naval service in World War II took him away from his office again, but upon his discharge, he reassumed the career that would keep him occupied to the end of his days.

Ibert's catalog includes three concertos, all for woodwind soloists: one for oboe, one for alto saxophone, and most famously, one for flute, written in 1934 for the internationally respected French flutist Marcel Moÿse. Moÿse himself premiered the work in Paris, and then, as professor of flute at the Paris Conservatoire, ensured that it would have many more performances by declaring it the institution's designated test piece for would-be graduates in flute. Each flute student, playing before a panel of judges, would need to navigate the score's intricacies successfully before earning a diploma. Whether the students dreaded or relished this opportunity would have depended on individual personality, but indeed, the concerto so challenges a player's technique that it would be a fair test of mastery.

Like much of his music, Ibert's Flute Concerto is bright, varied, and full of character, with much deft usage of the contrasting timbres of instruments. Determinedly energetic phrases appear in contrast to gently lyrical ones, not only for the soloist, but also for the orchestra. The first and last movements give more prominence to the brass instruments than one might expect of a flute concerto, but Ibert may have been intrigued by the contrast of timbres between the flute and the brass. Whatever one is hearing at a given moment is likely quite different from what one will be hearing in the next moment. Ibert was a composer who wished to ensure that whatever an audience was hoping to hear would appear before long in a given composition. There truly is something for nearly anyone.

♪♪♪♪

Castelnuovo-Tedesco: Guitar Concerto no. 1
    in D major, op. 99

From Florence to Beverly Hills: such was the career path of Mario Castelnuovo-Tedesco (1895 – 1968). The Italian was just beginning his compositional career around the time of World War I. In Italy, these were the Puccini years, years in which the public image of "Italian music" often meant opera and little else. Indeed, Castelnuovo-Tedesco did compose a few stage works, but instrumental music proved to be closer to his heart, and it is upon his instrumental music, in a generally conservative, neo-romantic style, that his reputation stands.

Although Castelnuovo-Tedesco was himself neither a Spaniard nor a guitarist, he wrote his Guitar Concerto no. 1 in 1939 for a man who was both: Andras Segovia (1893 –

1987). The composer took care to evoke the Spanish spirit in this concerto, in part for the sake of the instrument's public image, but also for Segovia's sake.

Thus, in this concerto, we find various elements borrowed from Iberia, including the abrupt juxtaposition of rejoicing and lamentation, the repetition of melodic fragments lower and lower in pitch, and the use of intricate rhythms that speak of a Flamenco heritage. The work sings of Spain, and in so doing, allows the guitar to sing. It is an appropriate pairing, since to many ears, the guitar is the musical essence of Spain. Here, an Italian-born composer proves how effectively he can don the costume of a foreign land.

Not long after Castelnuovo-Tedesco completed his Guitar Concerto no. 1, World War II broke out, and the composer joined the tide of musical refugees on their way to the United States. He made his way to southern California where his conservative musical style won him a place in the realm of film music. Yet cinema was not his only occupation. He also devoted many years to teaching composition at UCLA, where his students included Jerry Goldsmith (1929 – 2004) and John Williams (b. 1932), both of whom appear in Chapter Nine.

♪♪♪♪♪

Korngold: Violin Concerto in D major, op. 35

Best remembered today as the composer of scores for Errol Flynn adventure films, Erich Korngold (1897 – 1957) began his career far from Hollywood. Born in Moravia (now part of the Czech Republic), he was the son of an eminent

Austrian music critic, who trained the boy well. By the time he was in his 20s, young Korngold was startling all of Europe with his musical gifts.

That path to success was interrupted by politics. In 1934, the Jewish composer was badly beaten by a gang of Nazi thugs. When the Viennese opera producer Max Reinhardt (1873 – 1943) subsequently suggested a move to Hollywood, Korngold jumped at the suggestion. In California, the young composer's operatic background revolutionized the art of cinematic music. Although he continued to write for the concert hall, it is these innovative film scores that are now the basis of his reputation.

Of Korngold's non-cinematic US compositions, his Violin Concerto has attracted the greatest notice. That attention came about in part from the composer's own reputation, as in 1938, he had won an Academy Award for his work on the film *The Adventures of Robin Hood*. That the acclaimed violinist Jascha Heifetz (1901 – 1987) consented to give the work its premiere also helped. Heifetz subsequently played the concerto in Carnegie Hall to the obvious delight of audiences and the evident despair of critics.

Korngold ensured that any listener would think of Hollywood, for the composer's film scores served as the mother lode of melodic material. The Concerto's opening theme is drawn from the film "Another Dawn;" a melody from "Juarez" also makes an appearance. The second movement relies on his score to "Anthony Adverse;" for the third and final movement, Korngold chose themes from "The Prince and the Pauper" and "The Private Lives of Elizabeth and Essex." The average film-going audience member loved it. The critics, however, were only reminded as to why they turned their noses up at Korngold. Yet the composer had the last laugh. Ever since its premiere, his Violin Concerto has enjoyed fair success, and has been recorded by the greatest violinists of the century.

♪♪♪♪

Gershwin: Piano Concerto in F major

Despite his phenomenal success in popular music, George Gershwin (1898 – 1937) did not overlook the realms of concert music. He viewed jazz styles as a means of enlivening the old classical genres, bringing to them a true American spirit. His first such cross-over work, *Rhapsody in Blue*, was written early in 1924. The *Rhapsody* is a piano concerto in all but name, though it spans only a single movement roughly a quarter hour in length. Once he had more experience under his belt – and the lessons he could glean from a variety of music textbooks acquired on an excursion to Paris – Gershwin set out to tackle something bigger.

Not fully confident of his skills, Gershwin arranged a private tryout two weeks before its planned premiere, hiring an orchestra and recruiting a conductor friend but performing the solo part himself. "You can imagine my delight," he later recalled, "when it sounded just as I had planned." The formal premiere occurred at Carnegie Hall December 3, 1925, repeated the following evening. Gershwin had formally arrived in the classical world.

In crafting his concerto, Gershwin was drawing on a lengthy heritage, yet to that tradition, he added his own personal touch with the spunky sounds of jazz. For all its similarities to the concertos of history, this is a concerto that could only have been written by an American, with its jazzy rhythms and bluesy harmonies.

Gershwin's Piano Concerto sets about its business much as one of Mozart's would have done, with the expected three movements of fast, slow, and fast tempos. In each movement, it is the orchestra that begins, with the piano soloist joining after the orchestra has set the stage; Mozart would have done the same thing. Gershwin takes care to give substantial prominence to various members of the orchestra at times, rather than saving all the notable music for the pianist. Just as the final page of the final movement approaches, he ensures that no one is inattentive for the finale by adding a powerful stroke on the gong. Mozart might have left out the gong, but otherwise, it is just the sort of work that Mozart would have written had he lived at the height of the Jazz Age.

♪♪♪♪

Shostakovich: Piano Concerto no. 1 in C major, op. 35

Soviet composer Dmitri Shostakovich (1906 – 1975) was a gifted pianist who achieved world notice at the keyboard even before his compositions began to attract attention. He continued to appear as a concert pianist throughout his career, and took the stage for the premiere of his Piano Concerto no. 1 October 15, 1933, in the city in which he had been born. When Shostakovich had grown up there, it was St. Petersburg; by the time of the concerto's premiere, it had become Leningrad. That political sea-change would affect Shostakovich to the end of his days, as he struggled to keep Soviet authorities off his musical back.

His Piano Concerto no. 1 is striking for several reasons. First of all, it is almost a double concerto, with the featured piano, frequently sharing the spotlight with trumpet. Double concertos were not unknown; however, to pair a pianist with a brass instrument was a startling decision. At the first performance in 1933, Shostakovich and his trumpeter colleague, Alexander Schmidt, acted as virtual co-soloists, in an unprecedented combination of instruments.

Also notable is the frequent appearance of musical quotations, some well-known, others less familiar. Toward the beginning of the concerto, there is an echo of Beethoven's "Appassionata" Piano Sonata no. 23; later, another work by that master, the *Rage Over a Lost Penny*, is quoted in a cadenza near the end of the piece. There are also bits of Haydn sonatas, themes from other Shostakovich compositions, and an Austrian folk-song, that of itself evoked a scandal.

The song "Ach, du lieber Augustin" concerns a folk-hero who can survive any catastrophe as long as he consumes enough alcohol. The Soviet musical authorities found the presence of such a melody in an allegedly serious composition to be shocking. They claimed that the use of such a song hinted at a certain lack of decorum on the composer's part, but other members of the audience apparently were not offended. Besides, one of the notable characteristics of early Shostakovich works, such as this one, is an ironic sense of humor, and it may have served the composer well in later years, when he found himself under strict government opposition.

♪♪♪♪

Barber: Violin Concerto, op. 14

Barber began his Violin Concerto in the summer of 1939 on a commission from Samuel Fels, a Philadelphia businessman who was also a board member of Barber's alma mater, the Curtis Institute of Music. Since Fels' adoptive son, Iso Briselli, was a talented violinist, he asked the composer to write a piece that would showcase the young man's abilities. Trouble arose when Barber submitted to the intended soloist the first two movements of the composition-in-progress. "Too easy!" young Briselli responded, and Barber, secretly piqued at the criticism, promised to correct the problem. In a classic case of "be careful what you ask for; you might get it," the composer provided a final movement far more dramatic than the first two, too difficult, apparently, for the soloist-in-question, who now declared the concerto to be unplayable. Fels, annoyed on behalf of his protégé, insisted that Barber return the commission fee.

Refusing to believe it could not be played, Barber was disinclined to give a refund. He decided to vindicate himself, organizing an impromptu performance of that problematic final movement to be given before a panel of judges at the Curtis Institute. Herbert Baumel, a Curtis student, was given a few hours to look over the score, after which he performed it with no particular difficulty. That demonstration should have proved Barber's point, but he built an even stronger case, by arranging for a private performance to be given for Fels. That performance, too, went off perfectly, thus effectively demolishing contentions that it was unplayable. Unfortunately, historians have not yet discovered whatever discussion subsequently took place between Fels and his young protégé, who had said the piece was unplayable.

The question of playablility is always a judgment call. In this particular case, all three movements are challenging, yet in different ways. The first two movements, the ones declared to be "too easy," are expansive and lyrical, with rich, flowing melodies like the best of Brahms and Tchaikovsky. Here are no fireworks à la Paganini, no fingerboard gymnastics with which a soloist can dazzle an audience. The notes themselves are quite easily played. Challenges arise mostly in the interpretation, in bringing musicality to those little black dots on the page. As all the finest violinists admit, interpretation is no less vital than technique. It's just less obvious. Perhaps young Briselli damned these two exquisite movements because he was not yet mature enough as an artist to understand that difference. Significantly, he never did achieve any measure of fame.

♫♫♫♫

Bernstein: *Prelude, Fugue and Riffs*

The most influential of all names in American classical music, Leonard Bernstein (1918 – 1990) was a first generation American, son of Eastern European Jewish immigrants who had found a better life in the US. Long before his death, Bernstein had built a reputation as the most recorded, most media savvy, and one of the most gifted composer/conductors of the century, a man who could communicate in the rarified halls of art music as well as he could in the wider realm of popular sounds.

The two worlds intersect in Bernstein's *Prelude, Fugue and Riffs*, written in 1949. A short, high-spirited showcase for jazz-style clarinet with ensemble, it had first been intended for Woody Herman (1913 – 1987), who had also earned a concerto from Igor Stravinsky (1882 – 1971). Yet it would be Benny Goodman (1909 – 1986), whose performing repertoire ranged through Mozart and Bartók as well as swing, who would premiere the piece in a television broadcast October 16, 1955.

Strict jazz purists will point out that it is not actually jazz, as it contains no off-the-cuff improvisation, but Bernstein did not intend to write straight jazz. Rather, he borrowed jazz rhythms and inflections and set them within overall classical music structures. JS Bach (1685 – 1750) did not swing, yet even he would recognize the central fugue as doing exactly what fugues need to do. In this brief work, as he would soon achieve with *West Side Story*, Bernstein proves that two otherwise divergent realms can co-exist.

♫♫♫♫

Rautavaara: Violin Concerto

The most prominent Finnish composer since Jean Sibelius (1865 – 1957), Einojuhani Rautavaara (b. 1928) grew up in Helsinki. Having begun music studies at the Helsinki Academy, Rautavaara first came to attention outside his homeland in 1955, when the American-based Koussevitsky Foundation decided to honor Sibelius' 90th birthday by awarding a Juilliard scholarship to some young Finnish composer whom Sibelius was to select. His choice fell to Rautavaara, who then spent two years studying in the US, both at Juilliard and at the Tanglewood Music Center, where he attracted the favorable attention of Aaron Copland (1900 – 1990). Since that time, Rautavaara has rarely been out of the spotlight.

Rautavaara's Violin Concerto premiered August 23, 1977, at the Helsinki Festival in Finland, with soloist Eugen Sarbu, conductor Leif Segerstam and the Finnish Radio Symphony Orchestra. The composer himself says of the work that the solo part is meant to evoke a journey through diverse situations and experiences. Although the first of the two movements alleges in its tempo markings to be tranquil and the second energetic, in fact both offer their shares of tranquility and energy.

At times, the concerto is haunting and mystical in mood, at others strong with purposeful outbursts, like the on-rush of an avalanche surging forth during an otherwise restful afternoon. Of the dynamic final pages, Rautavaara attests that he was thinking of the busy streets in Manhattan that he observed during his Juilliard years, suffused with the restless energy of a great metropolis. It is a concept that drives the concerto toward its insistent conclusion.

Rautavaara's fondness for sudden assertive statements which appear out of a quiet, chorale-like texture brings to mind images of a brightly painted sleigh that pops into view from time to time as it crosses an austere snowy landscape, seizing one's attention and instilling a strong measure of energy. Overall, the work takes the spaciousness and drive that one usually finds in Sibelius' orchestral works and infuses them with an element of more modern harmonies, blending beauty and vigor into a single score.

♪♪♪♪

Williams: *Escapades* for saxophone and orchestra

No name is more identified with film music than that of John Williams (b. 1932). With well over 100 films to his credit, including the *Star Wars* and *Indiana Jones* franchises, he has, for decades, been the standard against which other film composers have been measured. However, despite being ever in demand in Hollywood, Williams has not neglected the concert hall. He has written numerous works specifically for it, sometimes adapting his film scores for concert use. In this latter category, one finds *Escapades*.

Escapades derives from the 2002 film "Catch Me If You Can." The Spielberg film tells of Frank Abagnale, Jr., a skilled and charming con man (played by Leonardo di Caprio), ever pursuing new adventures; in that context, Williams' new title *Escapades* is ideally suited to the source material. Much of the film is set in the early 1960s, which Williams chose to evoke with soft jazz moods. Sometimes these are bluesy, at others, more nimble of expression, and regularly featuring prominent saxophone lines.

Those characteristics led to a score readily adapted into the form of an alto saxophone concerto, a fact perceived by two great minds of music. Upon seeing the film, saxophonist Branford Marsalis took it upon himself to call Williams and suggest the creation of a concerto from the score. Williams responded that such a work was already in process, and offered it to Marsalis for its premiere.

Its three movements allow for more substantial orchestral support than in the original film, though one still finds prominent use of jazzy percussion, especially the vibraphone. Its shimmery voice played a prominent role in much of '60s jazz, especially in the care of Lionel Hampton, and is ideal for evoking the scenes Williams had in mind.

The first movement, "Closing In," is intended by Williams to represent the hunt by the FBI to solve the mystery of Frank and bring him to justice. In mood, it's slinky, finger-snapping cool jazz, rather nocturnal in nature, though with passages of stronger intensity. "Reflections," the second movement, brings out a bluesy, wistful atmosphere; Williams imagines this as capturing the spirit of Frank's fractured family. Jaunty and energetic moods arrive for the final movement, "Joy Ride," with Frank not just making off in a sporty stolen car but embarking on a large range of fraudulent adventures. Here one finds the most overtly virtuosic solo writing of the entire work.

Even without the accompaniment of cinematic images, the music stands gracefully and evocatively on its own. The first movement has a smirk, the second a sigh, and the third hearty laughter. Whether or not that reflects DiCaprio, it certainly captures the varied voices that an alto saxophone can express.

♪♪♪♪♪

Zwilich: Trombone Concerto

Unless one is Mozart – and who is? – one is unlikely to compose a dozen concertos without starting to branch out into less frequent choices of solo instruments. Mozart never ran out of new things to say with the combined forces of piano and orchestra; others are more likely to look for variety in the solo roles. That thought leads to the many concertos of Ellen Taaffe Zwilich (b. 1939 in Miami). She has written a piano concerto, and one for violin, one for violin and cello, one for piano, violin, and cello, and a great number of other solo concertos. Her catalog contains one concerto each for flute, oboe, clarinet, bassoon, horn, trumpet, trombone, and bass trombone. She has also produced scores that are in all but name percussion concertos, so there is no section of the orchestra that she has overlooked.

Of all those solo instruments, one that has most rarely found a place in the spotlight – at least outside of the jazz world – is the trombone. Usually relegated to adding color in bold orchestral passages, it has been given few opportunities to stand center stage. However, that is exactly where Zwilich placed the trombone in this work. It was commissioned by the Chicago Symphony and premiered there February 2, 1989.

As Mozart or Vivaldi would have done, Zwilich structures the work in three movements, beginning quickly before introducing more relaxed moods for the middle movement, then returning to lively ideas for the finale. The first movement is often bold and stirring, with the soloist given nimble, articulated lines as well as more lyrical, flowing ones. The second movement might seem restful, though eerie harmonies contributed in part by the xylophone bring a more unsettled mood than might otherwise be expected. With the last movement, those ideas of nervous energy and thoughtful reserve appear in turn, with fragments of the soloist's lines reappearing in the orchestral parts. In all, it is a work that proves the varied capabilities of the trombone, and its ability to stand out from the orchestra when the chance arises.

♪♪♪♪

MacMillan: *Veni, Veni, Emmanuel* –
    concerto for percussion and orchestra

One may not know the Latin of that title, but cast it into English – "O come, o come, Emanuel" – and many observers will immediately recognize it as the opening phrase of an ancient Christmas hymn. That fact does not make this work by Scottish composer James MacMillan (b. 1959) specifically a Christmas piece, though it does point out the identity of the melody upon which the piece is based. The composer attests that he wrote it between Christmas and Easter in the winter of 1991/92. It premiered in London's Royal Albert Hall August 10, 1992, with the Scottish Chamber Orchestra, for which it had been specifically commissioned. MacMillan dedicated the work to his parents.

In all but name a percussion concerto, *Veni, Veni, Emanuel* featured at its premiere the nimble virtuosity of soloist Evelyn Glennie. Ms. Glennie was kept ever on her toes, moving steadily between a host of percussion instruments, including (but not limited to) snares, congas, tam-tams, tom-toms, gongs, cowbells, tubular bells, marimbas, and cymbals of varying types. There are also two orchestral percussionists who add further effects late in the work, and an orchestra richly provided with an abundance of varied woodwinds (from piccolo to contrabassoon), allowing subtly varied coloration of the supporting lines. Since many of the percussion instruments in use are "pitched," that is, able to play distinct pitches, not just rhythms, even the percussion can contribute to these shifting colors.

MacMillan notes that the soloist and the orchestra are treated as "two equal partners," so that both sides of that equation have significant melodic and rhythmic material. Often, the music flows as if there is an active conversation in progress, with focus shifting quickly from one speaker to another. Attentive ears may notice that rhythmic fragments pass from one directly to another, as though they were completing each other's sentences.

As one might expect of a work with prominent percussion, one finds a steady, pulsing beat, sometimes slower, sometimes faster. The composer himself attests that he imagines this beat as symbolic of the "human presence of Christ," evoking both the Christmas hymn that recurs throughout the work and also the sacred season in which he was at work on writing it. *Veni, veni, Emmanuel* is not specifically a sacred composition, but MacMillan – a prolific composer of church music – wished his faith to echo here as well.

Chapter Five: Chamber Music

It is the opening of what nearly any violinist will admit is the most intimidating piece of solo violin music ever composed: the Chaconne of Johann Sebastian Bach (1685 – 1750). From this simple beginning – rather less simple when the player includes the harmonies that underlie this melody – the German master builds a quarter hour of violin soliloquy. Given that "chamber music" is a small group of players, here is the smallest of all: exactly one. Yet Bach found plenty to say with that single player.

Most of the other works in this chapter call upon more than one player. There are trios, quartets, quintets, and some works called "sonatas," which generally have two players, one of them using a keyboard instrument. One also finds a serenade, in which the ensemble may include up to a dozen or so players. However, even those are written so that each performer has an individual voice in the music. Unlike in a larger scale work, such as a symphony, no one is duplicating someone else's contribution to the overall sound. It's what is called "one to a part;" leave any one performer out, and an empty space appears in the music. Since everyone is an equal participant, listeners can enjoy focusing on one performer and then another, so as to sense how each person adds a unique element to the tapestry of sound. The composer will have attended to how the individual threads of that tapestry weave together.

Sometimes, chamber music is written for the composer to play with a few friends, or for several of his or her friends to tackle together. At other times, chamber music is intended for amateur players, so that non-professionals might also find pleasure in joining together for musical expression. Many a young composer new to the business has chosen to begin with chamber music works. The decision is not driven by an idea that these are easier to compose than symphonies; indeed, there are fewer parts to manage, but any shortcoming of that management becomes ever clearer when there are only a few persons playing. Rather, a young, unknown composer will likely have an easier time persuading a few friends to perform a new work than convincing an entire orchestra to take the plunge. That is true today in the 21st century; it was also true for Mozart and Beethoven.

♪♪♪♪

Corelli: Trio Sonatas, op. 1, 3, and 4

In a logical world, a trio sonata would be performed by an ensemble of three persons. In fact, it takes four: two primary soloists and two persons who together provide the supporting "basso continuo" lines. This continuo part, a standard presence in all music of the Baroque Era, was usually managed by a harpsichord and a cello or double bass, though a lute might replace the harpsichord and a bassoon could cover for the cello/bass.

More Classical Insights

All the principal Baroque Era composers wrote trio sonatas, sometimes as music for domestic diversion, though also for entertaining royalty. As for Italian composer Arcangelo Corelli (1653 – 1713), well more than half of his compositions are trio sonatas. That fact is influenced in part by the fact that Corelli, the youngest son of a wealthy family and one of the most highly praised violinists in Rome, kept so busy performing that he had little time to devote to composition. His entire published catalog includes only six sets of works of twelve pieces each. So in sixty years, Corelli composed just six dozen compositions, none with voices, all instrumental, most of them trio sonatas, and every single one including prominent parts for violin. He was willing to share the stage, but not willing to stand by idly while others had all the fun.

Corelli's trio sonatas were published in 1681, 1689, and 1694. Each uses different keys for the various sonatas, allowing the composer to explore how one key might sound quite distinct from another, even at similar tempos. Most of his trio sonatas have four movements, usually beginning with a slow one, before proceeding to a faster one, another slow one, and then a final one that is fastest of all. The two solo lines are always for pairs of violins – a fact that wouldn't stop an ambitious oboist from taking up one of them. Usually, the soloists are relatively balanced in prominence, and frequently, one will start a melodic idea that then passes on to the other. Corelli's trio sonatas offer a fine glance into the world of domestic musical entertainment in the Baroque Era.

♪♪♪♪

Betsy Schwarm

Marais: *La Sonnerie de Ste. Geneviève du Mont de Paris*

Paris-born Marin Marais (1656 – 1728) spent his musical career on the grandest of stages: that of the royal court at Versailles with King Louis XIV and his great-grandson and successor, Louis XV. Much of what Marais composed was chamber music for the monarch's casual entertainment, and in these years of the Baroque Era, that generally meant a string ensemble, with or without harpsichord support. As Marais himself played the bass, he had an innate sensitivity to the characteristics of string instruments, which are well showcased in his music. Moreover, one can rely on there always being something interesting for those lower voices.

Of Marais' dozens of works for string ensemble, the most memorable is *La Sonnerie de Ste. Geneviève du Mont de Paris (The Bells of St. Geneviève of Mt. Paris)*. The score is a masterful example of what Marais' Baroque contemporaries would have called a "ground bass," that is, a repetitive low rhythmic figure that underlies all manner of other melodies. The ground bass appears from the work's opening: a three-note falling pattern in the bass and harpsichord, which will continue almost uninterrupted throughout the score. Yet that statement is far from a complete summary of the action. Above it lies a flowing, brightly ornamented violin melody which grows and evolves as the work progresses, sometimes acquiring dance-like dotted rhythms of a sort of skipping pattern. In all, it is a work with far more variety than one would expect of a chamber composition usually played by only four musicians and based upon a repeated set of exactly three notes.

♪♪♪♪

More Classical Insights

JS Bach: Violin Partita no. 2 in d, BWV 1004 – Chaconne

The list of Bach's string compositions includes a half dozen Partitas and Sonatas for solo violin. These were composed in the late 1710s and early 1720s while Bach was employed at the court in Cőthen, Germany, not long before his move to Leipzig to accept a position with the church. In Leipzig, there was little need for instrumental works; the focus was on church music. However, in Cőthen, young Prince Leopold loved music and was always eager to hear what Bach had to say.

Atypically for court music of the period, Bach did not always restrict himself to scores for light entertainment, but indulged his love of musical intricacies, both for the challenge of writing it and for the challenge of performing it. This situation is never clearer than in the famed Chaconne from the Partita no. 2, arguably the most difficult solo violin piece ever penned by any composer.

The last movement of a five-movement set, it is also the longest of the movements by far, spanning roughly half of the entire Partita. It draws upon the Baroque form known as a chaconne, in which a basic theme stated at the opening is then repeatedly restated in gradually varying ways. To fully follow the intricacies, listeners are advised to focus upon the open measures in which one first encounters the basic theme, so as to better recognize what is happening to it as the work progresses. In this specific case, Bach's basic theme is all of four measures long, short enough to allow nearly endless room for variation, finally totaling sixty-four variations. The melody line for it stands at the head of this chapter.

From a stern and commanding mood at the beginning, Bach gradually increases the complexity of his theme, mixing in more and more varied compositional effects. Some twists upon the theme are spacious; others flow nimbly. Fast runs and large interval skips are frequent, requiring much dexterity from the performer. Bach also calls upon changes of emotional intensity, as some variations are dominated by long notes and others by many, more urgent short notes. Bach builds up his work over 256 measures, finally restating the theme at the end with new, even stronger, harmonies.

Of Bach's work, Johannes Brahms (1833 – 1897) – not himself a violinist but certainly a composer intimately familiar with the most intricate compositional techniques – would observe, "The Chaconne is to me one of the most wondrous, incomprehensible musical works... a whole world of the deepest thoughts and more powerful feelings." For many generations, violinists have agreed with him, choosing this work above all others when they had a statement to make in performance. It is not for the faint-hearted, only for those who have confidence in their abilities. For listeners, the Chaconne offers the best of all possible ways to find out what a true master (either performer or composer) can get out of a violin.

♪♪♪♪

Haydn: String Quartet in D major, op. 64, no. 5,
  "The Lark"

Throughout his career, Joseph Haydn (1732 – 1809) kept busy composing music for the diversion of his employers: first the aristocratic Esterhazy family, then eager fans amongst the middle class. Sometimes, these works were of larger scale, such as symphonies, of which he composed over 100. Others required only a handful of performers, and here one finds his string quartets, nearly six dozen in number.

Haydn's opus 64 quartets (a set of six) were composed in the spring and summer of 1790 near the end of his lengthy period of service with the Esterhazys. The quartets have a connection to Johann Tost, a violinist also employed at the Esterhazy court. In 1789, Tost had journeyed to Paris, presumably on some personal business matter; amongst his luggage were the scores of a previous set of Haydn's quartets, along with several other Haydn compositions. It was Tost's appointed duty to place the works with a Parisian publisher, which he duly did, though the publisher's fees seem to have spent an inordinate time in Tost's own pocket before eventually making their way to the composer himself. Yet Haydn, typically a good-natured man, does not seem to have held a grudge, since the opus 64 quartets, written a year after this incident, were nonetheless dedicated to Tost.

The best-known of the opus 64 quartets is the fifth of the set, known as "The Lark" for the soaring violin melody with which the first movement opens, a theme that vividly evokes a songbird singing on the wing. The other movements also have their delights: a song-like second movement, an eagerly dance-like third movement, and an even livelier fourth movement, with some of the spirit of a hornpipe. As a whole, the quartet proves how well Haydn understood string instruments and how best to bring varied moods out of their otherwise similar voices.

♪♪♪♪

JC Bach: Six Sonatas for keyboard with violin, op. 10

Of the twenty children of Johann Sebastian Bach (1685 – 1750), barely half lived to adulthood. Of the survivors, four boys would carry the family name on into the next musical generation, the elder ones early enough that their father could proudly observe their progress. These four musical offspring were Wilhelm Friedmann (1710 – 1784), Carl Philip Emanuel (1714 – 1788), Johann Christoph Friedrich (1732 – 1795) and Johann Christian (1735 – 1782).

Such a proliferation of composers with the same last name might have been confusing at the time, but fortunately each brother pursued his career in a different city. For the youngest brother, it was London, where he settled in 1762. There, JC Bach became known as the "London Bach," spending twenty years at the heart of its musical community. His death in 1782 was described by Mozart, whom JC Bach had befriended years earlier as "a loss to the musical world." Many more famous composers would have paid a high price to earn a similar tribute from such an authority.

Amongst the works that JC Bach composed during his London years are a set of six sonatas published in 1773 as his opus 10. In fact, he had composed far more music than that numbering would indicate, but at the time, different publishers would choose their own system of numbering without reference to what a rival might be doing.

Note the arrangement of the words in the collective title of these sonatas. That "keyboard" might have been either a harpsichord or a pianoforte, the latter of those an early version of the modern piano. Both were in use in London in the 1770s. As for the violin being named after the keyboard, rather than before, as would later become preferred form, the fact is that the keyboard part is significantly more demanding than the violin part, and usually takes the lead.

These were not sonatas designed for a pair of equally skilled professional players. Rather, the target audience was reasonably talented amateur players, making music for domestic entertainment. In those circumstances, pianists were frequently more experienced than their violinist colleagues. JC Bach knew well where the largest quantity of music was likely to sell, and that is the market that he specifically targeted.

♪♪♪♪

Mozart: Clarinet Quintet in A major, K. 581

A relative newcomer to the musical scene, the clarinet did not come into existence until the early 18th century, when one is first mentioned in a purchase order to a Nuremburg instrument maker in 1710. By late in the century, Wolfgang Amadeus Mozart (1756 – 1791) had come to appreciate the richness that the instrument added to the middle voices of the orchestra. Moreover, once he relocated to Vienna in 1781, he had at his disposal one of the finest clarinetists of the day, Anton Stadler (1753 – 1812), for whom Mozart would compose two of the finest works of his last years: the Clarinet Quintet of 1789 and Clarinet Concerto of 1791, the latter completed only months before Mozart's death.

The quintet is scored not for five clarinets, but rather for a string quartet plus clarinet, so two violins, one viola, one cello, and the woodwind instrument. The clarinet is not necessarily the principal voice. It stands out in part because its timbre is so different to that of the strings, even to that of the viola, closest to it in range. Rather, Mozart gives thematic material to all the players at various times, and though the clarinetist rather frequently earns the honor of playing the splashiest music, the others are not long neglected.

One may find that the opening of the first movement is particularly familiar. Its melody was prominently featured in the final episode of the television series *M*A*S*H* in 1983, when a group of Chinese prisoners-of-war decides to prove to one of the American doctors that they know Mozart. The melodies of the other three movements are equally charming, especially in the finale, when Mozart sets about crafting a set of variations on what had begun as a rather simple tune.

After Mozart's passing, manuscripts of both works fell into Stadler's care. When the widowed Constanze Mozart (1762 – 1842) attempted to retrieve them, the clarinetist claimed they had been stolen from him during a tour of Germany; she, for her part, was convinced Stadler had pawned them. To this day, the manuscripts have never reappeared. Extant versions are based solely on early copies and first printings in Mozart's own day, which contain apparent copyist's errors that musicologists have labored to correct.

♪♪♪♪

More Classical Insights

Mozart: Serenade in D major, K. 250, "Haffner"

The word "serenade" means "night music," and in classical Vienna, musical serenades were a highly popular diversion. At the end of the 18th century, it was the custom in that city for ensembles to perform in the parks and gardens. Composing serenades for such purposes was a good source of income, and Mozart took to the genre with delight. He wrote over a dozen such works. The best-known is *Eine kleine Nachtmusik*, but the grandest is the "Haffner."

The so-called "Haffner" serenade is by far the longest of his serenades. Indeed, nearly an hour in length, it is the most expansive of all his instrumental compositions, even including the symphonies. Perhaps its breadth says something of the young composer's regard for the person for whom the music was intended, or perhaps he simply found himself with time enough on his hands to explore a diversity of ideas. Whichever reason applies, the fact is that it was written in the summer of 1776, when the young composer was twenty years of age.

It was intended for the wedding of Elisabeth Haffner, daughter of a wealthy Salzburg banker known to the Mozarts. Six years later, Mozart would compose for the family again, for a ceremony celebrating the fact that Elisabeth's brother Sigmund was being raised to the nobility. The brother, too, would receive music, that which becomes the "Haffner" Symphony, though that work was less grand than the sister's piece. By then, Mozart was more in demand, and did not always have time to complete every request that came his way. So Fraulein Elisabeth, with the benefit of Mozart's relative youth and lesser reputation, received the most magnificent of wedding gifts.

The grand scope of this serenade is reflected in several ways. Its orchestra includes more woodwinds and brass than were normally used. Often, serenades were scored only for string ensemble (as in the famed *Eine kleine Nachtmusik*), but here one finds also flutes, oboes, bassoons, trumpets, and horns; there are no clarinets, as this new invention was not yet present in Salzburg. There are also more movements than the standard, eight rather than the usual three to four.

Mozart provided three dance-like minuets, a pair of graciously lyrical andantes, a perky rondo midway (with a violin solo that scampers nimbly), and both an expansive introductory movement and a spacious finale. Any other composer would have pared this mix down by half, but Mozart was always his own man. He had a wealth of ideas and understood well that this particular set of musical thoughts offered fine contrast with one another, yet still fit together as a perfect whole. There is exactly as much music as is required, and if the whole happens to be of generous length, all the better for a post-wedding celebration.

♪♪♪♪

Beethoven: Three String Quartets, op. 59, "Razumovsky"

Count Andreas Razumovsky (1752 – 1836) was neither a composer nor a performer. Yet he played an important role in Viennese music at the beginning of the 19th century. Having come to Vienna to serve as Russian ambassador to the Austrian Imperial Court, the Count fancied himself as a leader of aristocratic society and was determined to live in the highest style. He ordered the construction of a magnificent palace. Then, anticipating the grand occasion that the palace's first ball would represent, he commissioned three quartets from Ludwig van Beethoven (1770 – 1827). The plan was that the works would premiere at the palace, but Beethoven, perhaps unwilling to risk his music being lost in a social whirl, outfoxed the Russian count. He finished the quartets quickly, and arranged a premiere in February 1807, even before the palace was completed. The works were published together the following year.

Despite Beethoven's reputation as perhaps the greatest composer in all of Vienna, the three quartets were not immediately beloved. Violinist Ignaz Schuppanzigh, who had performed many of Beethoven's chamber works, insisted they were too challenging, that few violinists would be able to play them. The composer supposedly responded that he saw no reason to take such trivialities into consideration. If you can't play it, he seemed to say, it's your problem, not mine. Indeed, in this period of his life, the composer might have had little patience for other people's burdens, as his deafness had grown extreme, leaving him oblivious to all but the loudest sounds.

Although Beethoven had brushed off Schuppanzigh's remark, the violinist was right in one respect: these quartets do reflect a sharp departure for the composer. His earlier quartets, dating from the first decade after his arrival in Vienna, were composed with the city's talented amateur ensembles in mind. They are finely crafted, yet make no wicked demands on the players, for there was money to be made in catering to a more general audience. Yet in the Razumovsky quartets, Beethoven seems to reject such concerns, choosing instead to write music that is rich and varied, with intricate layering of parts and ambitious development of themes. Nothing lies quietly on the page for more than a few moments; Beethoven always has plans as to what to do with that theme next. One finds both sorrow and rapture; the intellect of a fugue is soon offset by the verve of a Russian country dance. In these three quartets, Beethoven revealed his versatility that one finds in this so-called "middle-period" of emotionally varied compositions. What one hears in the Razumovsky quartets would soon take massive orchestral form in the Symphony no. 5 and Symphony no. 6.

♪♪♪♪

Schubert: String Quintet in C major, D. 956

By the last year of his all-too-short life, Franz Schubert (1797 – 1828) had completed over a dozen string quartets and one quintet for piano and strings – the beloved *"Trout"* Quintet – but had not yet attempted a string quintet. His inspiration at this late date apparently stemmed from Mozart. In 1824, Schubert borrowed copies of Mozart's string quintets from a friend and studied them closely.

Mozart's quintets were scored for a standard string quartet with an additional viola, adding further richness to the middle layers. However, when Schubert began his own quintet, he chose instead to use an additional cello, giving his composition a weightier, richer tone than the Mozart works that had so triggered his imagination. He completed the quintet early in the fall of 1828.

In an October letter to a publisher, he mentions that the piece had been given its first rehearsal, but one month later, when Schubert died on November 19, there is no evidence that the quintet had been performed, even in private, in the interim. In fact, its premiere would not take place until 1850; publication would not occur until 1853. Thus, the quintet shares the fate of most Schubert masterworks: utter neglect during his lifetime, unsurpassed acclamation decades later.

The lyrical and expansive first movement belies its tempo marking of "Allegro ma non troppo" with a leisurely opening before gliding into a determinedly energetic main section. It is as if Schubert wished to offer a maximum of varied moods, for more themes will follow; here was a man who was never at a loss for a fine tune. The second movement Adagio is leisurely of pace and deeply mournful, so somber in mood that pianist Arthur Rubenstein (1887 – 1982) requested it for his funeral. The third movement Scherzo clears the clouds with exuberant rhythms in the spirit of folk-dancing. For his final movement, Schubert chooses a vibrant mood of swirling rhythms and lively energy hardly less dance-like than its predecessor. Despite all the melancholy of the earlier movements, he seems determined to end with optimism, an encouraging message from a man who was in the last months of his abbreviated life.

♪♪♪♪

Verdi: String Quartet in e minor

Few composers have demonstrated a talent for both opera and chamber music. The dramatic demands of the former seem somehow to preclude the intimate requirements of the latter. Thus, though the great kings of opera conquered the dramatic stage, chamber music remained apparently ill-suited to their skills. Since Mozart's passing, strikingly few composers have produced masterpieces in both fields. Yet opera specialists have occasionally delved into the realm of sonatas and quartets, sometimes producing strongly imaginative works. At the height of his fame, Giuseppe Verdi (1813 – 1901) spent a few otherwise idle days creating a string quartet. It was one of only three works he ever produced that did not make use of the human voice.

His String Quartet might never have come to life were it not for a fortuitous illness, not the composer's, but that of a singer. In 1873, Verdi had come to Naples for that city's first performances of his newest opera, *Aida*. Unfortunately, before rehearsals could begin, Teresa Stolz, the soprano scheduled to sing the title role, fell ill and was unable to perform. Rather than recasting the part, Verdi chose to await her recovery, and it was during that three-week period of idleness that he wrote his only quartet, composing it, in his own words, "solely for my own amusement." The work may have offered welcome relief from the pageantry of an operatic score, yet even here Verdi was not immune to his favorite muse. One of the themes heard in the first movement is adapted from a melody belonging to Aida's nemesis, Amneris.

The quartet premiered privately April 1, 1873 (curiously, the date of composer/pianist Sergei Rachmaninoff's birth), one day after *Aida*'s belated launch. Of the occasion, Verdi later recalled, "I had it performed one evening in my house, without attaching the least importance to it and without inviting anyone in particular. Only the seven or eight persons who usually come to visit me were present!" All these years later, it is embraced by chamber music performers, who find delight in this rare opportunity to explore a composition by a man who was a master of vocal melody.

♪♪♪♪

Brahms: Horn Trio in E-flat major, op. 40

The French horn as it is known today is a relatively recent invention: a second-generation descendent of the hunting horn, used by fox and deer hunters to signal their dogs and each other. Function led to form, the coiled shape being better suited to horseback than would have been a straightened instrument.

Hunting horns were later adapted for orchestral use. However, since those early horns had no valves, the player could only change notes by altering the position of the lips and of the right hand tucked into the bell: matters of great finesse that made the instrument notoriously difficult to play. It was, thus, a brave composer who dared to write difficult solos for the recalcitrant creature. Those who loved the horn's mellow voice must have rejoiced when, in the early 19th century, the idea developed of adding valves to control the pitches. This new instrument came to be called the French horn (not that it was French at all). The earlier valveless instrument, by then called the natural horn, soon faded from popularity.

By 1865, when Johannes Brahms (1833 – 1897) composed his Trio for Horn, Violin, and Piano, the natural horn had been absent from the musical scene for half a century, displaced by its more amenable cousin; few performers could have anticipated that anyone would ever again compose for the instrument. Yet Brahms was a master of the retrospective, always fond of earlier forms and styles. For this trio, Brahms specified that he wanted a natural horn, not a French horn, and advised that the performer practice the piece only on that old instrument, so as to become more accustomed to the different technique.

His choice of instrument seems to stem from the trio's inspiration, which came to him while he was walking in the Black Forest above Lichtenthal. In such a sylvan setting, the natural horn, with its hunting connotations, came immediately to mind, and it is to this instrument that Brahms gives the lyrical opening melody. Although modern performers of the trio almost without exception choose French horns, not natural horns, even today's listeners can imagine that melody ringing out across the hills and valleys of southern Germany. If at all possible, hear the trio played in the open air.

In the trio, the horn is matched with violin and piano. Practical enough to desire a wide audience for the work, Brahms noted that he would not object to a viola or a cello taking the horn melodies, if a satisfactory horn player could not be found.

♪♪♪♪

Saint-Saëns: Sonatas for woodwinds and piano

Late in his life, Camille Saint-Saëns (1835 – 1921), having dominated the conservative side of French music since the mid-1800s, decided to speak up against the stark and, to his ears, chaotic directions in which music was heading. He took himself back to the roots, writing a series of sonatas drawing upon the old ideas of structure and lyricism. Three of these sonatas he completed in his last year: the Oboe Sonata in D major, op. 166, the Clarinet Sonata in E-flat major, op. 167, and the Bassoon Sonata in G major, op. 168. In each case, the woodwind instrument was paired with piano. Barring one last short solo piano piece, these three sonatas would be his last completed works.

Of the sonatas – intended to be six in number, though he had too little time remaining to complete the entire series – Saint-Saëns declared that he wanted to bring attention to otherwise neglected instruments. Oboes and bassoons had much repertoire from the Baroque Era, but little thereafter. Clarinets had been slower to come to attention, but other than Brahms, no notable composer of the late 19th century had bothered to bring them into the spotlight. Here, Saint-Saëns gives due attention to all three.

Each of the three sonatas alternates gently reflective moods with others of more sparkling energy. By and large, the music lies neither perilously high in pitch nor uncomfortably low, instead focusing upon what the instrument does best, so as to show it in the best possible light. Saint-Saëns himself was a pianist, so he ensures that his own instrument always has something of interest to add, without overwhelming the woodwind instrument with which it is paired. Taken together, these three sonatas prove that, even in the early 20th century, there was much grace and elegance to be found in music.

Betsy Schwarm

♪♪♪♪

Dvořák: Piano Trio in e minor, op. 90 "Dumky"

A piano trio is not a work for three pianos, but rather one for three instruments, one being a piano, the others a violin and a cello. Although it represents his fourth attempt at the genre, the Piano Trio in e minor of Antonìn Dvořák (1841 – 1904) is never known as his "Trio no. 4." It is, rather, always called by its nickname, "Dumky."

"Dumky" is the plural of "dumka," a traditional Slavonic lament popular throughout all of Eastern Europe. The dumka came to personify the spirit of Slavic folk music, in the same way that the waltz was viewed as the essence of Vienna. Thus, many Eastern European composers worked with dumky styles in hopes of more vividly evoking their homelands. Dvořák, as a Bohemian, would never have ignored its possibilities for emotional expression.

Having had the advantage of dumky in his blood, thanks to growing up in a small village, Dvořák concocted his own original melodies intending to achieve an authentic effect. Thus, in one moment, we may be sure that we are hearing a lark soaring over a wheat field at dawn, but in the next, the scene is of peasants at a harvest celebration, and both images are directly from Dvořák's imagination. In each of the trio's six brief movements, one can imagine these kaleidoscopic visions of the composer's beloved Bohemia.

Of all his chamber works, Dvořák's *Dumky* Trio was the most successful during his lifetime. The piece was completed early in 1891, and premiered in Prague April 11 of that same year. Soon afterward, the composer was invited to New York City to direct the National Conservatory of Music. He then embarked on a farewell tour of Bohemia, a five-month series of forty chamber concerts during which the composer, more frequently occupied as a violist or violinist, performed as pianist in this new masterpiece.

Having said that a dumka is a lament, and noting that the trio is in a minor key, it is worth pointing out that, these points to the contrary, the trio is not a somber work. There are, indeed, passages of tears, but these are carefully balanced with passages of delight, and along with the key changes are changes of tempo so striking that it is as if dancers, frozen in a spotlight, have suddenly burst again into frenzied activity. The agile alterations are typical of the folk music of the region.

♪♪♪♪

Ysaÿe: Sonatas for Solo Violin, op. 27

Belgian-born Eugene Ysaÿe (1858 – 1931) had a great advantage from the beginning: as the son of a violinist, he began learning the instrument at the age of four and three years later, entered the Liège Conservatory. By the time he had reached his 20s, he was regarded as one of the most exciting violinists of his day, and important composers of the day were writing works specifically for him.

However, Ysaÿe did not always stand about waiting for gifts of new repertoire. He also composed for himself. His compositional catalog includes a set of six fiendishly difficult solo violin sonatas (with no piano accompaniment), a quintet, a trio, and a variety of colorfully virtuosic violin works with orchestra, some of which were later transcribed for smaller ensembles, to suit them better to his own concert schedule.

The solo sonatas came into being when Ysaÿe heard his younger colleague, violinist Joseph Szigeti (1892 – 1973), perform one of the JS Bach sonatas, similarly for unaccompanied violin. The earlier works had had little following in earlier generations, except as practice pieces, for with Romantic Era fondness for grand statements, the sight of a single violinist standing alone on stage seemed bizarre. Yet Szigeti proved the worth of the music and thereby inspired Ysaÿe to try his own hand. He completed six solo sonatas in 1924.

Each is dedicated to a different violinist of Ysaÿe's acquaintance – the first to Szigeti – and each attempts to evoke stylistic techniques most identified with that soloist. Ysaÿe himself also played them, but attested that he meant them as tributes to the men to whom they were dedicated. As such, they recall for listeners today the sorts of playing for which those men were renowned. One can also suppose that, in showcasing techniques associated with other players and then playing the sonatas himself, Ysaÿe managed to show that he was as gifted as these other violinists.

♪♪♪♪

Debussy: Sonata for flute, viola, and harp

In the summer of 1915, French composer Claude Debussy (1862 – 1918), together with his wife and daughter, took refuge from the wartime bombardment of Paris in Pourville, a village near the English Channel. He kept busy with composition, stating that he wished to prove that the Germans could not interrupt French artistic thought. Toward this goal, he decided to compose a series of six sonatas for diverse instruments: cello and piano; flute, viola, and harp; violin and piano; oboe, horn, and harpsichord; trumpet, clarinet, bassoon, and piano; and, lastly, a larger ensemble including double-bass.

The diversity of specified instruments was unusual, as was the fact that he was writing sonatas at all; the genre had long been associated with the German/Austrian style, far remote from Debussy's own tastes. Yet precedent for his decision dates from the era of the French Baroque. During the 1600s and early 1700s, such music thrived during the reign of Louis XIV, dubbed "The Sun King" for the supposed brightness of his court; Louis XV continued that tradition. Amongst the leading composers of the day, François Couperin (1668 – 1733) and Marin Marais (1656 – 1728) both wrote sonatas, though not in the expansive duet style that would become popular a century later. Rather, Baroque sonatas were envisioned as light chamber works for several players, often performing on a mixed variety of instruments. It is this type of sonata, not the more recent Germanic model, which Debussy sought to recall.

His project was an ambitious one, particularly for a man slowly succumbing to cancer. Yet Debussy worked as long as strength permitted, dedicating each completed sonata to his wife and daughter. Of the six intended works, Debussy would only manage three: the Cello Sonata of August of 1915; the Flute, Harp, and Viola Sonata later that fall; and the Violin Sonata of 1917. These and a set of piano etudes would be his final compositions. On March 25, 1918, Debussy passed away with his wife and daughter by his side.

Of the three completed sonatas, the most unusual is that for flute, viola, and harp. Although the smooth timbres of the three instruments blend well together, few composers have taken the time to make use of the combination. Debussy produced a sonata in three movements spanning about a quarter hour, with the emphasis of gently floating lines, occasionally rising into greater levels of animation. Often Debussy allows fragments of one player's music to reappear in one of the other parts. As a whole, it is a light-hearted and playful work belying both the war during which it was composed and also the composer's failing health. Here, music rises above circumstance.

♪♪♪♪♪

Bartók: *Contrasts*

Béla Bartók and Benny Goodman: it sounds at first like an unlikely pairing. Bartók was a renowned master of Eastern European folk music, the roots of which strongly affect many of his works. By contrast, Goodman was one of the most respected clarinetists in the world of jazz, that most American creation, but also cared for the classical realm, having the Mozart Clarinet Quintet in his repertoire. They intersected for exactly one work, Bartók's *Contrasts*.

The work was commissioned by Goodman together with violinist Joseph Szegéti, like Bartók a native Hungarian, but one who had resettled in the US. It was Szegéti's idea that Bartók should write a piece for the three of them to perform together, initially asking that the piece be planned to fit on two sides of a 78rpm record, which could accommodate not quite four minutes per side. Bartók agreed to the assignment and produced two movements, which premiered in Carnegie Hall January 9, 1939; as Bartók had been unable to accommodate the date in his schedule, the piano part was played by Endre Petri.

The following year, Bartók managed the trip to New York. He, Szegéti, and Goodman performed the piece again, now with the addition of a middle movement to stand between its two elder brothers, April 21, 1940, and recorded it soon afterward. With the additional movement, the work was now too long for two sides of a 78; four were needed, thus two full records.

Each movement toys with the rhythms of Hungarian folk music – especially the *verbunkos* and *czardas* dances – though flavored with the harmonies of jazz. Bartók was no scholar of jazz, but Szegéti had mailed him some of Goodman's records to give him the general idea of how to proceed.

♪♪♪♪

Tailleferre: String Quartet

Born near Paris, Germaine Tailleferre (1892 – 1983) studied music at the Paris Conservatoire, though her parents had not sent her there with a future career in mind. Rather, the presumption was that a girl who played the piano well was somehow more marriageable than a girl of lesser talents. However, someone neglected to relate this theory to Germaine, who much against her parents' will, determined to make music her life. She became the only female member of the group of early 20th century French/Swiss composers known as "Les Six." Members of that loose assemblage who appear in this collection include Darius Milhaud (1892 – 1974), Francis Poulenc (1899 – 1963), and Arthur Honegger (1892 – 1955).

Having first dabbled in composition in 1897, when as a precocious five-year-old, Tailleferre decided to write an opera, she continued to compose until her health failed just one month before her death at the age of 91, having long survived her male colleagues. The intervening 86 years – almost three times the length of Mozart's compositional career – had been devoted to writing concertos, sonatas, ballets and operas, songs and solo piano works, a piano trio, and a single string quartet, composed in 1919.

Like all her best works, the quartet is a fascinating mixture of moods and styles, from naïve to boisterous, from rhythmically jazz-like to vaguely dissonant. It is as if Tailleferre had set out to create a graceful amalgam of all the best musical developments of the early 20th century: imaginative, inventive, sometimes jazzy, often humorous, and always very individual.

♪♪♪♪♪

Hindemith: sonatas

German composer Paul Hindemith (1895 – 1963) lived through a difficult time in his nation's history, with two world wars and the turmoil of National Socialist rule. Young enough to serve in the first of those wars, he spent his time of service with his viola under his chin, performing in a string quartet formed for the diversion of the officers. With the rise of the Nazis, Hindemith found himself on the wrong side of a political divide, expressing ideas in his concert works that the new government found not to its tastes. Sometimes, those works were banned from performance in Germany, leaving Hindemith not only short on income and artistic expression, but also concerned for his own continued freedom of movement. In 1938, he left for Switzerland, and then in 1940 for the US. He would not return to Europe until after the war.

Hindemith's catalog of works includes an abundance of symphonic and stage works. However, especially notable are his sonatas, some with piano accompaniment and some for solo instrument alone. Perhaps it was his personal experience as a chamber music performer that led him to decide he had something to say with small groups of players. Indeed, his own instruments – principally the viola, but also the violin – are well-represented in the list. However, he does not neglect other families of instruments. His list of sonatas also includes works for cello, bass, harp, flute, oboe, English horn, clarinet, bassoon, trumpet, French horn, trombone, and tuba.

Most of the sonatas date from 1938 and '39, just after Hindemith left for Switzerland. None of the sonatas is intensely ferocious in a virtuosic manner. Rather, they tend to be pleasantly lyrical and well-balanced. Hindemith had come to feel that music should have some practical value, not merely rely upon pyrotechnics or compositional finesse to make its point. He believed that anyone should be able to appreciate good music, and his sonatas are a fine example of that view. One need not be an insider to appreciate what it has to say, and a decent performer on almost any instrument has a fair chance to include the German master in his/her repertoire.

Ullmann: String Quartet no. 3

Had he been of an earlier generation, Viktor Ullmann (1898 – 1944) might have had a long and happy life. A native of Prague, he had gone to Vienna in his early twenties to study with the progressive composer Arnold Schoenberg (1874 – 1951), but returned to his hometown for work as a conductor and accompanist. His string quartets, piano sonatas, orchestral pieces, and operas found mostly favorable notice. Unfortunately, Ullmann's Jewish heritage also earned attention, in his case from the Nazis who had come to Prague in 1938.

In 1942, Ullmann was arrested and sent to the Terezin concentration camp (the Germans called it Theresienstadt), where many other musical figures had been confined. Together, they kept active in music, composing and performing whenever possible, and Ullmann composed his last works. In October of 1944, he was sent on to Auschwitz, where his life came to an end.

One of Ullmann's Terezin compositions is his String Quartet no. 3. Its two predecessors vanished, but this one survived, in the care of Ullmann's fellow prisoner Dr. Emil Utitz. Dr. Utitz remained at Teresin, rather than going on to Auschwitz, and Ullmann dedicated the quartet to him, before leaving it in Utitz' hands.

About a quarter hour in length, the quartet is ostensibly in four movements, though there are no breaks between the movements, so the effect is more of changing moods than of separate movements. Melodic fragments are more the rule than broad expansive melodies, as if Ullmann sensed there would be insufficient time to develop more extended musical expressions. Throughout the work, one finds reference to musical ideas both old and new, with astringent modern harmonies shading intricate weaving of musical lines. The former technique would have puzzled JS Bach, even as the latter made sense to him, but both worked for Ullmann.

♪♪♪♪

Shostakovich: Piano Quintet in g minor, op. 57

Dmitri Shostakovich (1906 – 1975) was not only a composer. He was also a superb pianist who, during his student years, had helped to support his family by playing piano in silent movie houses. As his career moved in more artistic directions, his flair for the keyboard continued to influence his music, resulting in compositions that are both virtuosic and perfectly suited to the instrument.

In 1940, Shostakovich was asked by the members of the Beethoven Quartet – who, in years to come, would premiere nearly all of his 15 string quartets – to write a work that all five friends could play together. At this point in his career, Shostakovich, whose catalog included six symphonies and a quantity of stage and film music, had written very little chamber music. It is perhaps that limited experience that caused him to rely on Classical models, planning the work somewhat as Haydn or Mozart would have planned it, even though the melodic structures tended in more modern directions. With this quintet, Shostakovich produced a work reminiscent of that bygone era, yet still mindful of his own 20th century milieu.

The quintet was remarkably successful. At its premiere in Moscow November 23, 1940, the third and fifth movements were encored, and it soon earned a Stalin Prize from the Board of the Leningrad Composers' Union. Along with the award came prize money of 100,000 rubles: a significant sum. Remembering the political furor that his opera *Lady Macbeth of Mtsensk* had attracted only six years earlier, nearly costing Shostakovich his career, this victory must have seemed especially sweet.

To be sure, there were some skeptics. Shostakovich's elder colleague Sergei Prokofiev (1891 – 1953) commented on his own astonishment that so young a composer should be, in his phrase, "so very much on his guard," that is, he wondered why Shostakovich had bothered to retain any elements of the Classical style. Yet those words may have been flavored by a bit of sour grapes, for few of Prokofiev's compositions achieved the immediate acclaim of this one quintet by his younger colleague.

♪♪♪♪

Takemitsu: *Toward the Sea*

Despite coming of age in Tokyo during World War II, Toru Takemitsu (1930 – 1996) was enamored of Western musical concepts. Take the flow of Debussy and the modern harmonies of Messaien, flavored by only a touch of the Oriental, and one finds Takemitsu's very personal style. His music shows a strong interest in subtle shifts of tone color, and often reveals connections with non-musical art forms, especially poetry, painting, theater, and film. His was a wide-ranging imagination, giving listeners much scope for their own interpretations.

Toward the Sea is one of numerous Takemitsu pieces evocative of water. In this case, it is specifically the ocean, a fact emphasized by more than just the overall title. Each of its three movements bears a subtitle derived from the ultimate sea-faring novel, Herman Melville's *Moby Dick*. The music becomes more a sequence of mood pictures than depictions of specific scenes from the tale. One does not hear the harpoons swishing through the air, nor even Ahab raging at his crew, but one can certainly sense the atmosphere with which the novel is occupied.

The opening "Night" is gently haunting in atmosphere; "Moby Dick," the second movement, gradually becomes more restless in character, perhaps evocative as much of Ahab's thoughts as of the whale itself. The piece concludes with "Cape Cod," the most spirited of the three movements, with dance-like rhythms that alternate with more melancholy ideas, as if the sailors are thinking of home.

Takemitsu composed *Toward the Sea* in 1981 for alto flute and guitar. Later that year, he reworked it for alto flute, harp, and string orchestra, then in 1989, created a third version for alto flute and harp duet, but without orchestra. In each version, there is a melodic fragment that represents the sea itself in its notes upon the page. The second and third letters of the word "sea" are readily rendered musically. As for the S, Takemitsu knew that in old German notation, S stood for that which is commonly thought of as E-flat. So this three-note rising pattern, the first two of those three notes very close in pitch, is intended to sing out "sea" in the most literal sense.

♪♪♪♪

Glass: String Quartet no. 2, "Company"

For the general public, the hypnotically flowing lines of the music of Philip Glass (b. 1937) are most familiar through his film music, notably *Koyaanisqatsi, Mishima, The Thin Blue Line,* and *The Hours* (see Chapter Nine). However, his music takes many forms, including symphonies, songs, stage works, and operas. He has also composed numerous string quartets, and the second of those derives from his stage music for *Company* of 1983.

Glass had been commissioned to provide incidental music to accompany a dramatization of Samuel Becket's *Company* (not to be confused with Steven Sondheim's musical of the same name). Upon completing that score, he thought it would work well for string ensemble and named the new quartet after the original stage work. Whether in its quartet setting or in a grander version for string orchestra, in either realization, one finds a haunting and reflective work rich with the pure minimalistic style that Glass popularized.

Steady pulsing effects underlie long phrases that float above, and whether the tempo is slow and reflective or fast and driving – both of which are found here – there is always that pulsation acting as a heartbeat for the music. Even with the simple scoring of a work for strings alone, Glass finds a kaleidoscope of colors through the interactions of his musical forces. Just because all the instruments are of the same family does not mean Glass cannot find contrasting effects within those families to juxtapose against one another.

♪♪♪♪

Golijov: *Dreams and Prayers of Isaac the Blind*

Born in Argentina to parents of Eastern European Jewish origin, Osvaldo Golijov (b. 1960) often reflects upon his heritage in his music. This is particularly clear in *Dreams and Prayers of Isaac the Blind*. Isaac was a Medieval rabbi who lived in Provence and asserted that all of existence throughout the universe derives from a single source, in this case, the letters of the Hebrew alphabet. This concept of the connectedness of things relates well to music of all kinds, as the performers must work together to achieve the desired results. Golijov maintains this is especially true of chamber music in which, in the composer's words, "groups of four souls dissolve their individuality into single, higher organisms, called string quartets."

Golijov's *Dreams and Prayers of Isaac the Blind* began as a work for string quartet with klezmer clarinet, drawing upon the styles and sounds of much traditional Jewish music. In that form, the work premiered in Germany August 10, 1994. A version for string orchestra and klezmer clarinet followed in 2005. Both are structured with three central movements bracketed by a prelude and a postlude.

The opening prelude is thoughtful and prayer-like, its melodic material derived from an ancient Hebrew prayer. With the next movement, marked "Agitato," moods shift to a dance-like spirit, with both the clarinet and the string ensemble evoking klezmer styles. Each of the following two movements contrasts reflective passages with others of frenetic energy, often in close order, as if to suggest that life is changeable in nature. For the finale, the calm and flowing atmosphere of the prelude returns, bringing the work full circle.

Throughout, the clarinet tends to offer the rather mournful atmosphere of the quieter side of klezmer style folk music. It is not a style that all fine clarinetists can magically call forth. However, when one can, and when the string players are equally inspired, it is a work of impressively shaded colors and attitudes.

♪♪♪♪

Newman: *Pennipotenti*

Musical gifts sometimes run in families. Consider the great number of German Baroque and early Classical composers of the name Bach, or, in the same generations in France, the Couperins. Closer to home – both in geography and in time – there are the Newmans of southern California. Family founder Alfred Newman (1901 – 1970) was one of the major names of film music, with a catalog of works that included *Song of Bernadette* and *Love is a Many-Splendored Thing*, both of which earned for him Academy Awards. The next generations of Newmans includes Alfred's nephew, the famed singer-songwriter Randy, as well as two sons who followed their father into film music, and youngest daughter Maria (b. 1962), who shifted the family's music focus from cinema to the concert hall.

More Classical Insights

Ms. Newman's *Pennipotenti* dates from 2005. Note that this title is not quite the political term "plenipotentiary," though the two words have a Latin root in common. Ms. Newman's title speaks not of sweeping political powers, but of the sweeping powers of feathers, as in birds, and each of the four short movements bears as subtitle the name of a bird. In the work, she attempts to represent the essence of various birds through the contrasting timbres of flute, violin, and viola. Ms. Newman plays both the string instruments on a professional level, and understands the characteristics of the flute well enough to allow it to contribute much beyond simple warbling of bird song.

The first movement, "The Dipper," portrays both the chirping of the waterside bird and the restful aura of the environments it inhabits. "The Snowy Owl" of the second movement bears all the serenity of that regal bird's soundless flight – serenity, that is, unless one happens to be a field mouse. The third movement brings the restless motion of "The Hummingbird." To close the four-movement suite, Ms. Newman chose to represent "The Falcon," with varied melodic ideas that capture both its effortless, soaring flight and its lightning quick dives upon its prey. Each player is asked at times to bend the pitch subtly from one note to a nearby one, as if one were imagining the deft manipulation of the edges of the wings in flight. All in all, despite having only three players, *Pennipotenti* manages to bring to its listeners a great variety of imagery.

♪♪♪♪

Frank: *Leyendas – An Andean Walkabout*

The family of Gabriela Frank (b. 1972 in Berkeley, California) has roots from Peru to China to Lithuania. Perhaps unsurprisingly, her music has a highly varied character, reflecting elements of the styles of various lands. Ms. Frank has been called a "musical anthropologist," an idea that places her in the best company, as composers from Edvard Grieg (1843 – 1907) to Béla Bartók (1881 – 1945) similarly explored national musical traditions. Ms. Frank is rediscovering those approaches, blending rhythmic/melodic elements of her own culture into a classical framework.

Frank wrote *Leyendas* in 2001 for string quartet, then reworked it for string orchestra. She envisions it as a blend of the traditions of Western classical music, with its expectations of scope and structure, and Andean folk music, with its vibrant rhythms and personalities. Each of the six short movements – spanning rather less than half an hour together – has a particular scene to portray, drawn from the cultures and folk instruments of the Andes. Languid, haunting moods appear in turn with restless, nervous ones, and though the instruments involved are all strings, this fact does not prevent Frank from evoking the particularly Andean aura of the panpipe. Taken as a whole, it is a vibrant and colorful musical journey into the high peaks of the Andes, though with tools Bach and Mozart would have known. The accent is new, but the medium familiar.

More Classical Insights

Chapter Six:
Keyboard and Guitar Works

In his time, Wolfgang Amadeus Mozart (1756 – 1791) was one of the greatest pianists in Vienna, and here is one of his most famous melodies for that instrument. It opens not the very beginning of the work in which it appears, but the rather the third movement, and the composer specified that it was meant to sound rather Turkish. Why was an Austrian composer bothering with Turkish sounds, and why with a piano? We'll find out, not only why Mozart did what he did, but also why other composers for keyboards wrote their music the way they did. For an 18th century Austrian such as Mozart did not use the piano at all similarly to a 20th century Frenchman such as Olivier Messaien (1908 – 1992).

We'll also find solo guitar music in this chapter. Pianos and guitars are not entirely interchangeable: not only is one is much larger and the other much more portable, but their playing techniques are quite different. However, both represent ideas of how a single player can present melodies and harmonies simultaneously in music of impressive complexity. Besides, guitarists in search of new things to play have been known to borrow music from the piano repertoire, so we'll let them co-exist here.

Of the keyboard music, it is not solely for piano. Before the piano came into wide usage in the late 18th century, the keyboard instrument of choice was the harpsichord, possessed of a more delicate mechanism and a lighter, rather plucky sound. It is not an instrument that could have survived the touch of Jerry Lee Lewis (b. 1935), nor even Ludwig van Beethoven (1770 – 1827). However, it was the stand-by keyboard instrument of the Baroque Era, and it was the voice of that instrument that composers had in their ears prior to the time of Mozart. One can play that music on a modern piano, and even on a modern synthesizer, but it will not sound quite as it was imagined by the composer. Similarly, though there is no law preventing one from playing guitar works on the electric version of the instrument, it was the acoustic one that these composers had in mind for their music.

Terms that often appear in the context of piano or guitar music are "prelude" and "etude." One might suppose that a "prelude" would be an introduction to some other, grander creation: not in this case. Often, "prelude" was a word used for a short, one-movement solo piece, often highly expressive in nature. "Etude" derives from the French verb étudier, meaning "to study." An etude was a study piece or practice piece, intended to help hone a particular technical skill, perhaps playing notes of a specific interval or rhythm. Etudes do exist for other instruments, and even for singers, but they rise to public attention most frequently in the realm of keyboard and guitar music. This fact should not be taken to suggest that they need more practice than other musicians; more likely is that a larger number of composers have perceived a market for such pieces, and most of those included in this chapter themselves played the instrument for which they were writing.

♪♪♪♪

François Couperin: Pieces de clavecin, Book 2:
    6th Ordre in B-flat major

The Couperins were to French music as the Bachs were to German music: for 200 years, one of the most prominent names in the field. Throughout the 1600s and 1700s, their names and music were ever-present and ever-respected. For the Bachs, Johann Sebastian (1685 – 1750) was the greatest; for the Couperins, it was François (1668-1733). Even in his own time he was known as "Le Grand," in part to distinguish him from his Uncle François, who was also active in music, but also in recognition of the quality – and quantity – of his music. Couperin published four separate collections of harpsichord music, each including four to five dozen descriptively named solo pieces. Within these "Books" were separate sections called "Ordres," into which pieces were sorted according to the key in which they were composed.

Book Two of Couperin's harpsichord pieces was published in 1717, four years after the first book and thirteen years before the fourth and last. In its sixth Ordre, one finds eight different pieces, amongst them one of the most often encountered of all solo harpsichord pieces. Fifth of those eight pieces is *Les baricades misterieuses*, the French title of which means exactly what it would appear to mean to

English speakers. Its fame may be due in part to its memorable title, but its music is also notable, with a brisk and airy opening theme that gradually evolves. It seems not to be exceptionally "mysterious" nor certainly a "barricade" in any traditional sense. However, Couperin might have been thinking figuratively, perhaps of a coquette who slyly puts off her admirers. The other seven pieces of the Sixth Ordre offer a variety of moods and impressions. Taken together, it is a suite of pieces that demonstrates the range of expression that one can summon from a harpsichord. At least, one can if one is a master like Couperin.

♪♪♪♪

JS Bach: *Goldberg Variations, BWV 988*

Difficult though it is to understand now, Johann Sebastian Bach (1685 – 1750) was sorely neglected during his own lifetime. His nearly three decades in Leipzig – from 1723 until his death in 1750 – brought him little income and less admiration. In such a situation, it is no surprise that Bach began to look beyond Leipzig for appreciation. He found it in Dresden, where his eldest son, Wilhelm Friedemann (1710 – 1784), who worked as a church organist, had managed to bring the family name and reputation to the attention of Count Hermann Karl von Kayserling, the Russian ambassador to the court at Saxony.

A great devotee of music, the count suffered from insomnia. The combination of those two influences led to the count to commission from the elder Bach a set of harpsichord variations lengthy enough to amuse the sleepless ambassador in the small hours of the night. The resulting piece, the *Goldberg Variations*, reputedly was named for Johann Gottlieb Goldberg, a young pianist protégée of the Count's. Supposedly, Goldberg would be the designated performer. Some scholars suggest that that part of the story may be apocryphal, but since Goldberg acquired little fame on his own account, and died before he was 30, it seems a small matter to let his name stand in this case.

The lengthy score – roughly an hour complete – is a set of variations upon a simple theme which is stated at the opening, then taken through thirty alterations to rhythms, harmonies, and textures, before returning simply at the end. Over two and a half centuries later, it stands as proof of how much a gifted composer can make of limited materials.

It was published in 1742 as part of the *Clavier-Übung (Keyboard Exercises)*, making it one of all too few Bach compositions to come into print before his death. That it was published without a specific dedication to the Count has led some historians to question whether the work was actually written at his request. However, it is possible that the Count, for his reasons of his own, declined public acknowledgement of his connection to the score. Whoever stood behind the work's creation, it remains a magnificent testament to the composer's finesse.

♪♪♪♪

Mozart: Piano Sonata in A major, K. 331, "Alla Turca"

Wolfgang Amadeus Mozart (1756 – 1791) was not just an inspired composer but also a gifted pianist. Famed for his effortless playing, he consistently offered performances which in his own words would "flow like oil," and ridiculed melodramatic players for "flopping about and making grimaces." From Mozart's point of view, the beauty of a composition should never be disguised by theatrics. It should look easy, even when it isn't, indeed, especially when it isn't. As he remarked in a letter to his father in 1784, "I had to work hard so as not to need to [let it look like] work anymore."

Evidence of his preferred style of piano music survives in his Piano Sonata in A, K. 331, completed around 1782. This was after the composer had left his native Salzburg for the bright lights of Vienna, but as he was sometimes out of town on concert tours, he may not have finished the work in the imperial capital. However, it would have caught much attention in that city, so fond of fine piano playing.

The sonata's first two movements have their charms. However, it is upon the third and last movement that the sonata's reputation hangs. In the final movement, Mozart draws upon a popular trend in Vienna at the time for Turkish-flavored music. With the Austrian Empire so close to Turkey, and the latter nation's armies occasionally making their way as far as Vienna's walls, Turkish styles always caught attention. In cuisine, that meant coffee. In music, that meant the Janissary bands of the Turkish military, with their strong percussion and jangling bells. Here there are no bells or drums, yet a pair of hands on the keyboard can evoke much of the same effect, with great exuberance and energy. This one movement has acquired a life of its own, in various transcriptions, as the Rondo alla Turca. A 'rondo' was a pattern for composition in which various contrasting melodies take turns with one another for dramatic effect.

More Classical Insights

♪♪♪♪

Beethoven: Piano Sonata no. 14 in c-sharp minor,
    op. 27, no. 2 "Moonlight"

Dating from 1801, the so-called "Moonlight" Sonata was one of Beethoven's first works in a new century. The composer himself, his hearing still adequate at this early date, gave the work's premiere; the friend who had been recruited as page turner remembered later that during the last movement, strings were breaking and getting tangled in the hammers, that he spent much of his time reaching inside the piano to try to rectify the situation. The sonata is dedicated to Countess Giulietta Guicciardi, a 16 year old aristocrat whom the thirtyish composer would have married had she been willing. In 1803, she would marry another composer, Count Gallenberg, who was not only of her own social set but also her own age.

Its official subtitle, chosen by the composer himself, is "sonata quasi una fantasia," which he had also adopted for its immediate predecessor, the Sonata no. 13. The reference serves to remind listeners that the piece lies between a formal sonata and a free-flowing fantasia in mood and structure, and that one should expect the unexpected. Indeed, contrary to usual practice, the first movement is the gentlest of the three with a reflective melody floating over progressions of arpeggios. The second movement offers more forward motion, though still in a mostly restful mood. All the sonata's storms are saved for its highly dramatic last movement, a turbulent and swirling storm of pounding chords and charging melodies. Here, Beethoven offers a Niagara Falls of music that overwhelms the listener, though hopefully not the pianist.

The familiar nickname "Moonlight" originated at the work's publication thanks to the German Romantic poet Rellstab, and can only be imagined as referring to the first movement. For if there is moonlight in the angry third movement – strong with the storms of Sturm und Drang – it can only be breaking through a tempest, and the second movement, though mellower, is still a rather domestic mood with none of the mystery that moonlight generally inspires.

♪♪♪♪♪

Schubert: *Wanderer Fantasy* in C major, D. 760

Franz Schubert (1797 – 1828) was one of the finest pianists in piano-hungry Vienna. Unfortunately, few beyond his own social circle knew it; even he wasn't entirely sure of it and was ever hesitant to put himself in front of the public. However, examination of his many solo piano works reveals an innate understanding of what can be made of the instrument. That understanding can come from a finely honed grasp of musical concepts, and such a sense was, indeed, in Schubert's bag of tricks. Yet being able to try out different effects one's self at the keyboard is also useful, sometimes leading to ideas that are not standard practice. Schubert was no wild radical, but his piano works offer ideas that even his elder contemporary Beethoven had not tried at the piano.

This is exactly the case with the *Wanderer Fantasy*. Its colorful name derives from the composer's 1816 song "The Wanderer," a melancholy narrative of a homesick traveler. Schubert borrowed its melody for re-use in this solo piano work in 1822. Unlike the vast majority of this composer's music, it found publication quickly, appearing in print the next year as his opus 15: a shocking under-estimation of how much music he had actually composed. The catalog compiled most of a century later by musicologist Otto Deutsch attests that, in fact, Schubert's works were already nearing 800 in number.

By calling the piece a "fantasy," rather than the more usual term "sonata," Schubert left himself room to indulge new ideas. A sonata would be expected to be in three or four movements of different tempos, each featuring the expected structures of the music. Schubert knew how to follow the rules, but here chose not to do so. His *Wanderer Fantasy* has tempos that accord with protocol. However, he based the entire work upon elaborations of a single theme and supporting rhythm borrowed from that song, though here much varied and colored in far more vivid shades. All of it could be broken into separate movements, but this need not be done. Spanning only twenty minutes as it does, and with the first two "movements" fading to a gentle close, it is even more effective to slide smoothly from one section to the next, forming a vividly shaded tapestry of sound.

Beethoven had used fragments of melodies to tie together symphonic works; most famously, his Symphony no. 5 does exactly this. However, his piano works tend to offer distinctly new ideas as they progress. At the time that Schubert composed his *Wanderer Fantasy*, Beethoven was living right across town. One wonders what the elder composer would have made of the piece, but Schubert was simply too shy to seek out the great master for consultation. Schubert's new ideas for music came entirely out of his own imagination.

Betsy Schwarm

♪♪♪♪

Mendelssohn: *Songs without Words*

There is a vintage *Peanuts*® comic strip in which Schroeder, playing his piano while Lucy lounges nearby, remarks, "This is Mendelssohn's *Song without Words*." She listens for a moment, then asks, "Couldn't he think of any?" It's a good joke, but though Schroeder has no reply, the composer himself, Felix Mendelssohn (1809 – 1847), would have had a ready answer for her.

The composer, in a letter written to his friend Marc-Andre Souchay October 15, 1842, observed as follows: "If you ask me what I was thinking of when I wrote it, I would say: just the song as it is. And if I happen to have particular words in mind for one or another of these songs, I would never wish to tell them to anyone, because the same words never mean the same things to different people. Only the song can say the same thing." So we are not meant to ask what the *Songs without Words* are about, only to find what the music says to us as individuals.

Mendelssohn composed about four dozen short, abstract piano pieces that have come to be known as *Songs without Words*. The first set of six appeared in print in England in 1832 under the title "Original Melodies for the Pianoforte." Five more collections appeared in the course of Mendelssohn's abbreviated life (he died at age 38), two further collections posthumously.

Two of the most famous *Songs without Words* are the op. 62, no. 6, having become known as the "Spring Song" and the op. 67, no. 4, labeled "Spinning Song." Neither subtitle originated with the composer, but they do serve to help these two sunny and charming pieces to stand out from their fellows.

In each set, the various pieces had been composed over the course of a few years, as time and ideas came to him, and it cannot be assumed the Mendelssohn originally intended them to belong together. As a set of several short piano pieces would likely sell better than a single work, there was logic in collecting together a few otherwise unrelated items. Therefore, contemporary pianists have no obligation to play a single book straight through beginning to end. Choosing a variety of pieces that speak to the performer's heart not only makes practical sense, but also seems to suit Mendelssohn's own view that the songs, words or no words, are individual expressions.

♪♪♪♪

Robert Schumann: *Carnaval*, op. 9

Published in 1837, three years before Robert Schumann (1810 – 1856) and Clara Wieck (1819 – 1896) married, Schumann's *Carnaval* is not strictly a piano sonata. Rather, it is a set of so-called "character pieces:" short movements intended to convey a mood or personality to the listener.

Their effectiveness depends not only on the player's dexterity with the actual notes, but also in that player's ability to change expressive mood from one moment to the next, for the various movements differ greatly from one another. The work became a favorite in Clara's repertoire;

she was considered one of the very finest pianists of the day, and, outliving her husband by forty years, continued to include his works in her recitals. It also attracted favorable attention from Franz Liszt (1810 – 1886), whose playing style, though very different from Clara's, also had devoted admirers at the time.

Each of the pieces – nearly two dozen in all – has a subtitle to clarify what image Schumann had in mind as he wrote it. Space does not permit an explanation of each movement, but some deserve clarification. The fifth and sixth pieces, "Eusebius" and "Florestan," bear pen names that Schumann used in his critical writing, the former even-tempered in mood and the latter tending toward exuberant expression.

The eleventh piece, "Chiarina," is the teenaged Clara, already an object of Schumann's interest. One also finds Ernestine von Fricken, two years older than Clara, captured in the tenth and thirteenth pieces. Schumann greatly admired Ernestine and would have married her. However, within another year, Ernestine would be displaced in Schumann's heart by Clara.

The last piece in the sequence, the Davidsbűndler (Band of David), pays tribute to a group of musically inclined friends and colleagues of Schumann's; their opinions and reactions to music were often referred to in his critical writing. At the time *Carnaval* was published, Schumann was better known as a music journalist than as a composer; it was in part through Clara championing his works that the balance of Schumann's reputation began to shift.

More Classical Insights

♪♪♪♪

Liszt: Piano Sonata in b minor

Hungarian born Franz Liszt (1811 – 1886) was a showcase pianist: the pop idol of his day, offering flamboyant recitals to crowds of adoring women and stunned colleagues. Sometimes, critics took him to task for having more glitter than substance, but regardless of his public image, the man himself was well-read. He had a preference for religious and philosophical texts, and his ideas gradually came to influence his compositions. Liszt's music, like the man himself, is an intricate blend of showmanship and idealism.

Although Liszt composed hundreds of solo piano pieces, he seems to have preferred the more abstract and less constraining forms, as only once did he bother to create a full piano sonata. This work, his Sonata in b minor, was finished in 1853 and published the following year.

At the time, Liszt had set aside his original career of traveling piano virtuoso in favor of a conducting appointment in Weimar, Germany. At first, skeptical critics refused to believe that the flashy ladies' man had what it took to be a serious artist, but his conducting work with both orchestral pieces and operas won over the detractors. The new focus of his career seems to have flavored his own compositions, too, as nearly all of his large-scale ambitious works date from the Weimar years.

As for this lone Sonata, Liszt dedicated it to his colleague Robert Schumann (1810 – 1856) whom he had come to know through Schumann's virtuoso pianist wife Clara (1819 – 1896). The sonata would not have figured prominently in Clara's repertoire, as her journals reveal that she found Liszt's music to be excessively showy. However, many other virtuosos reveled in its challenges, with sharply varied dramatic moods and distinctly contrasting themes. Unlike his predecessors, Liszt does not bother with the standard three or four distinct movements, but rather creates an uninterrupted flow of music in which tempo changes hint at the more usual division into movements.

♪♪♪♪

Gottschalk: *The Union*

Born in New Orleans to parents of English and French heritage, Louis Moreau Gottschalk (1829 – 1869) was a musical prodigy. At seven, he was playing the organ at his hometown's cathedral. In adolescence, he concertized in Europe. Even Chopin was impressed by the boy's skills at the piano. Although Gottschalk had been refused admission to the Paris Conservatoire due to his American birth, a French publishing house offered to print all his future compositions, whatever he might choose to write. The popularity of his works, and his own personal charisma, made him the best-known American pianist of his generation.

Gottschalk's own compositions, largely though not exclusively for solo piano, sometimes draw upon his own Creole background, and at other times upon a broader American perspective. Dating from 1862, Gottschalk's *The Union* is a patriotic tribute written by a native of the American South then resident in the North. Its inherent American voice might have been lost on his European fans, but not upon the American ones.

Here, one finds an amalgam of American melodies, including "The Star Spangled Banner" (at the time, not yet the national anthem), the old military tune "Hail Columbia," and even "Yankee Doodle." Rolled chords in the lower notes of the left hand suggest drum-rolls, and Gottschalk takes the time to combine his melodic materials into simultaneous expression. Ultimately, one finds "Yankee Doodle" dancing in the right hand while "Hail Columbia" struts in the left. In so doing, Gottschalk deftly shows how much can be made of even the humblest melodic materials.

♪♪♪♪♪

Tárrega: *Recuerdos de la Alhambra*
 (Reminiscences of the Alhambra)

Francisco Tárrega (1852 – 1909) was the Andres Segovia of his day: internationally regarded as the greatest of all guitarists. That Tárrega achieved this reputation in a time when the guitar, too quiet to stand out against massive orchestras, was generally little noticed, further enhances his achievements, for in his hands, the guitar became worthy of attention. Studies at the Madrid Conservatory gave him a thorough knowledge of composition and the piano, skills that he used to enhance the complexity and the impact of his works for his own instrument.

Although an active composer of original works for guitar, including an expansive set of solo Preludes, Tárrega also transcribed piano pieces by Beethoven, Mendelssohn, Chopin, and others. Moreover, he adapted the works of some of his fellow Spaniards, especially Isaac Albeniz (1860 – 1909) and Enrique Granados (1867 – 1916). Just because a piece had been imagined for the 88 keys of the piano did not keep Tárrega from fitting it to the six strings of the guitar.

His most famous original work, *Recuerdos de la Alhambra* was inspired by the magnificent Moorish palace in Granada. One might imagine it as reflective of the architecture, or of the people who used to live there, or, more broadly speaking, of the fact that the guitar – having roots in Arabic culture – would have been a favored instrument there. Whichever of those images one favors, Tárrega flavored the piece with thoughtful melodies and a steady tremolo technique – trilling upon a single note so as to create a longer tone – to evoke his impression of the ancient royal palace.

♪♪♪♪♪

Chaminade: *Etudes de concert*, op. 35 *(Concert Etudes)*

Influential neighbors can be useful. When Cécile Chaminade (1857 – 1944) was growing up in Paris, her parents saw to it that she had piano lessons, as it was considered appropriate for elegant young ladies of the upper class. A career in the arts, or even university studies of any kind, was <u>not</u> considered appropriate, so Cécile's music training might have ended there. However, the Chaminades were neighbors of Georges Bizet (1838 – 1875), then not yet composer of *Carmen*, but respected for his previous stage works. Upon hearing Cécile at the piano, he persuaded her parents that it would be a loss to the musical world if she did not attend the Paris Conservatoire, and so she went.

Chaminade developed a successful career as both a pianist and a composer. That she happened to be an attractive and fashionable woman may have helped; certainly, her publishers were fond of putting her picture on the cover page of her music, a strategy that might not have worked for her gentlemen colleagues. Yet the quality still needed to be there, and critical commentary at the time agreed that she was not just a woman who composed, but rather someone who had something to say in music, whatever her gender.

Chaminade's six *Etudes de concert* strike the perfect balance of sweetness and storms, with gentle, lyrical passages alternating with others more markedly dramatic. Consider the contrast between the light but steady motion of "Fileuse" (Woman Spinning) and the strongly dramatic energy of the central pages of "Autumne" (Autumn). Neither etude would be likely to suit a pretty young society woman playing to entertain her family. They are rightly called *Concert Etudes*: designed for the sterner demands of the concert stage.

♫♫♫♫

MacDowell: *Woodland Sketches*, op. 51

Born in New York City, Edward MacDowell (1861-1908), like many of his American contemporaries in music, received the bulk of his musical training in Europe. American music schools of the time were widely considered inferior to their counterparts in France and Germany.

Returning to the US in 1888, MacDowell soon became professor of music at Columbia University, though he always reserved time for his own composition projects. Although he had learned his trade abroad, the inspirations for his music generally lie in American soil, particularly the countryside of New England, for he owned and loved a summer home in Peterborough, New Hampshire.

Although his catalog contains everything from songs to symphonic works, it is for his piano pieces that MacDowell is best known, particularly for one specific miniature: "To a Wild Rose," one of the ten pieces that together compose his *Woodland Sketches*. The continued existence of the graceful little piece is due to the attentiveness of the composer's wife, Marian. One day, as she was emptying the wastebasket in his studio, she happened to unfold a discarded scrap of paper and found that it was a page of used manuscript paper. As a music student herself (formerly one of MacDowell's own students), she found her curiosity piqued and sat down at his piano to play it. Immediately, she was struck by its value and persuaded her husband that it should be kept, adding that it made her think of the wild roses near their New Hampshire summer home. Thus, "To a Wild Rose" was saved, and eventually would become the opening movement of the more extended suite *Woodland Sketches*, when it was published in 1896.

Each of the ten pieces is brief, a character piece of particular mood. Some, like "To a Wild Rose," are sweet and wistful; others, like "From an Indian Lodge" are bolder of expression. In each, the best approach seems to be for a listener to glance at the title, then seek to find in the music what that phrase might have meant to MacDowell. It is music that speaks to the mind's eye, and if many a beginning pianist has tried to tackle "To a Wild Rose," one rapidly discovers that, in the hands of a fine pianist, there is more beneath the surface of the music.

♪♪♪♪

Debussy: Preludes

It is on his orchestral score *Prelude to the Afternoon of a Faun* that the reputation of French composer Claude Debussy (1862 – 1918) mostly rests. Yet he was also a piano devotee, and it was as a piano student that he was admitted to the Paris Conservatoire in 1873 at the age of eleven. Composition studies soon took precedence, but he never ceased to play, and always continued to write for piano, producing dozens of solo pieces.

Debussy's piano Preludes were published in two books, each including a dozen pieces, the first book in 1910, the second in 1913. He was far from the first composer to write solo keyboard pieces and call them "preludes;" even JS Bach (1685 – 1750) had done so, as had the more recent example of Frederic Chopin (1810 – 1849). Yet Debussy went one step further than his predecessors, designating each piece not just by number and key, but also by a vividly descriptive title. So one finds such scenes as "Footsteps in the Snow", "The Girl with the Flaxen Hair," "Fireworks," and "Sounds and Perfumes Swirl in the Evening Air."

Interestingly, he placed the titles at the ends of the pieces, not the beginnings, as if he did not want either players or listeners to feel too constrained by his imagery. "Art," he once observed, "is the most beautiful deception of all... Let us not disillusion anyone by bringing too much reality into the dream." In their individual ways, each of Debussy's Preludes offers a fleeting glimpse of some imagined scene.

♪♪♪♪♪

Granados: *The Maiden and the Nightingale,*
   from *Goyescas*

Despite the high profile of the guitar, the piano has rarely been far from the attentions of Spain's greatest composers. Enrique Granados (1867 – 1916) was one of his nation's finest pianists, attracting strong international interest. He flavored his performances with dash and flair, and his own solo piano works make the most of the instrument's varied abilities. Along with the occasional Spanish rhythms, one also finds richly varied expressive colors.

Granados' most ambitious solo piano work is the six-movement suite he called *Goyescas*. The name comes from the masterful Spanish painter Francisco Goya (1746 – 1828). Goya was fond of painting emotionally vivid portraits of aristocratic ladies and gentlemen, and Granados was inspired to bring the spirit of those paintings into the piano suite. It premiered in Barcelona March 9, 1911, and immediately attracted such favorable attention that Granados expanded it into an opera.

The opera premiered five years later at New York City's Metropolitan Opera, and, in an unexpected fashion, led to the composer's death. So much attention had been granted to the opera that President Woodrow Wilson invited Granados and his wife to a state dinner at the White House. The occasion caused them to change their intended ship home to Spain. The original ship reached port safely;

the ship that carried the Granados couple was torpedoed by a German U-boot in the English Channel, and both the composer and his wife drowned.

Of the original solo piano suite, the movement most often heard on its own is *The Maiden and the Nightingale*. Granados evoked the bird with fluttery trills, and the girl with a melancholy, song-like melody. For the finale, he expanded upon the warbling effects to give the nightingale the final word in the dialog.

♫♫♫♫

Rachmaninoff: Preludes

Tall and lanky, Sergei Rachmaninoff (1873 – 1943) was one of the greatest pianists of his generation, with an unusually expansive reach to his hands. As the Russian wrote piano pieces specifically for his own performance, players of more humble proportions have great difficulty playing Rachmaninoff's music, let alone playing with the expansive drama the man himself managed.

One of his very early solo piano pieces, the angrily determined Prelude in c-sharp minor, op. 3, no. 2, would achieve stupendous popularity. Unhappily for its composer, at the time he had been a young unknown who sold the piece off to a publisher at a pittance, so it was the publisher who made the subsequent fortune. His other preludes include 10 in the set published as op. 23 (1903) and 13 in op. 32 (1910). The total for all of these preludes together came to 24, exactly the number of preludes that Frederic Chopin (1810 – 1849) had written, and exactly half the number that JS Bach (1685 – 1750) had written.

Thus, the fact that Rachmaninoff wrote 13 preludes in that last set: he needed to even off the overall total.

Of that ever-famous Prelude in c-sharp minor, Rachmaninoff became thoroughly tired of it. Not only was it requested of him nearly every time he neared a piano, but also its popularity served to remind him of how much income he was missing from having sold it off when he was young. Perhaps in writing the other preludes, he was not only seeking to match his predecessor's totals, but also to recapture the astonishing demand for that early piece. If nothing else, now when people said 'play the prelude,' he could pretend sardonically he didn't know which one they meant and indulge himself with another.

♫♫♫♫

Villa-Lobos: Preludes and Etudes for guitar

Heitor Villa-Lobos (1887 – 1959) was the guiding light of Brazilian classical music. Fascinated by the traditional music of his country, he saw within its diversity the spirit of a new nationalism that might inspire new styles of concert music. Travelling throughout his homeland, he studied the varied rhythms, melodies, and harmonies of folk music, later incorporating the essence of those elements in his classical compositions. From orchestral works and concertos to intimate solo pieces, Villa-Lobos created a vast repertoire of some 2000 works, all flavored with the irrepressible spirit of Brazil.

Villa-Lobos' interest in the guitar is natural, given his heritage. The guitar is central to all Latin American folk music, and the composer himself had spent some of his youth playing guitar in street bands in Rio de Janeiro. His love for the instrument lasted throughout his career.

In 1912, Villa-Lobos composed a set of guitar pieces in the popular Brazilian style. A collection of *Twelve Etudes*, written for Andras Segovia (1893 – 1987), dates from 1929. In the 1940s, Villa-Lobos composed six preludes for guitar. Each of the 18 pieces offers varied challenges to the player, with intricate rhythms set one against another and singable melodies overlying all the supporting action. They are the spirit of Brazilian folk music tuned up for the concert hall.

♪♪♪♪

Shostakovich: 24 Preludes and Fugues, op. 87

Piano studies began for early for Dmitri Shostakovich (1906 – 1975). He first studied with his mother, herself a professional pianist. At 13, he enrolled at the newly-renamed Petrograd Conservatory first as a piano student, and only later adding composition studies. During these years, the future star supported himself, his mother, and his sisters by playing piano in silent movie theatres, but before long, his keyboard skills would attract favorable international attention performing works by great composers from Mozart to Prokofiev, the latter of those names still alive and busy in music at the time. Shostakovich's last public performance of other composer's works was in 1930, when he was 24, yet his own keyboard pieces remained in his repertoire. Shostakovich personally premiered nearly every piano work in his catalog.

It was rather later in Shostakovich's career that he found occasion to pay tribute to JS Bach (1685 – 1750) in his piano music. In 1950, on the 200th anniversary of Bach's death, Shostakovich traveled to Leipzig, Germany, where Bach had spent his last 28 years. The visit inspired Shostakovich to produce a series of piano pieces reminiscent of those of Bach, works complex in melodic structure and demanding in technique. He hoped that his 24 Preludes and Fugues, like the 48 Preludes and Fugues of Bach, would aid in developing facility at the keyboard, and indeed, the pieces were sufficiently challenging as to lead toward that goal.

Shostakovich's preludes, like those of Bach, span all 24 keys, major and minor alike. Each introductory prelude is followed by a fugue in the same key, usually somewhat faster in tempo than the prelude itself. A "fugue" is a pattern for composition, particularly popular in Bach's day, in which melodies are layered one over another simultaneously. The composer strives to balance all these components without falling prey to musical train-wrecks. In Bach's day, it was a common task. In Shostakovich's day, fewer composers were writing fugues, but clearly he was fascinated by the challenge.

♫♫♫♫

Messiaen: *Vingt Regards sur l'Enfant Jésus*
(Twenty Views of the Infant Jesus)

Written in 1944 by Olivier Messiaen (1908 – 1992), *Vingt Regards* is one of the grandest things ever conceived for solo piano. With 20 widely divergent 'views' of the Christ child, virtuosic in their demands on the performer, the work spans roughly two hours. One might suppose that the composer, long organist at La Trinité in Paris, had much to say about the nativity, though *Vingt Regards* is not entirely Christmas music. Little of it has to do with stars in the sky, shepherds in the fields, and a baby in the manger. One might also imagine that Messiaen was inspired by the pianist for whom he intended the suite, Yvonne Loriod, who later became his second wife, and perhaps he wished to give her ample space to display her talent.

Radio Paris had requested 15 minutes of music to accompany a dramatic reading of a text called *Les Douze Regards*: that is, 12 views, not 20. As a whole, Messiaen's final product was too much for the demands of radio at Christmastime and *Vingt Regards* did not premiere until the spring of 1945. With Paris then newly released from German control and the composer freshly returned from time in a German prisoner-of-war camp (he had been captured at the Battle of Verdun), the varied moods of the music, ranging from serene to almost confrontational, did not exactly fit the festive mood of the day.

Critics were uncomplimentary and remained so for some years. Yet pianists and piano aficionados recognized the work for what it is: an epic achievement to write, to learn, to perform, and to absorb. On first approach, *Vingt Regards* may be best taken two or three views at a time, as long as one remembers to return later for another visit to the banquet.

♪♪♪♪♪

Brouwer: *El Decamerón Negro*

The original *Decameron* was a Medieval collection of stories by the Italian writer Giovanni Boccaccio (1313-

1375). The premise was that travelers fleeing the plague take shelter in the countryside and amuse themselves with storytelling. Here, however, is a work declaring itself to be "The Black Decameron." It derives from an anthology of African stories collected by the 19th century German anthropologist Leon Frobenius. Cuban composer Leo Brouwer (b. 1939) borrowed elements from three of those stories for this solo guitar suite written in 1981 specifically for American guitarist Sharon Isbin.

There are three movements, each with a sub-title that hints to the listener as to what sort of story might be involved. The suite begins with "Harp of the Warrior," proceeds through "Flight of the Lovers Through the Valley of Echoes," ultimately concluding with "Ballad of the Maiden in Love."

The melodies are not African, only the inspiration and perhaps the varied moods, from energy to lamentation, urgency to meditation. Throughout, one finds more focus upon the interweaving of rhythmic elements than upon conventional melodic development. However, the simultaneous layering of various rhythms is something a guitar does particularly well, and Brouwer has chosen to make the most of that characteristic.

♪♪♪♪

Adams: *Hallelujah Junction*

Born in Massachusetts, John Adams (b. 1947) spent much of his youth at a lakeside resort in New Hampshire: far from the capitals of music, but not far from music itself, for both of his parents were musical and his grandfather ran a lakeside dance hall where Duke Ellington once played. From there, Adams went on to study music at Harvard on scholarship, then shifted his base of operation to San Francisco. He has come to be regarded as one of the most highly esteemed of all current American composers, a Pulitzer Prize winner whose works for nearly all musical media attract both performances and admiration around the world.

Although it is for his operas and orchestral works that Adams is particularly known, he has not ignored keyboard music. His *Hallelujah Junction* (1998) is a fine example of how his style can still be effective and affecting even with only a small number of performers, here specifically two pianos. It is bouncy and buoyant with driving, repetitive fragments of rhythm underlying a richer sense of color and energy than one might find in the works of other composers using minimalist techniques. Adams regularly finds more to do with music than just rework a single idea, a tendency that rewards his listeners with exuberantly varied sounds. It is a work that meant so much to its composer that, when he published his autobiography in 2008, he chose to name the book *Hallelujah Junction*.

Chapter Seven:
Lieder and Art Songs

Anyone playing it or singing it will almost certainly recognize the tune, and probably also know words that go with it, at least English ones. However, the composer Johannes Brahms (1833 – 1897) thought of it with German words, and those of this opening phrase do not translate literally as "Lullaby and good night." Brahms' *Lullaby* is a fine example of how a composer more often associated with grand musical expression could also focus his inventiveness down into something suitable for the cradle-side, the parlor, or possibly the stage of a recital hall. Any of those settings would be appropriate for art songs.

In English, they are called art songs. Other languages have other terms, though the one most frequently encountered is "lieder," pronounced "LEE-der." That's the German word, the wide usage of which is due to the fact that many of the finest song composers had German as their native language. Certainly, that's the case for Brahms, but also for Franz Schubert (1797 – 1828), Gustav Mahler (1860 – 1911), and Richard Strauss (1864 – 1949), amongst this chapter's offerings. However, there are also composers here who worked in Norwegian or French or Spanish or Italian and even several in English. Language is no barrier to the effectiveness of an art song.

On a basic level, one might have a solo singer, with a solo pianist providing accompaniment. Some composers preferred larger accompanying forces, so with several of the offerings in this chapter, there is a small chamber group, or even a full orchestra. It depends on how richly the composer wished to shade the words of the text, and that may depend on what those words have to say.

Most art song texts are pre-existing poems, ones that the composer or perhaps the singer for whom the song is being written particularly like. By and large, poems that are rather simple in construction make the most effective art songs, as the words do not get in the way of the music.

No composer has yet been so brave as to set all of TS Eliot's "The Wasteland" to music, and it seems unlikely that anyone ever will. It is too long, too dense, and too obscure in its imagery. What is it about? Eliot may have known, but no one else can be completely certain, and composers like to know what they are expressing in music. Similarly, singers and audiences alike seem most comfortable with less abstract concepts in their music; if they can identify with the ideas, the composer has a better chance of reaching them musically.

♪♪♪♪

Schubert: *Winterreise*, D. 911, op. 89
    (A Winter's Journey)

Inspired in part by friends who were talented singers and also by the regrettable fact that most of his music was heard only by groups of friends at private musical gatherings rather than in public concerts, Schubert consistently turned out art songs, combining his era's fascination for poetry with its interest in music on a domestic scale. Ultimately, he would compose over 600 songs. Many are free-standing, individual songs, setting a single poem for one singer and one piano. Others are collections known as "song cycles," with a number of songs, often all with texts by the same poet. Such is the case with *Winterreise (A Winter's Journey)*

It is music of uncommonly intense power, despite being written for only two performers. One male voice – most often, a baritone – and one pianist hold court for two dozen songs spanning a bit more than an hour. In lesser hands, it would be too great a span of music for two performers to maintain the interest of the audience. However, in Schubert's hands, the music shifts in color, sometimes subtly, sometimes dramatically, to impressive effect. If one ever wondered how much one can get out of how little, here would be a fine place to seek an answer.

The song cycle sets 24 poems by Wilhelm Müller (1794 – 1827), Schubert's contemporary and nearly as short-lived as the composer himself. The imagery is of a young man who, upon seeing his sweetheart marry another, sets out on foot in the deepest winter to escape memories of her. His heart is broken, life is empty, and Schubert's music captures that aura, richly rendered through the harmonies and the melodic flow. Some of the songs are rather less shadowed, but even there, the mood is rather that of whistling in the graveyard: however determinedly one might whistle, the graveyard is still there.

Schubert completed the songs in the summer of 1828 and performed them for a gathering of friends, managing both the singing and the piano playing himself. Some remembered being rather taken aback by the darkness of the cycle. Others shrugged it off with a sort of "That's our Franz" reaction, for his songs often set somber texts. Additionally, in these days of the early Romantic Era, the image of a melancholy wanderer was much in vogue; few could capture that image as well as Schubert, and none better. *Winterreise* was one of his few works that found a publisher relatively quickly, a fortunate fact given that, when Schubert was reviewing the publishing proofs later that year, he was already so unwell that he had only weeks to live. He would not make his 32nd birthday.

One could sum up the general atmosphere of *Winterreise* with a few lines from the 18th of the 24 songs, "Der stürmische Morgen" (The Stormy Morning):

> Mein Herz sieht an dem Himmel
> Gemaht sein eignes Bild –
> Es ist nichts als der Winter,
> Der Winter kalt und wild!
>
> My heart sees its own image
> Painted in the heavens –
> It is nothing but the winter,
> Winter cold and wild!
>
> (Translation by Betsy Schwarm)

♪♪♪♪♪

Betsy Schwarm

Schubert: *Der Hirt auf dem Felsen*, op. 129, D. 965
(*The Shepherd on the Rock*)

Composed barely a month before his tragically early death, *Der Hirt auf dem Felsen (The Shepherd on the Rock)* is virtually the last of roughly 600 songs by Franz Schubert (1797 – 1828) and, to a significant extent, his most ambitious single song. Some would go so far as to cite it as his best, a strong statement, not only because he composed so many, but also because, two centuries later, Schubert still is the mark against which other song composers are measured. In *Der Hirt auf dem Felsen,* there is no orchestra, and yet, the music packs all the dramatic punch one could possibly desire.

Schubert composed *Der Hirt* in October 1828 specifically for soprano Anna Milder-Hauptmann, a leading star of the day and a champion of Schubert's music. That it was written with her in mind reveals much about Frau Milder-Hauptmann's voice, as the song calls for both gentle, melancholy lines and nimble ones of celebration, with much coloring of the voice along the way.

Der Hirt is longer than most of Schubert's individual songs, little short of a quarter hour in length. It also differs from nearly all of the others in that, rather than being intended just for one singer and one pianist, there is also a prominent part for solo clarinet. One might suppose that the clarinet represents the pipes of the shepherd of the title, though if so, it is a shepherd of formidable skill.

The clarinet begins before the singer, provides numerous interludes between verses, and often picks up phrases from the singer's music. The two of them sometimes echo each other, as if the shepherd's calls are bouncing back to him across the valley to his perch upon the rock.

Text for *Der Hirt* is partially drawn from a poem by Wilhelm Müller (1794 – 1827), with additional verses provided by Helmina von Chézy (1783 – 1856), author of the play *Rosamunde* for which Schubert had provided incidental music (see Chapter Nine). In Müller's verses, the shepherd laments the distance between him and his sweetheart; Chézy's contribution allows for the arrival of spring and the rejoicing that comes with it. Schubert's music masterfully conveys those evolving feelings: languid and generally lower pitched in the opening pages, agile and moving higher in pitch for the last pages. It is impressive musical shading, particularly from a composer who was in far from strong health. His body was failing, but his musical ability was still up to the task.

♪♪♪♪

Berlioz: *Les nuits d'été*, op. 7 *(Summer Nights)*

One most often hears the music of Hector Berlioz (1803 – 1869) in the form of highly charged orchestral works. However, he was of diverse intellectual interests. A product of a broad liberal arts education, Berlioz was devoted to literature and also forged connections in Parisian literary circles. Such a background will often lead a composer to the realm of art song, and Berlioz was no exception. The poet Théophile Gautier (1811 – 1872) shared Berlioz' neighborhood in Paris. Soon after Gautier's poetic collection *La comédie de la mort (The Comedy of Death)* came to print, the composer was at work on setting some of the verses to music.

When Berlioz first wrote these songs in 1840 and '41, he intended them for mezzo-soprano or tenor with piano. After completing all six, he decided to rework their keyboard accompaniments into orchestral parts, a process that he did not complete until 1856. At that time, the songs were published together under the collective title *Les nuits d'été* (*Summer Nights*), though they did not specifically deal with either summer or night. Four of the six reflect upon the loss of a love, in most cases to death, recalling Gautier's own original title. The other two, "Le Spectre de la rose" and "L'ile inconnue," are more hopeful in tone, but still ambiguous as to what will come of this romantic experience.

All are richly tinted, with the nuances of the words shaded by vocal and instrumental colors alike. Long, flowing lines are more the rule than short, nimble ones; only the first and last songs of the set lean toward vibrant energy, as if the composer wished to capture his audiences' attention as the music began and ended, yet trusted the music to hold its own for the middle songs. Even with the leisurely, sometimes melancholy pace of the other four songs, the emotional colors are vivid enough to capture the ear.

Here, rather than the grandiose impact of the same composer's *Symphonie fantastique* commanding one to attend, one finds instead a whispered invitation to glance through the door. The opus number is deceptively low; in fact, in their final form, the songs date from the middle of Berlioz' career.

♪♪♪♪

More Classical Insights

Robert and Clara Schumann:
  12 Songs from *Liebesfrühling (Love's Springtime)*

For German speaking composers, there were three especially popular poets from whom to borrow inspiration for art songs. Most senior of the three was Johann Wolfgang von Goethe (1749 – 1832); not far behind him in popularity were Heinrich Heine (1797 – 1856) and Friedrich Rückert (1788 – 1866). The last of these is likely the least familiar to those who do not read German, but he was widely read and admired, particularly for his own translations of and imitations of Oriental verse. Gustav Mahler (1860 – 1911), Johannes Brahms (1833 – 1897), Richard Strauss (1864 – 1949), and numerous other great composers found in his poems imagery begging for musical expression; add to this list both Robert Schumann (1810 – 1856) and Clara Wieck Schumann (1819 – 1896).

Clara is principally remembered now as one of the greatest pianists of the 19th century. However, she had also studied composition, and when not otherwise occupied, enjoyed writing not only solo piano works for her own concerts, but also song settings. The latter were often intended as birthday gifts for her husband, and it was for his 31st birthday – June 8, 1841, only nine months after their wedding – that she composed song settings of several Rückert poems. The impetus for those songs had come from Robert. The couple had been reading Rückert's love poems together, and came to feel that it would be a pleasure for each of them to write a handful of Rückert songs to be combined into a single collection.

Ultimately, there would be nine songs by Robert and three by Clara, all published together on Clara's own 22nd birthday that fall – one day after their first anniversary. The set was given the collective title *Liebesfrühling (Love's Springtime)*. The title was apropos, not only to this early period of their marriage, but also to the verses themselves, most of which are gently rapturous love songs, rarely shadowed by troubles. It is exactly the sort of music that a pair of newlyweds ought to be creating for each other's birthdays, and makes for sunny listening. At publication, the set was given two opus numbers: no. 12, referring to Clara's contributions, and no. 37, referring to Robert's. Clara's songs were placed second, fourth, and eleventh in the collection, with Robert's occupying the intervening positions.

♪♪♪♪

Brahms: Five Songs, op. 49

Johannes Brahms (1833 – 1897) is best known for his orchestral works. These include four symphonies, four concertos, and a variety of shorter symphonic pieces. These selections may get the largest number of performances, but they are not the most numerous items in his catalog, especially early in his career. Fearful of being compared to his great predecessor Beethoven, Brahms was forty before he dared to bring a symphony before the public. Until that time, he kept busy with piano music and songs. Of his first fifty opus numbers, 60% are vocal works of some type, and 25% are solo songs.

Brahms tended to gather his songs into sets, generally of five or six songs each. The collected songs were not necessarily all settings of verses by the same poet. Rather, they were songs that he apparently felt fit together by mood, with none startlingly different from the others.

The five songs that one finds in his opus 49 collection – published in 1868, six years after he had moved to Vienna – are all gently reflective in character. This is especially true of the fourth of the set, the ever-famed "Wiegenlied" (*Lullaby*). The tenderly rocking motion of the song, not far dissimilar from its companion songs, is just the right mood for tucking in a small child. The others – "On Sunday Morning," "To a Violet," "Longing," and "Evening Twilight" – would serve nearly as well.

♪♪♪♪♪

Dvořák: *Gypsy Melodies*, op. 55

Antonin Dvořák (1841 – 1904) was Bohemian to the core, not Gypsy. However, in the mid to late 1800s, the Gypsy culture seemed to have a certain élan and Europeans who otherwise had not much to do with Gypsies – the Roma, as they call themselves – might be inspired to think well of those people. The fact that they were somewhat nomadic seemed appealing in the face of society's growing urbanization, and the Gypsy life was often seen as the epitome of freedom, despite the fact that they had no nation of their own. Although Dvořák more often wrote music inspired by his own Bohemian heritage, he would not have ignored a popular trend of the day. In 1880, he published a set of songs he called *Gypsy Melodies*.

The original title, *Cigánské melodie*, was the Czech form of the title by which the songs are now known, and he had set Czech poems about the carefree spirit of the Gypsy life.

However, when the songs came to print with the composer's German publisher Simrock, it was with German language texts: Simrock was apparently sure that they would sell far better in a language more widely familiar than Czech. Sometimes meanings had to be altered to make the German words fit phrases that had been originally be intended for Czech words. In either version, however, the point of most of the songs is how delightful it is to be a Gypsy.

One of the few truly poignant songs in the set is the most famous of them all, that known in English as "Songs My Mother Taught Me." The gist of its text is that when the singer's mother taught her to sing, the mother would often cry. Perhaps they were tears of memories of a distant childhood; specifically whence the tears came is not specified. However, the music carries well that greyer tone, whether in the original voice-and-piano version, or in one of the many transcriptions. Just because Dvořák did not intend it for a cello, or a clarinet, or any other instrumental soloist, does not mean that a gifted interpreter cannot make it work.

*****

Grieg: *Hjertets melodier (Heart's Melodies)*, op. 5

Norwegian composer Edvard Grieg (1843 – 1907) is most frequently encountered through his incidental music for *Peer Gynt,* his Piano Concerto, or perhaps his many Lyric Pieces for solo piano. However, most numerous in his catalog are songs for solo voice with piano, of which he composed many dozens, the first dating from his late teens and the last from the final year of his life. By Grieg's own admission, his inspiration was less the poetry he was setting than the voice of his cousin Nina Hagerup, who in 1865 became his wife. "For me," he wrote in a letter to a biographer, "she has been – dare I admit it? – the only genuine interpreter of my songs."

Perhaps it was for Nina's sake that Grieg often chose to set love poetry, particularly that of his fellow Scandinavian Hans Christian Andersen (1805 – 1876). *Hjertets melodies (Heart's Melodies)* dates from 1864, the year that Nina agreed to marry Grieg, and offers four short songs, all with texts by Anderson, from whose own published edition the collective title was taken. The cycle includes his single most popular song, "Jeg elsker Dig" (I Love You), widely performed and recorded, often in translation to ensure that the audience grasped every nuance of the affections it expresses. Together spanning little more than five minutes, the four songs yet offer an impressive range of expression, the first and third being delicate feelings of love, the second and fourth being significantly more restless and troubled. Grieg had barely reached his twenties, yet had already learned what varied ideas one could bring out in music.

♪♪♪♪

Tosti: songs

Although his current reputation lies in his abundant catalogue of songs, Paolo Tosti (1846 – 1916) began music studies in Naples in 1858 as a twelve year old violinist. Composition came to him somewhat later, and he owed his success in the field in part to a period of ill health that sent the young man home from school for convalescence. His songs soon became popular, particularly in Rome where Princess Margherita, the future Queen of Italy, appointed him as her singing teacher. Other royal appointments would follow, including a post with the English royal family starting in 1880, through which Tosti would earn a knighthood from King Edward VII. He remained in England for three decades, though he returned to Rome for his last years.

Tosti's songs include settings of texts in Italian, French, and English, depending on the audience he had in mind at the time. Roughly 200 in number and all with piano accompaniment, the songs became international favorites both with professional singers and with amateurs; many a family evening of home-grown music has included Tosti's music. Whether the sunny moods of "Mattinata," the forlorn spirit of "Tristezza," or the bright and buoyant joy of "La Serenata," somewhere in Tosti's catalog is a song right for the mood of the moment. These parlor songs, as they were known for the setting in which they were usually heard, are relatively unchallenging of technique, especially for the singer. However, a superior artist can shade the simple texts for more subtle emotional colors, and some of the finest opera singers – especially Italian tenors – have troubled themselves to do so.

♪♪♪♪

Chausson: *Chanson perpétuelle*, op. 37 *(Unending Song)*

Music was not a first career for Frenchman Ernest Chausson (1855 – 1899). Rather, he began with legal studies and was sworn in as a Parisian barrister in 1877. In that same year, however, he wrote his first composition, and soon exchanged the legal profession for the musical profession. His first composition instructor was Jules Massenet (1842 – 1912). Later, he studied with Cesar Franck (1822 – 1890), and exhibited a long-lasting fascination for the works of Richard Wagner (1813 – 1883). From those varying influences, Chausson developed a deep love of rich melodies and lofty emotions, expressed in a lyrical style that was uniquely his own. He might have become the leader of a new generation of French composers, but tragically his life was cut short when he died in a bicycling accident, not yet 45 years of age.

Although Chausson had too few years to compose a quantity of music, he did produce several works that have earned lasting admiration. The *Chanson perpétuelle*, though not his grandest work, is yet a strong candidate for his most rapturous. It sets most of the verses (no. 1-5, 7-9, and 11-14) of the poem "Nocturne," from Charles Cros' collection *Chansons perpétuelle.* The text deals with a woman whose lover has left her for distant lands. The woman's shifting emotions are deftly captured in Chausson's gently shaded music. First, there is tender melancholy. Then, as she recalls how they met and became lovers, the music shifts into brighter colors. Once he departs, the woman becomes increasingly anguished, imagining her own death. As the text has her supposing that she will await him in this imagined afterlife, Chausson's music fades softly both in tempo and in dynamics. The pitch of the vocal lines soars to its highest reaches, yet one is left with the sense that this represents her soul drifting away.

Composed in 1898 and bearing one of Chausson's very last opus numbers, the song was first scored for soprano, piano, and string quartet, though one may sometimes hear it with full string orchestra. Including the strings with voice and keyboard allows for even more subtle tinting of the accompaniment; often melodic fragments will move amongst the members of the ensemble, expanding and evolving as they go. He may have been a late starter in music, but Chausson clearly understood how to achieve proper musical effect.

♪♪♪♪

Mahler: *Lieder eines fahrenden Gesellens*
   (Songs of a Wayfarer)

With conspicuous vocal parts in half his symphonies, it should come as no surprise that Gustav Mahler (1860 – 1911) was a devoted composer of songs. He wrote his first songs at the age of twenty, setting some of his own poetry, something which even the greatest song composers rarely dared to do. In the 31 years that remained to him, Mahler produced several dozen more songs; intense conducting duties kept him from being more prolific.

One of his earlier song cycles, the *Songs of a Wayfarer*, was completed early in 1885, when the composer was 24. The texts, all by Mahler himself, are of lost love, not that the beloved has died, but that she has chosen someone else. The world around this wayfarer is bright and the birds sing, but such views serve mostly to bring his sorrow into starker relief. Mahler's traveler, like Schubert's in his epic song cycle *Der Winterreise*, is aware of the beauties around him, but finds therein no balm for his soul. In the composer's personal life, he had just been jilted by a young singer, Johanna Richter, and perhaps with her voice in mind, he set the songs much lower than would have suited her own voice.

Once it was completed, the cycle existed in both voice/piano and voice/orchestra forms. Yet the richness of the harmonies suggests that the orchestral setting was his principal intention, with the piano version perhaps undertaken to increase likelihood of performance. At the time, Mahler was still an up-and-coming figure finding more success as a conductor than as a composer. That the orchestral version was closer to his heart is proven by the fact that its influences – particularly the main melody of the second song – are prominent in his Symphony no. 1 (see Chapter Two). The first verified performance of *Songs of a Wayfarer* came March 16, 1896, in Berlin, when the orchestral version reached the public.

♪♪♪♪

Richard Strauss: *Vier Lieder*, op. 27 *(Four Songs)*

From the age of six until the last months of his long life, Richard Strauss (1864 – 1949) was ever composing lieder. Short musical settings of poetry for one singer with accompaniment, art songs suited his tastes, in part because he was an avid reader rarely at a loss for a text. Additionally, his wife of over fifty years, Pauline de Ahna (1863 – 1950), was a talented soprano whom he had come to know through his work as an opera conductor. Of the hundreds of songs in Strauss' catalog, many were written for and first performed by Pauline, often with Strauss himself providing the piano accompaniment.

On their wedding day (September 10, 1894), Strauss presented Pauline with a set of four songs that would soon be published as his opus 27. Most of his preceding published works had been songs, although standing next in his catalog, as opus 28, is the sardonically tinged orchestral piece *Till Eulenspiegel's Merry Pranks*, so Strauss was already proving himself as a composer of varied imagination.

At first, these songs were intended for voice with piano accompaniment. However, he later reworked several of them for orchestral accompaniment, giving greater richness and expressive power to the songs. As befits the occasion for which Strauss composed them, they are largely love songs, particularly the last of the set, "Morgen" (Morning), in which a rapt couple strolls down to the beach to lose themselves in one another's eyes. It is, in small scale, a love scene worthy of a Puccini opera.

♪♪♪♪

Ravel: *Sheherazade*

For Maurice Ravel (1875 – 1937), the year 1889 represented a turning point in his life. He would enter the Paris Conservatoire at age 14, and would attend the Paris World Exhibition. There, he (and most of Europe) heard for the first time the bell sounds of Javanese gamelan music, from which the aspiring composer learned of alternate harmonic systems: different ways of structuring chords and harmonies. This knowledge brought a certain exotic flavor to Ravel's early compositions, a flavor of which his conservatory professors did not approve. Ravel was the despair of his professors, and the toast of the town.

More Classical Insights

In 1898, Ravel first considered composing an opera after the Arabian-themed *Tales of a Thousand and One Nights*. The seed of inspiration may have been planted years earlier when Ravel heard the music of Nicolai Rimsky-Korsakov (1844 – 1908) conducted by its composer at the Exhibition. It is, after all, the Russian master who usually comes to mind when one hears the name *Scheherazade*. However, Ravel, too, opted for using the name of that enchanting Arabian as the title of a new work.

The following year, Ravel's overture *Sheherazade* (spelled in the French manner) was given its premiere, only to earn the disdain of the critics. The composer, too, would later dismiss the piece, but was not entirely put off the idea of Arabia. Rather, he changed his focus, deciding upon a set of orchestral songs in place of the original concept. For texts, Ravel recruited his friend, the poet Tristan Klingsor (1874 – 1966), who provided three poems evocative of the East. As he was at work on the music, Ravel asked Klingsor to recite the texts, so that he might better echo the poetic line in the music. Completed in 1903, the *Sheherazade* song cycle premiered the following spring.

The first of the songs, "Asia," concerns itself with the allure of Eastern lands. Ravel took care to use in this song some exotic percussion and an affecting interplay between voice and flute. In the second song, "The Enchanted Flute," a slave girl listens to her lover playing his flute outside her window while she remains confined, attendant upon her master. The final song, "The Indifferent One," speaks of a glimpse of androgynous beauty.

Betsy Schwarm

♪♪♪♪♪

Falla: *Siete canciones populares españolas*
(Seven Popular Spanish Songs)

Manuel de Falla (1876 – 1946) was born in the coastal city of Cadiz, not far from Gibraltar. The city's previous musical claim to fame had been the commissioning of Haydn's *Seven Last Words of Christ*, which, 80 years later, was still performed locally each Easter week. As a boy, Falla was so impressed by the powerful and evocative sacred work that he became devoted to classical music and eventually chose a career in the field.

Like many of his countrymen, Falla received most of his composition training in Paris, but never banished his nation's musical spirit from his heart. Often, he made a conscious point of evoking the musical traditions of Spain in his original compositions. That Spanish flavoring resonates especially clearly in the *Siete canciones populares españolas*.

Composed in 1914 and 1915 and intended for either mezzo-soprano or baritone with piano, the songs are rich with folk rhythms and harmonies, at times evoking the trills and sobs of flamenco. Plaintive moods and restless ones appear in turn, the latter particularly in the fourth of the seven songs, the "Jota." The fifth movement "Nana" is a lullaby; the others tend toward lyrics of love, though here love does not always run smoothly. Busy accompanying lines may be paired with more languid vocal lines: an idea borrowed from some styles of Spanish folk music. Clearly, Falla had studied his musical models closely.

More Classical Insights

♪♪♪♪

Butterworth: *Six Songs from A Shropshire Lad*

Their lives overlapped, but it would be misleading to consider composer George Butterworth (1885 – 1916) and poet AE Houseman (1859 – 1936) to be true contemporaries. Houseman was well into his 20s when Butterworth was born and lived two more decades after Butterworth's death in combat at the Battle of the Somme. So the two Englishman had very different world views, but Houseman's reflective verses still spoke strongly to Butterworth, as they did to many British composers at the turn of the century.

Houseman's poetry – especially the 1896 collection *A Shropshire Lad*– was so popular that he gave up asking composers for payment in return for use of his verses. His view seemed to be that if the lines could be given musical expression, so much the better, and in Butterworth's hands, they take on an aching beauty.

For this cycle, Butterworth chose six poems from Houseman's collection: numbers 10, 21, 23, 53, 28, and 31. Mostly gentle in mood, though the fourth of the set has greater rhythmic energy, they prove the melodic gifts of this often overlooked composer, making it all the more poignant that he died so young, and that, before his departure for war, he had destroyed most of his music, intending to write better works later. At least these songs were allowed to survive. The main melody of the first, "Loveliest of Trees," earned a second existence, in his orchestral rhapsody *A Shropshire Lad* of 1912. That work would be one of Butterworth's very last, written just before he left for the war from which he would not return.

♫♫♫♫

Copland: *Twelve Poems of Emily Dickinson*

Born in Amherst, Massachusetts, Emily Dickinson (1830 – 1886) spent most of her life in seclusion, reading widely but otherwise isolated from modern developments, interacting principally with her immediate family. Having time on her hands and a mind that explored existence, she wrote over 800 poems, none of which were published until after her death. Her inner life emerges in her poetry: reflective, deeply personal, musing upon moods more than scenes. Rarely does she delve into realism, as Robert Frost (1874 – 1963) would in a later generation, but more often a person's reaction to experience. She has remained enduringly popular with composers, who clearly find much room for musical interpretation in Dickinson's perspectives on life and death.

The poems that Aaron Copland (1900 – 1990) chose for this song cycle, published in 1950, are from various collections of her works, brought together only by his thought that the images would lend themselves to music. In setting the poems to music, he occasionally made small alterations to phrasing so as to make the piece more suited to singing. The changes, however, are so small that only a Dickinson scholar would notice them, and even then would not likely be troubled by the alteration. They remain in the spirit of the original author, Copland's music serving to

More Classical Insights

underscore her imagery and make the visions that much more powerful.

The twelve chosen poems are "Nature, the Gentlest Mother," "There Came a Wind like a Bugle," "Why Do They Shut Me out of Heaven?," "The World Feels Dusty," "Dear March, Come In!," "Sleep is Supposed to Be," "When They Come Back," "I Felt a Funeral in My Brain," "I've Heard an Organ Talk Sometimes," "Going to Heaven," and "The Chariot." The last of those is perhaps Dickinson's best-known poem, beginning with the lines, "Because I could not stop for Death, He kindly stopped for me." Copland rendered its ideas with delicately floating lines, both for singer and for accompanist. At times, the music turns in a gently playful mood, but never becomes boldly declamatory. It is a mood that Copland uses frequently in the set, as it often fits Dickinson's imagery. This most American of composers and most American of poets seem ideally suited to one another.

♪♪♪♪

Barber: *Knoxville: Summer of 1915*

> "... It has become that time of evening when people sit on their porches, rocking gently and talking gently and watching the street and the standing up into their sphere of possession of the trees, of birds' hung havens, hangars. People go by; things go by. A horse, drawing a buggy, breaking his hollow iron music on the asphalt; a loud auto; a quiet auto; people in pairs, not in a hurry ..."

Betsy Schwarm

The words of American author James Agee (1909 – 1955). Words of a subtler time, slower paced, softly reminiscent, a time recalled visually in photographs in sepia tones, aurally in the music of some of America's finest composers.

Agee's prose poem *Knoxville: Summer of 1915* had the good fortune to fall into the hands of Samuel Barber (1910 – 1981). Barber grew up in small town Pennsylvania. Agee was from Tennessee, but when Barber encountered the text of *Knoxville*, he observed, "Agee's poem was vivid and moved me deeply ... It expresses a child's feeling of loneliness, wonder, and lack of identity in that marginal world between twilight and sleep." It proved to be an ideal focal point for a new work.

In 1947, renowned Metropolitan Opera soprano Eleanor Steber (1914 – 1990) asked Barber to compose something for her. What she wanted was not a full opera but rather a concert work, something she might perform in a recital with orchestra. Barber knew well how to work with vocal music; he was himself a skilled baritone and his aunt, Louise Homer, sang with Miss Steber at the Met. So he was delighted by the invitation to write something that would allow him to make use of this text that had so moved him.

Knoxville: Summer of 1915 premiered April 9, 1948, with Miss Steber joining the Boston Symphony and its conductor, Serge Koussevitzky. The music, like the text it seeks to convey, is often gentle and lyrical, though a palpable sorrow underlies that quiet mood. Barber's hallmark lush harmonies and flowing melodies are here in full force. In fact, though the work is less well-known than others of the composer's creations, it yet may sound familiar, for it blends the serenity that opens his Violin Concerto with the tragedy that infuses his *Adagio for Strings*. Here is another work in which Barber was at his best.

♪♪♪♪

Britten: *Winter Words*, op. 52

Few great composers could have been better suited to writing art songs than Englishman Benjamin Britten (1913 – 1976). Firstly, he was an avid reader with a clear sense of how particular words and phrases might be evoked best in music. Additionally, his life partner – spending over 30 years at the composer's side – was the acclaimed English tenor Peter Pears. The majority of Britten's songs were written with Pears' voice in mind, and a significant number of them premiered with Pears as the singer and Britten himself as the accompanying pianist. It was they who gave the first performance of *Winter Words* at England's Leeds Festival late in 1953.

Winter Words sets eight poems by Thomas Hardy (1840 – 1928), all mood pictures set in frosty days and nights in England's West Country, so closely associated with Hardy. That Britten himself was from England's east coast, growing up within sight of the North Sea, did not prove a handicap in setting Hardy's words evocatively to music. People and nature, it seems, are largely similar wherever one goes, and those are the images at hand in these songs.

Listen for train whistle effects in the accompaniment to the second song, relating as it does to a late night railway journey, a hymn tune as a choirmaster is laid to rest, and an aura of warbling and twittering as young thrushes and finches give voice. Throughout, one finds recurring shadows as if of England's West Country melancholy. With only two performers at his disposal, Britten yet finds a thousand shades – some muted, others vibrant – within his music. Between his own skills as pianist/composer and Pears' as singer, Britten had all the resources he needed to mine the richness of Hardy's imagery.

♪♪♪♪

Bolcom: *Cabaret Songs*

The most famous years for cabaret songs predate not only the offerings to the genre by William Bolcom (b. 1938 in Seattle), but, in fact, predate Bolcom himself. However, aware of the fond place that such music has held in public attention, Bolcom has long delighted in crafting his own cabaret-style songs, some bright and humorous, others wistful and melancholy. Just because one is a Pulitzer Prize winning composer of piano music, orchestral works, and operas does not mean one cannot indulge in other sides of musical expression.

Bolcom has published four books of *Cabaret Songs*, totaling about two-dozen individual songs. All are settings of modern lyrics by Arnold Weinstein (1927 – 2005); he and Bolcom set out to give a new voice to the familiar genre. The 1930s are long gone, but one can still imagine how that musical style might have evolved over the years to reach the present day.

The first book of *Cabaret Songs* premiered July 18, 1978, the second in April of 1983. The third and fourth books premiered together December 2, 1997. All the premieres were given in New York City with Bolcom himself at the piano and his wife, mezzo soprano Joan Morris, as the singer. By Bolcom's own account, they are songs best suited for a voice of middle range: neither particularly high nor particularly low. Whether sung by a woman or a man, the songs require a voice that can deftly shade the color of the voice for the meaning of the words, bringing out whimsy or melancholy, as the moment demands.

♪♪♪♪

Laitman: *Four Dickinson Songs*

Of her vocal music, which includes hundreds of songs and several operas, Washington D.C. based composer Lori Laitman (b. 1955) says, "I try to compose music that is kind to both singer and audience... I work from the words out: the music is in the service of the text... Approaching the composition from this angle allows the words and music to become completely entwined." That debate between music and words has resounded for centuries. One can hope that those composers of the past who have wrestled with it would be impressed by the solution Laitman has reached and the results she has achieved.

Laitman's many songs include roughly three dozen to texts by the American poet Emily Dickinson. Dickinson's verses may be ideally suited for song settings, as they tend to be shorter, inward of expression, and more prone to emotional allusions than intense action. Laitman herself says she is fascinated by Dickinson's way of "examining the human condition," and by "the uniqueness and truth of her insights as well as the mastery of the language."

The cycle Laitman titled *Four Dickinson Songs* begins with "Will There Really be a Morning?," largely wistful of mood, though with some more fervent passages when the text suggests more assertion. Second is the jaunty "I'm Nobody," most high-spirited of the songs in this cycle. Fragile and plaintive moods return for the third song, "She Died," tending toward use of mid-range notes, without emphasizing exceptionally high or low pitches. The final song, "If I," blends thoughtful and hopeful moods, evocative of the poem's assertion, "I shall not live in vain." Here, and at times in the earlier songs, one finds the pianist picking up and elaborating on the vocalist's lines. As in the best art songs, the two performers are full partners in expressing the imagery of the text.

♪♪♪♪

Muhly: *Far Away Songs*

Since graduating from Julliard in 2004, Vermont native Nico Muhly (b. 1981) has become a prominent member of the musical community, first as an assistant to Philip Glass and then as a composer in his own right. His catalog already includes works written for the American Ballet Theater, the New York City Ballet, the New York Philharmonic, the Chicago Symphony, the Boston Pops, and on the grandest scale, the Metropolitan Opera and the English National Opera, which co-commissioned his full-length opera *Two Boys*. The opera premiered in London in 2011 and will come to New York in the fall of 2013.

That very partial list of those commissioning Muhly's music reveals that he has attracted favorable notice at the highest level. Here is a composer who can work evocatively with the singing voice and with instruments alike, ensuring that both will play a substantive role in a composition, thereby communicating vivid emotional ideas to the audience.

One of Muhly's most recent compositions is the song cycle *Far Away Songs*. Setting several poems by the early 20th century Greek poet Constantine Cavafy, the quarter-hour long set is scored for soprano, piano, and string quartet and premiered November 29, 2012. The soprano for the premiere was Jennifer Zetlan, for whom the music was specifically written at the request of Muhly's alma mater, the Julliard School.

There are three songs in the cycle, though Muhly himself admits that the last of these, "Voices," is a "refinement" of the first, "Sweet Voices," its musical expression being more developed and focused, as a person may become more developed and focused over time. The central song, "Hours of Melancholy," tends toward moodiness, emphasized by the manner in which the instruments may find themselves in opposition to the singer.

Muhly attests that this allows him to bring a measure of sarcasm into the work, so as to comment upon the text. Schubert may have never set out to be specifically sarcastic. However, he, too, used the music to shade words, and in recognizing the effectiveness of that approach, Muhly proves his familiarity with the classic ideals.

Chapter Eight: Opera and Operetta

It is a bold little theme, galloping across the page. Similarly, it gallops through the imaginations of many millions of persons, even those who would swear that they had never heard an opera, for as it hastens along, it likely does so accompanied by imagined cries of "Hi-ho, Silver!" The composer, Gioacchino Rossini (1792 – 1868), created it for no such purpose, but so it has come down in the mind of the public. So why did he create it? That's what we'll find out in this chapter: that and much more.

Opera was the original multi-media entertainment, combining vocal and instrumental music with a plot, props, and sets. It began as diversion for the Italian royalty in the early 17th century. However, by Mozart's time in the late 18th century, it had also become popular in theaters for the general public. About this time, opera went through a transition from largely serious productions with an emphasis upon elaborate singing techniques to sometimes comic pieces in which the singing is used more to tell stories of believable characters than to spotlight the singers' individual talents. It is at this point that the works profiled in this chapter begin: when the transition from the older idea of *opera seria* and the newer one of *opera buffa* is beginning to occur.

More Classical Insights

By the mid-1800s, musical tastes began to move away from the light and bright spirit of late 18th century music and onward to something more strongly dramatic. This change affected opera composers as well as others, and new ideas arose that came to be termed *grand opera* for the splendor they brought to the stage. Grand they were, though not necessarily realistic. By the end of the 19th century, there was a strong backlash that drove opera into the realms of realism, or, as the Italians called it "verismo."

Throughout these years, there was a cousin of opera that refused to take itself too seriously. This type, known as "operetta," mixed spoken dialog with sung portions of music. This style eventually produced its own offspring in the line of musical theater, but all come from the same root stock. Another century hence, *Les Miserables* may come to be viewed more as an opera and less as a Broadway extravaganza.

In the 20th and 21st centuries, opera composers are less easy to categorize. Their works may be serious, or comic, or both, or not quite either. They may be grand in scale or humble of scope. Often, they are based on stories borrowed from cinema or newspaper headlines, proving again that opera is an art form with something to say to modern audiences.

Admittedly, opera and operetta now have competition for the entertainment dollar from musical theater, as well as from film and from countless other activities. However, opera continues to have relevance. Two of the 20 operas profiled in this chapter are 21st century works. Another dates from 1998, and six others originated between 1910 and 1960, so that roughly half of the chosen operas are less than 50 years old.

Every year, new operas come to the stage throughout the world; the best of those begin to attract wider attention, beyond the headlines that come with a premiere. It is one thing to get an opera performed once by the company that paid for it to be created; it is entirely another thing for that work to have other opera companies – and other audiences – clamoring for it as well. The second situation is harder to achieve. However, composers are managing it: proof that there is demand for what they are writing.

♪♪♪♪

Mozart: *La Clemenza di Tito*, K. 621
    (The Clemency of Titus)

Standing at the far end of Mozart's operatic catalog, *La Clemenza di Tito* was written for the coronation in Prague of Austria's Emperor Leopold II as King of Bohemia, a ceremony that was set for the fall of 1791. The request had come to Mozart a few months in advance, but as he was already busy with *The Magic Flute* and the *Requiem*, this newest work progressed slowly. He was still at work on the score when he arrived in Prague that fall, and finished it there, literally the day before the September 6 premiere. Before leaving Vienna, he had already managed to complete *Flute*, though it would not premiere until September 30. In later years, *Flute* would earn the slightly lower Köchel number (K. 620), since, spending longer in rehearsal, it premiered after *Clemenza*.

More Classical Insights

Like many of Mozart's less familiar operas, *Clemenza* is an example of what was called 'opera seria.' A holdover from Baroque days, opera seria tended to be not only of sober mood, but also most often employing settings in ancient Greece or ancient Rome, perhaps even mythological settings. Biblical tales might also appear, as they, too, were sufficiently distant from mundane contemporary scenarios. *Clemenza* has a historical setting, dealing with an actual Roman emperor, who, reigning at the time of the eruption of Vesuvius, was perhaps not quite so saintly as he is made to appear in the opera. However, as the work was connected to an emperor's coronation, one could not allow a ruler to be anything less than perfectly admirable.

Opera seria were also more focused upon showcasing singers than in telling a story. In this last characteristic, Mozart was one of the first to diverge. He clearly viewed opera as more than just a concert in costume and was determined to explore the personas behind the characters. He still allowed them to be called 'opera seria,' but he went the extra mile for dramatic purpose, especially here with the mercurial leading lady Vitellia, who from one scene to the next changes from wanting to murder the emperor to wanting to marry him, with music to support those widely divergent moods.

The story of a Roman ruler's nobility and forgiveness of his enemies was based upon a 1734 libretto by the respected court poet Pietro Metastasio (1698 – 1782) and revised for Mozart by Caterino Mazzola (1745 – 1806). The story would have been familiar to many, as Metastasio's original version had already been given operatic form over three-dozen times. In this new telling, there are fewer arias, more group action, and indeed, more action in general, a different approach well suited both to modern tastes and to Mozart's own preferences in opera. At its opening in Prague September 6, 1791, it was not a huge success. However, Mozart's death just three months later launched it into popularity, as audiences became suddenly determined to discover what they had missed from the lost genius.

One challenge in performing the opera since Mozart's time is that the leading male role, Sesto, was composed for a male soprano. At the time, male sopranos, known as castratos, were popular in Italy and tolerated in the Austrian empire, for the way their voices blended the bright, high tones of a female voice with the power of a male one. Mozart was asked to write the role specifically to feature one of these gentlemen and did as requested. Occasionally, one can find a natural male countertenor who can handle the role as written. However, even a high tenor voice isn't high enough for these roles, so lacking suitable countertenors, the roles are given to female singers in masculine costume.

The success of a performance then lies in how convincingly this woman can play a male role; the same issue comes into play with one of the other male roles, Annio, who is Sesto's friend. With women in both of those roles and also in the roles of the two female characters, one needs four exceptionally good female voices at once, sometimes all appearing in the same scene. The only characters written for male voices are the tenor role of Emperor Tito and the bass role of the prefect Publio. Here is an opera that is a festival for the female voice, which likely suited Mozart, as many of his best professional friends were sopranos, as was his wife Constanze.

Rossini: *Guillaume Tell* (*William Tell*)

The composer was Italian, the playwright upon whose drama it was based was German, the story is Swiss, and the language in which it is sung is French. Taken together, it equals the opera *Guilllaume Tell (William Tell)* by Gioacchino Rossini (1792 – 1869). Of all operas that only a minority of opera audiences has witnessed in their entirety, this one is the best known by name, thanks to its ubiquitous overture. Ironically, the overture did not even originate with this opera, and decidedly, its composer had no intention of it coming to be the theme song of a masked avenger of the Wild West.

When *William Tell* premiered at the Paris Opéra August 3, 1829, its Italian-born composer had been based in Paris for about five years. He had chosen Paris in hopes of having more creative control over his music with less exposure to opera house politics than was usual in his native Italy. By the time of *William Tell*'s premiere, Rossini had realized that neither hope had entirely come to fruition. He was immensely successful at everything other than his original goal, and so, with *William Tell*, the 37-year-old composer announced his retirement. He would live nearly 40 more years, devoting his time to composing occasionally – as long as it wasn't opera – and to hosting acclaimed dinner parties with live musical entertainment. Only those of the highest social or artistic rank could hope to obtain one of those coveted invitations.

For this farewell to opera, Rossini chose a drama by Friedrich von Schiller (1759 – 1805). The play was Schiller's last completed drama, coming to the stage only one year before his death. Rossini had it adapted to his own specifications, which did not include much in the way of brevity. Running most of five hours in length, *William Tell* is the most spacious of Rossini's 39 operas. Moreover, it requires an immense cast of Swiss patriots, Austrian oppressors, and others, even in addition to the half-dozen principal roles.

Those facts are part of what has worked against the work receiving much in the way of modern performances. Additionally, there is the fact that few who are not Swiss know anything about the title character other than the shoot-the-apple-off-your-son's-head episode. That event does occur in the opera, midway through the third of the opera's four acts. However, much else happens as well, and the central love story – few operas can survive without one – does not involve William Tell himself.

As to that overture, finding himself pressed for time, Rossini borrowed it from one of his many earlier operas, *Elizabeth, Queen of England*, composed 14 years and 24 operas before *William Tell*. So its melodies are not drawn from *William Tell* itself, and if one were to listen attentively through the opera itself seeking that famed Lone Ranger theme, one would listen in vain. Yet much of the music is bold and exciting, and if one is seeking fervent choruses of patriotism, here they are aplenty. As a swan song, it stands as a worthy summary of a storied career. Rossini was drawing down the curtain in very grand scale.

♪♪♪♪♪

More Classical Insights

Bellini: *I Capuleti e i Montecchi (Romeo and Juliet)*

In the 21st century, the name of Vincenzo Bellini (1801 – 1835) stands rather less prominent than that of his contemporary Gioacchino Rossini (1792 – 1868). At their time, however, Bellini's fame was no less than Rossini's and if his catalog of operas is shorter, that is largely due to the fact of his premature death, leaving him less than half as much time on earth as Rossini would be given. Of the ten operas Bellini lived to complete, three are held in particularly high regard, and each of those premiered in 1830 and 1831. Rossini had retired, and Giuseppe Verdi (1813 – 1901) was still but a youth.

So amongst the Italian opera specialists of lasting reputation, only Gaetano Donizetti (1797 – 1848) stood as competition. As for Donizetti, he spent most of his time in the opera houses of Naples and those of Paris, so Bellini usually had northern Italy to himself. That's where these three acclaimed operas – first *I Capuleti e i Montecchi*, then *La Sonnambula* and *Norma* – premiered. All three had librettos written by the same man, Felice Romani (1788 – 1865); he and Bellini clearly agreed as to how best to structure a drama for musical expression.

Of those three mid-career Bellini operas, the one with the most familiar story is *I Capuleti e i Montecchi*. Gaze closely at that Italian title and one will likely perceive those familiar names of literature, Capulets and Montagues; indeed, this is a Romeo and Juliet tale. It is not, however, one quite like Shakespeare's. Rather, Bellini and Romani were working from an Italian play on the subject, an 1818 version by Luigi Scevola, and Scevola himself was drawing upon an Italian Renaissance version of these famous lovers' tragedy. Shakespeare may have known of the Italian version, but Bellini and Romani cared nothing for Shakespeare's.

The action does take place in 13th century Verona, and there are two feuding families, the Capulets and the Montagues, with Juliet belonging to the former and Romeo to the latter. However, Romeo is not the son of that clan, but rather its leader, and so is unlikely to be a teenager. He has no friend Mercutio, whose murder serves in Shakespeare to escalate the violence, and there is no sympathetic nurse for Juliet. The Italian version lacks a balcony scene; rather, Romeo is smuggled into the Capulet home by their doctor. However, the principal elements of the love story play out in familiar fashion, with Juliet feigning death to avoid an undesired marriage, then waking in the tomb too late to save either Romeo or herself. So details vary, but the outline is substantially what one expects

I Capuleti e i Montecchi premiered March 11, 1830, at the La Fenice Opera House in Venice, and quickly gained an international following. Opera lovers today might wonder why, if the opera had an international following, they have not encountered it before. In fact, it is not often staged today because of a peculiarity of the writing: Juliet is a soprano, as one might expect, but Romeo is not a tenor. Bellini wrote the part as a "trouser role" for a female mezzo-soprano, and it is the last important opera in which a male protagonist was to be sung by a woman.

In the decades before the opera's premiere, women often took male roles, as many earlier operas had male castratos in leading roles, and by the early 1800s, there were few of these around to appear in revivals of such operas. So women were dressed in male costume and reveled in the opportunity to take on a different sort of character. Furthermore, Bellini knew that the mezzo-soprano at his disposal at La Fenice would be Giuditta Grisi (1805 – 1840), who had a strong reputation for her previous work in male roles. Holding Grisi's artistry in higher regard than that of the tenor in the proposed cast, Bellini made Romeo a trouser role. In the 21st century, it is less common for a woman to play the role, but if one has a mezzo at hand who is skilled in such portrayals – and in the flamboyant singing style required for the music that Bellini gives her – *I Capuleti e i Montecchi* is a fine choice for the program.

♪♪♪♪

Berlioz: *Les Troyens (The Trojans)*

Give a young man a strong liberal arts education complete with studies of Greek and Latin, and he will come to know the ancient tales of Homer and Virgil. Name that young man Hector and he will be fascinated with that tragic figure of Troy. Let him be Hector Berlioz (1803 – 1869), and he will develop the highly dramatic musical tastes and skills to make an opera of the Trojan War and its aftermath.

For *Les Troyens*, Berlioz crafted libretto and music alike, drawing largely upon Virgil's *Aeneid*. He began with the fall of Troy through the tactic of the Trojan Horse; the Trojan prince Hector, having already fallen in battle, appears only as a ghost. Berlioz then followed Aeneas and his men to Carthage for Aeneas' fateful encounter with Queen Dido.

The adventure was epic in scale, as was Berlioz' score: one of the grandest of all *grand operas*. The orchestra alone required 100 players; cast and chorus another 100 or more, as well as a cadre of dancers. Moreover, the two leading ladies – the prophetess Cassandra for the Trojan acts, and Queen Dido for the Carthaginian ones – are sufficiently different in their music that it would be a rare soprano who could manage both, even her voice were strong enough to handle four hours of singing. Therefore, numerous principal artists are also required.

So grand was *Les Troyens* that, although Berlioz completed it in 1858 – over a decade before his death – he never saw it staged in its entirety. An act here or there would be presented, but never the entire work. As the composer observes time and again in his autobiography, not only did he have to consent to the staging of individual acts without the rest of the work, but he also would have to alter the notes upon the page to bring them within the skills of the singers and the instrumentalists. More than once, he even paid out of his own pocket for the orchestra's size to be increased to something approximating his standards.

His ambition with *Les Troyens* was simply beyond the reach of opera houses of his time. Its five acts span over four hours in all, and even in Berlioz's time (as well as now), its music is most often encountered in orchestral excerpts. However, it stands as proof of how much action and drama a single creative mind can bring to the stage in a single magnificent work.

♪♪♪♪

More Classical Insights

Balfe: *The Bohemian Girl*

The legacy of history is a curious thing. Ask even a knowledgeable opera lover to hum something by Michael Balfe (1808 – 1870), and the only answer one is likely to receive, if any, is a few bars of 'I Dreamt I Dwelt in Marble Halls.' It is one of the lead soprano's arias from *The Bohemian Girl*, which premiered in London November 27, 1843. Indeed, it is a lovely tune, but *Bohemian Girl* was twelfth of Balfe's 29 operas, and his catalog also includes songs, cantatas, and chamber music. In his day, this Dublin-born composer was not only the most successful British composer of opera, he was also virtually the only Briton whose operas and operettas were being performed on the continent, even on the famed stage at Milan's La Scala. He was an important composer in his day and has deserved better of history.

If Balfe's works go unstaged today, that is in large part the fault of the stories, for even in his own day, they were sometimes mocked for their illogical plot developments. That a very young aristocrat should be stolen away from her household by gypsies, be raised by them, grow up to love one of them, but never quite forget the ghosts of her childhood, and finally be identified by a scar on her arm – all this happens in *Bohemian Girl* – does rather call for some suspension of disbelief. However, the same could be said of Verdi's *Il Trovatore*, and Balfe and Verdi were of the same generation, so it may be less a matter of the composers' tastes than the tastes of the day.

Balfe, however, had begun his career as a violinist and only afterward came to composition and vocal performance; a baritone, he once sang Figaro in Rossini's *Barber of*

Seville. So perhaps he thought of melodies first and regarded the plot as something to carry those melodies. Many another composer of his time would have made the exact same decision. Indeed, the melody of 'Marble Halls' deserves its fame, but much of the rest of *Bohemian Girl* is equally well crafted. If part of an opera's score is beloved, the rest is worth exploring.

♪♪♪♪

Wagner: *Parsifal*

At its premiere at the Bayreuth Festspielhaus in Bavaria, *Parsifal* was termed by its composer, Richard Wagner (1813 – 1883) to be "ein Bűhnenweihfestspiel," that is, "a theater-consecrating festival piece." That the Bayreuth house was not itself new that day, having opened in the summer of 1876 with the four parts of *The Ring Cycle*, is beside the point. Perhaps Wagner felt that in its half dozen years of use, it had yet to be truly "consecrated."

For this last of his operas (13 in all, if one counts the four parts of *The Ring Cycle* as four individual operas), Wagner set aside his usual fascination with German mythology and cultural history in favor of an even more universal tale: the quest for the Holy Grail. In truth, the composer was not deeply religious; in his 1880 manifesto "Religion und Kunst" (Religion and Art), Wagner asserted that neither of those two fields dealt with objective truth, but that art was at least honest enough to admit the fact. So he chose the Grail story less for its ties to Christ and the search for His chalice and more for what it said about a man's quest for any ideal. In the course of this expansive extravaganza (lasting the better part of five hours), young Parsifal undergoes all manner of temptation before ultimately emerging triumphant.

Most frequently encountered of its various scenes is the so-called *Good Friday Spell*, occurring near the end of the Parsifal's adventures, when he has been welcomed back by the Knights of the Grail in Act Three. Music of rapt beauty, it is the portion of the opera that Wagner composed first, only afterward expanding the work into a full evening's spectacle. The *Good Friday Spell* itself premiered December 25, 1878, also at Bayreuth, with Wagner himself conducting. The rest of the opera would not reach the public for nearly four more years, premiering July 26, 1882. In seven more months, the composer would be in his grave, having died in Venice, not quite 70 years old.

Wagner would not have minded this scene being extracted from the much more expansive full opera, as he often led programs of orchestral excerpts from his works. He appreciated the promotional value of gathering interest for the operas themselves by letting listeners sample the music in smaller doses; it was the 19th century equivalent of Hollywood trailers. Moreover, frequently finding himself in financial straits, the composer approved almost any event that could generate immediate income.

He rarely insisted that an opera be played complete, and usually specified that it should be sung in the local language, to ensure that the audience understood the story. Clearly, Wagner judged that some attention was better than none at all. This is especially true of *Parsifal*, which is rarely staged complete. In addition to the *Good Friday Spell*, the *Transformation Music* also merits note. Wagner placed it between the two scenes of Act One, so as to allow time for a change of sets. Both reveal that Wagner, though choosing to focus his career upon opera, was yet highly skilled at getting the desired effects out of an orchestra. Were that not the case, his operas would not work nearly so well as orchestral excerpts.

♫♫♫♫

Verdi: *Macbeth*

For most composers, the challenges of creating a Shakespearean opera are two-fold. There is the difficulty of focusing an epic drama down into something that can be sung in an evening of reasonable length. Then there is the formidable obstacle of crafting an operatic version of the tale so that it will still satisfy those many audience members who already know the story well. In the case of Giuseppe Verdi (1813 – 1901), the second of these issues did not exist at the time of his first Shakespearean opera. Other than *Romeo and Juliet* – a story known in Italy even before Shakespeare's day – the Bard's works were not widely familiar to Italian audiences. So in the place of satisfying knowledgeable observers, Verdi instead had to capture the attention of those many potential listeners – and, indeed, potential performers – who simply had no notion of the tale at hand. Even the Scottish setting of *Macbeth* seemed to them unutterably foreign, and Verdi would have his work cut out for him.

One of the small percentage of Italians who knew and loved Shakespeare, Verdi began by crafting his own prose summary of this epic of uncontrolled ambition. This he turned over to the librettist Francesco Maria Piave, asking for a singable text. Verdi and Piave had worked together before, and would do so again, most famously with *Rigoletto* and *La traviata*. In this case, however, Piave seemed somewhat uncomfortable with the task; he set to work well enough, but ran into repeated roadblocks, and eventually the libretto passed on to Andrea Maffei for completion.   Throughout the process, Verdi remained actively involved, corresponding with theater directors in London about how particular scenes were customarily staged. Clearly, what he envisioned was creating not just an Italian operatic reworking of the tale, but rather one that would be as faithful as possible to the original.

Verdi's *Macbeth*, tenth of his 28 operas and the first of three he would base on Shakespeare, premiered March 14, 1847, at the Teatro della Pergola in Florence. It was an immediate triumph, earning over three dozen curtain calls for the composer alone. That the Italians embraced it so fervently – despite the fact that, since it contains no romantic story whatsoever, the Italian press swiftly dubbed it "l'opera senza amore" (The opera without love) – is a tribute to Verdi's musical craftsmanship.   By setting Macbeth as a baritone rather than a tenor, he gave further gravitas to this dark-timbred persona. Lady Macbeth is a soprano, not a mezzo, but the part requires a strongly dramatic voice, not a bright coloratura, giving her, too, appropriately substantial weight.   Neither character is given an aria that casual audiences are likely to recognize; nor is the tenor role of Macduff or the bass Banquo.

However, there is much colorful ensemble writing. A group of Scottish villagers have "Patria oppressa," a rich chorus of devotion to their homeland fully as grand as the better-known "Va pensiero" from Verdi's earlier opera

Nabucco. Less majestic, though no less colorful, is the music for the witches. In Shakespeare's hands, they famously declare "Eye of newt and toe of frog... double, double, toil and trouble, fire burn and cauldron bubble." In Italian, the words are not literally translated, but are equally sinister. For the witches' scenes, Verdi crafted music appropriately dark and stormy. The root material is amongst Shakespeare's most theatrically compelling, and Verdi's telling is fully worthy of his source.

♪♪♪♪

Johann Strauss Jr.: *Der Zigeunerbaron*
(*The Gypsy Baron*)

King of the Viennese waltz, Johann Strauss Jr. (1825 – 1899) had to be persuaded to enter the world of operetta. His first wife, Jetty Treffz, conspired with a theater director of Strauss' professional circle to have words set to some of Strauss' melodies. In so doing, they managed to convince him that his music was favorable for singing, and the outcome of that discovery was the smashingly successful operetta, *Die Fledermaus,* which premiered April 5, 1874. A decade – and two wives – later, Strauss was still entrancing operetta audiences throughout German-speaking Europe.

The Gypsy Baron arose through several professional visits to Budapest, where Strauss became intrigued with the vibrancy of Gypsy culture. Knowing that all things Gypsy were enjoying popularity throughout Europe, Strauss met with the Hungarian writer Maurus Jókai (1825 – 1904) in search of subject matter for a new operetta. Jókai suggested his own short story *Saffi*, in which a gypsy girl is gradually proven to be the lost daughter of a nobleman, clearing the way for her to marry a Hungarian aristocrat. That the essence of the story was not dissimilar to that of Michael Balfe's 1843 operetta *The Bohemian Girl* did not trouble anyone, as Balfe's work was almost entirely unknown in Imperial Austria. The work premiered October 24, 1885, at Vienna's Theater-an-der-Wien, where early in the century some of Beethoven's works had received their first hearings.

The Hungarian setting and Gypsy characters inspired Strauss to craft a score rich with ethnic colors. Admittedly, there are Viennese waltzes as well. However, the Hungarian czardas and verbunkos are also present, and the buoyant character of Magyar culture is never long absent. Spirited marches, plaintive songs, and intricately balanced ensembles came together to result in a masterwork of comic drama. Although *The Gypsy Baron* is not often performed today, it was even more successful in its first season than *Die Fledermaus* had been, and is well worth discovery, even in part. If one cannot find a staged performance of the complete work, seek out at least its opening overture, containing as it does much of the spirit of the operetta as a whole.

♪♪♪♪♪

Tchaikovsky: *The Queen of Spades*

As William Shakespeare (1564 – 1616) is to English speakers, so Alexander Pushkin (1799 – 1837) is to Russian speakers: arguably the greatest writer in his language. A romantic, charismatic character, Pushkin lived a brief though dynamic life, born to a literary family, dying after a duel fought in defense of his wife's honor. His career, when not interrupted by politics, was devoted to creating dramatic poems and novels-in-verse, many of which are now classics of Russian literature. Pushkin's poetry was so appealing that six of his dramas became operas and two became ballets. Of those eight works, two of the operas are by Peter Tchaikovsky (1840 – 1893): *Eugene Onegin* and *The Queen of Spades*. Both blend obsession and passion into darkly emotional tales that, in their abundance of tragic lyricism, exhibit traits that seem particularly Russian.

"It was so sweet to weep." Thus Tchaikovsky described his reaction on composing the final fatal scene of *The Queen of Spades*. He had been at work on the opera for about two months, since early in 1890, when, while vacationing in Florence, he began setting a libretto prepared by his brother Modest from Pushkin's tale. That libretto alters the fates of some major characters. Pushkin allowed Herman to live out his tortured life in an asylum, whereas Lisa fades into obscurity married to a nice, if dull, man. Tchaikovsky thought suicide would be more dramatic; the libretto reflects his rather morbid decision. Perhaps this fact, that Herman's death was the composer's choice, triggered his tears on the completion of the scene. As he remarked at the time, "I believe that my warm, living feeling for the hero of the opera is also favorably reflected in the music."

A painstaking composer, Tchaikovsky took great care that his musical score would appropriately evoke the various scenes. His sense for pathos suffuses the scenes of death, as his gift for melody enriches the love scenes, particularly in Prince Yeletsky's exquisite Act Two aria to Lisa. Other scenes were given no less attention. The courtly setting of Act Two called forth regal music reminiscent of the late 18th century in which the opera is set. In Act One, when Lisa and her friends are amusing themselves by singing around the piano, Tchaikovsky produced sweet, unpretentious melodies well-suited to such a setting; minutes later, when the girls indulge in peasant songs, this master of the symphony proved that he could also call forth the vibrancy of a Russian village. Considered as a whole, the score reveals the breadth of Tchaikovsky's talent and of Russian music itself, as it ranges from the imperial court to the village square.

♪♪♪♪

Sullivan: *The Mikado*

So often – and so well – did William S. Gilbert (1836 – 1911) and Sir Arthur Sullivan (1842 – 1900) work together that their paired names serve as code for all that is best in late 19th century musical comedy. *HMS Pinafore* (4th of 14 G&S operettas), *The Pirates of Penzance* (5th), and *The Mikado* (9th) became the standard against which all other musical theater of their time would be measured. An abundance of skillfully crafted music, a quantity of witty dialog and sung text, and a bit of pointed social satire made a potent formula for success, much imitated but never surpassed.

A "mikado" is a Japanese ruler, and, as such, might seem an unlikely topic for this utterly English creative team. However, it was 1884 and the Knightsbridge area of London was hosting a Japanese culture exhibit that spurred strong interest in all things Japanese. Knowing a good hook when he saw it, Gilbert – who, as librettist, was responsible not only for the texts but also for overall concepts – proposed the idea to Sullivan. Receiving enthusiastic approval, Gilbert quickly drafted a scenario and then set to work on the words. By year's end, Sullivan had the music underway; rehearsals began in January. The premiere performance, given March 14, 1885, at London's Savoy Theatre, was a triumph, with numerous demands for encores. This magic team of musical theater had another hit on its hands.

As in much of the G&S canon, there is sharp commentary upon contemporary English society. Gilbert makes the character Pooh-Bah a government official in charge of absolutely everything, as a prominent man in an English town might fill all roles from chief librarian to mayor. That one who wished to protest the man's decisions would need to protest to the man himself is part of the comedy. Similarly, the plot revolves upon a law condemning a man to prison for the crime of flirting, which may be a spoof of outdated laws that had remained upon the books.

The music, too, is cleverly wrought. In the romantic leading man Nanki-Poo's entrance aria, he declares himself to be able to offer a song in any mood, from folksy to martial to nautical, and Sullivan sets each of those verses to music of suitable character. Later, in a trio for three other male characters, Sullivan gives each man his own melody. These are presented separately, then combined into intricate counterpoint that almost recalls Johann Sebastian Bach (1685 – 1750). It might be a light and comic tale, but there seemed no reason why Sullivan couldn't give the music a serious level of craft, which is part of what raised G&S operettas above the standard set by their competition.

More Classical Insights

♪♪♪♪

Massenet: *Cendrillon (Cinderella)*

Far from being the inventor of the Cinderella story, French composer Jules Massenet (1842 – 1912) was not even the first opera composer to tell the tale. Gioacchino Rossini (1792 – 1868) had beaten him to it in 1817, though the Italian master deleted the familiar magical elements from the story. Other operatic versions followed, German speaking composers usually drawing upon the Brothers Grimm's macabre reading of the story and French ones upon more genteel interpretations by their countryman Charles Perrault (1628 – 1703).

It was the latter version that intrigued Massenet, who had long talked of writing a Cinderella opera. Yet when *Hänsel und Gretel* of Englebert Humperdinck (1854 – 1921) came to the stage in 1893, Massenet almost set aside his idea, lest he be accused of producing a copycat fairytale opera. He took up the project again when presented with a fine libretto by Henri Cain (1857 – 1937), who had been a painter before turning to literature.

Cain's reworking of Perrault's tale builds in an opportunity for an additional love duet by contriving a scene after the grand ball in which Cinderella and the Prince meet in the countryside and pledge their love. Whether the encounter is actual or a dream sequence is not clarified by the librettist, leaving the question to the discretion of opera directors. Another unusual feature of the opera was that Massenet, wanting the Prince to sound young, wrote it originally as a "trouser role": a young male character sung by a woman. Most modern performances rework it as a tenor part, largely because otherwise there are very few men in the cast.

Cendrillon's premiere was given May 24, 1899, at the Paris Opéra-Comique, the management of which had spared no expense in preparing the production. Critics reported that magical effects appeared truly magical, and had as many kind words for the production's appearance as they did for Massenet's colorful score.

The Cinderella story seems ideal for Massenet's approach to music. Although he could and did select more exotic subjects (his famed *Thais* tells of a Middle Eastern courtesan who decides to become a nun, then does not survive self-imposed privation), he seemed most at home with sentimental tales in which simplicity and innocence figure prominently, though they are not always rewarded. Here, all ends well for the leading lady, and audiences delighted in Massenet's work. At his time, Parisians regarded opera as much a social diversion as an artistic event, and *Cendrillon* served both needs perfectly.

♪♪♪♪

Puccini: *La fanciulla del West*
   (The Girl of the Golden West)

Anyone who loves the music of the opera *Tosca* by Giacomo Puccini (1858 – 1924) but wishes it had a happy ending will delight in *La fanciulla del West*. In this later work from the same composer, one finds all the same character types: the soprano, beautiful, brave, and vulnerable; the tenor, charming, charismatic, and in need of rescue; and the baritone, darkly determined to win the soprano for himself, even at the cost of the tenor's life. It is as if Tosca, Mario, and Scarpia had all been reborn in Gold Rush California, this time intent upon surviving to the final curtain. Of Puccini's twelve operas, *Fanciulla* is one of only two without a single dead body on the stage, one of only two (a different two) in which the lovers are allowed to ride off together into the sunset, in this case, often literally. It is, moreover, the only Puccini opera in which one finds gold miners gathering in a saloon to drink whiskey.

Ironically, this American-themed love story was inspired by the same playwright whose Japanese-inspired tragedy was the source of *Madama Butterfly* in 1904, and that opera played an important role in the existence of this one. In January, 1907, Puccini traveled to New York City to witness the Metropolitan Opera premieres of his operas *Madama Butterfly* and *Manon Lescaut*. Both were enthusiastically received, and the ebullient Puccini, with a few free evenings on his hands, indulged in the theatre, seeing three plays by David Belasco, including *The Girl of the Golden West*. Despite strictly limited fluency in English, the composer was impressed by the highly atmospheric tale of a young woman's love for a desperado, and the sheriff who wants the woman for himself. Obtaining a copy of the play, he ordered an Italian translation, and when that document was in hand, Puccini set to work immediately. "This is it!" he proclaimed to his publisher Ricordi. "I have an idea for a grand scene, a clearing in the California forest with colossal trees, but it requires eight or ten horses."

The premiere of this most American tale occurred December 10, 1910, at New York City's Metropolitan Opera. Enrico Caruso sang the tenor role of a Western bandit: Italian-born and stocky, it might have been casting against type, were it not for his glorious voice. Arturo Toscanini conducted, as he had at *La Bohéme*'s premiere in 1896, as he would at *Turandot*'s in 1926. Despite the evening's grim winter weather, the house was packed, many of the audience members having braved not merely ice and snow, but also the demands of New York ticket scalpers. The production proceeded smoothly, and 52 curtain calls later, *Fanciulla* was declared a triumph. Writing to a friend while journeying home to Europe on the *Lusitania*, the delighted composer himself termed the opera "magnificent."

In its music, *Fanciulla* demands not only a tenor who can manage high, floating notes, and a baritone who can sing with a snarl, but also a soprano who can project, as the orchestra is one of the largest that Puccini ever used. Moreover, she needs to be able to hold her own against a stage full of male voices, for in addition to the bandit Dick Johnson and Sheriff Rance, there is a Wells Fargo man, a traveling minstrel, and a host of miners. For fans of masculine voices, *Fanciulla* is a treat, and Puccini manages the dashes of local color well, stopping just short of commanding the men to sing "Clementine." Italian opera can be cheerful, and here is Puccini's proof.

Incidentally, the original Italian title of the opera would simply translate as *The Girl of the West*, with no reference to gold. However, since the beginning, it has routinely been rendered in English as *The Girl of the Golden West*, as Belasco's play had had it.

♪♪♪♪

Richard Strauss: *Ariadne auf Naxos*

Few composers have ever had a more up-close-and-personal relationship with opera than Richard Strauss (1864 – 1949). Not only was he one of the busiest opera conductors in Europe, ever in demand not only for his own operas but also for those of other composers past and present, he also had an experienced and acclaimed operatic soprano in his own life. Pauline De Ahna Strauss, his wife for over fifty years, became engaged to the composer when both were involved in the same operatic production. Although she retired from the opera stage to raise their family, she continued to give song recitals, frequently including songs that her husband had written for her. She never performed any of his 15 operas, but it can be no coincidence that nearly all of those works include multiple prominent roles for women.

Such is the case with *Ariadne auf Naxos*, with three very different leading ladies. The title character is a strong and dramatic soprano. Another – the comedienne Zerbinetta – is a high and light coloratura. The third – the Composer – is actually a male character, but written for a mezzo-soprano, so as to make him sound younger. These same three voice types also appear in the Strauss opera that immediately proceeded *Ariadne, Der Rosenkavalier*. Here, as there, Strauss often sets one of those women's voices directly against another, so as to emphasize the difference in vocal types. Had he not already learned that trick as an opera conductor, he would have come to understand it through spending his life with Pauline.

Peripherally based on an ancient Greek myth, *Ariadne auf Naxos* had two premieres in two different forms. It was first crafted for Max Reinhardt (1873 – 1943), a theater director friend who wanted something to insert into a production of the Moliere play *Le bourgeois gentilhomme*. In the play, a nouveau riche pretended gentleman has an opera performed in his town house for his own amusement. That's all Reinhardt was expecting: a little half-hour bit of something suitable to Moliere's time period, along with some incidental music to go with the play itself. That's where Strauss began, but it is not where he and his librettist, Hugo von Hofmannsthal (1874 – 1929), stopped. By the time they were finished, they had a combination of play and opera that had far outgrown the resources of Reinhardt's Deutsches Theater in Berlin. So the creators transplanted *Ariadne* to the Court Theater in Stuttgart, where it premiered October 25, 1912.

Not only was that first *Ariadne* too much Reinhardt, with a running time of nearly four hours, most of it spoken dialog, it was too much for the Stuttgart audience. *Ariadne* would not become a success until Strauss and Hofmannsthal split it into two, making of it one full opera and one set of incidental music for a play. The opera came to the stage at the Vienna Court Opera October 4, 1916, in the form in which it is almost universally performed today.

As for the incidental music, that reached the stage separate from the opera and attached to an abridged version of the Moliere play back in Berlin in 1918. These two halves of what was once one single work are now two separate entries in Strauss' catalog of works. Both have much to recommend them, and one may choose depending upon whether wishes to have singers involved in the story, or simply instrumental selections conveying the changeable moods of this would-be gentleman entertaining his guests.

More Classical Insights

♪♪♪♪

Wolf-Ferrari: *The Secret of Susanna*

Although he was born and died in Venice, Ermanno Wolf-Ferrari (1876-1948), was a man of diverse roots and residences. His mother was Italian, his father Bavarian, and though the youth began his music studies in Rome, he continued them in Munich. From Munich, it was only a short trip up the road to Bayreuth to experience Wagner's operas in the theater that had been built for them. Wolf-Ferrari became intrigued with the modern German approach to harmony, though he never fell for Wagner's robust sense of high drama. Even as Wolf-Ferrari's elder Italian contemporaries were discovering the powerfully emotional dramatic possibilities of *verismo*, Wolf-Ferrari himself was more interested in the jolly comedies of the early Romantic days of Gioacchino Rossini (1792 – 1868).

Wolf-Ferrari's most successful work, and one that has enjoyed productions throughout much of its century of existence, is *The Secret of Susanna*, which premiered December 4, 1909, at the Munich Hoftheater, the composer still being of the opinion that the Germans understood him better than the Italians. A mostly cheerful work, it concerns the adventures of a young couple, of whom the wife is concealing a secret from her husband. In other composer's hands, such a plot line might lead to dark and scandalous developments, perhaps even a murder. In fact, the husband's first instinct upon smelling cigarette smoke in the house is to suppose that she must be having an affair, the smoke being leftover from her lover. But, no: the aroma is due to Susanna having taken up smoking, which she has been hiding from her husband. Once the husband realizes what is afoot, he not only forgives her for smoking and keeping secrets, but, relieved to have found no human rival, joins her in the habit.

The high-spirited opera does not sound quite like Rossini. Wolf-Ferrari indulged in more modern, so-called "chromatic" harmonies than his predecessor would have ever imagined. However, it can fairly suggest how Rossini might have sounded had he lived a century later.

♪♪♪♪

Weill: *Street Scene*

Street Scene is a tale of primal passions, of young lovers seeking directions for their lives, of a mature woman whose desires drive her down a path of destruction. Such a hot-blooded tragedy might have perfectly suited the tastes of Giacomo Puccini (1858 – 1924), yet it is not a product of the *verismo* movement. It is, rather, a thoroughly American piece by a German immigrant that premiered in New York City on Broadway January 9, 1947.

The opera's origins lie in the Pulitzer Prize winning play of the same name by Elmer Rice (1892 – 1967), a drama so successful that it reached an international audience within one year of its initial appearance on the stage. The composer Kurt Weill (1900 – 1950), already renowned for his controversial *The Three-Penny Opera*, saw *Street Scene* staged in German in Berlin in 1930. Five years later, when Nazi persecution drove him to abandon Germany in favor of New York, Weill began a decade-long campaign to win the rights to create a musical adaptation. Finally, in 1936, the composer and the playwright, together with poet Langston Hughes as librettist, set to work.

Weill, Rice, and Hughes all agreed that what they had created was an opera, yet they studiously withheld that term from their advertising. They called the piece instead a "dramatic musical," a subtle evasion that was not lost upon the critics. In fact, in his favorable *New York Times* review, Olin Downes pointed out the semantic dodge, then observed upon the cleverness of the practice: "audiences came to the show, as they probably would not have done if the operatic element in it had been stressed as such, and found themselves excited, astonished and entertained. Opera had crept up and caught them unaware... For it was as a play musically expressed that the work was taken – as opera always should be taken – and the sum of the two elements make opera."

Although *Street Scene* won critical acclaim, there was little a financial success. Both *Finian's Rainbow* and *Brigadoon* opened in the same Broadway season, causing some potential audience members to choose a pastoral Celtic romance over Weill's gritty urban drama. *Street Scene*'s run of only 148 performances was unimpressive by Broadway standards. Yet when one considers how few operas, even those of Verdi and Puccini, can claim a similar record in their initial seasons, it then becomes clear that, in its own context – as an opera, rather than a musical – the piece was no failure. Rather, it was as influential as any new opera to ever reach the stage, and has continued to move audiences for over half a century.

♪♪♪♪

Copland: *The Tender Land*

No one man was more responsible for bringing American music into the classical mainstream than Aaron Copland (1900 – 1990). He had an infallible sense of the spirit of traditional American music and a knack for evoking that spirit in the concert hall. Those talents, blended with a firm grounding in European techniques of composition, made him the perfect figure for bridging the Atlantic and convincing skeptical Europeans that the US had something to offer musically. Copland was respected both at home and abroad, and it would seem that he would be the best choice for confronting the Europeans on their own ground in composing the definitive American opera.

Copland's 1954 opera, *The Tender Land*, offers all that is best about his music. It is rich and lively and lyrical, filled with beautiful, folk-like melodies and nostalgic images of a slower pace of life. The work was commissioned by Richard Rodgers (1902 – 1979) and Oscar Hammerstein II (1895 – 1960). Those two names are more often encountered in the realm of musical theater, but both men were well familiar with fine music and admirers of Copland.

The story, concerning the love of the idealistic farm girl Laurie, and the romantic drifter Martin, is pure Americana. Its message concerning the strength one can derive from the land lies deep in the heat of the nation's best literature. Perhaps, however, that message was a bit too firmly rooted in the land, at least for sophisticated New York critics. When the opera premiered at the New York City Opera April 1, 1954, the critics treated it coldly, despite a warm reception from the public. The dichotomy of responses led the composer to muse the "the first night audience must have been a houseful of friends."

Today, *The Tender Land* stands as an admirable example of Copland's well-honed touch with folk-like moods. Just because the melodies are his own does not keep them from sounding as if they had emerged directly from American soil. It is an opera that only an American well versed in American musical roots could have produced, and one which, in its story, required a familiarity with those roots.

♪♪♪♪♪

Menotti: *The Saint of Bleecker Street*

Although Italian-born, Gian Carlo Menotti (1911 – 2007) lived in the US from 1928 until his death. As an Italian, he was strongly attracted to the realm of opera; as a naturalized American, he wished those operas to be sung in English. He composed some two dozen such works, both for professional performers and for children, in each case crafting both the music and the librettos. Menotti's best-known opera is *Amahl and the Night Visitors* (1951), which he wrote on a commission from NBC television. His works earned two Pulitzer Prizes (one for *Bleecker Street*), the New York Drama Critic's Circle award, and Kennedy Center Honors, as well as favorable international attention.

Bleecker Street was Menotti's first opera after the phenomenal success of *Amahl*. Choice of the story arose in part from the composer's visit late in 1951 to southern Italy, where he met a priest reputed by some admirers to be a saint. When the priest scolded Menotti for not having a deep enough faith, the composer determined to explore musically the nature of belief. *Bleecker Street* premiered at New York's Broadway Theater December 27, 1954, to strongly positive reception.

Some more skeptical observers were startled by the religious tone of the work, unusual on a Broadway stage. However, Menotti himself always claimed that the piece was less religious than broadly philosophical, as his operas tend to be. In his view, operas were "metaphors for moral or philosophical issues," and much the same can be said for many operas by Giuseppe Verdi (1813 – 1901) or Richard Wagner (1813 – 1883) or Giacomo Puccini (1858 – 1924). Opera composers have often moved beyond simple tales to choose instead stories that say something significant about the human condition and how we react to the world around us; that's exactly what *Bleecker Street* does.

Having penned his own libretto, Menotti then set out to develop a score that would accurately convey the words he had written, not just their specific meanings, but also the correct rhythms of those words as they would be spoken. The text is set to music much as it would be spoken, though with musical pitches to underlie those rhythms of speech. It's a nice trick from a man whose native language was not English. Focus on the patterns of delivery of the lines, particularly in the scenes in which several characters are conversing, and one finds the patterns of speech, with emphasis on correct syllables and especially important words. Menotti is not the only composer to assign himself such a task, but as the score is sung almost entirely in English (other than a few brief passages in Latin or Italian), it is here particularly clear to the English speaking listener.

More Classical Insights

In musical terms, the score is not tuneful in the manner of Puccini; it is not a work that sends the audience home humming the big tunes. In fact, there are few arias in the traditional sense, which means that listeners accustomed to opera recitals and opera highlight recordings will not find much that is immediately familiar. The fact is that the music is all part of the whole, flowing seamlessly from one moment to the next and does not extract well from its setting. There are no conventional love scenes; even the scene after Carmela's wedding is more festive than romantic. Yet *Bleecker Street* is not in any way a dissonant, modernistic work. Rather, Menotti chose to focus in his score more on power, drama, and characterization than on set pieces for vocal display. Although much of the music is beautiful, the overall emphasis of the piece is upon its strength of expression. It is a work that punches straight through to the heart, rather than first seducing the ears.

♪♪♪♪

Previn: *A Streetcar Named Desire*

The essence of opera is often grand personalities, made grander yet by the power of music. Some of the most iconic opera characters – the womanizing Don Giovanni; the Germanic hero Siegfried – become super-human when given musical voice. When it comes to grand personalities, it would be hard to outdo Blanche Dubois, from Tennessee Williams' play "A Streetcar Named Desire." A Southern lady of a certain age adjusting poorly to declining fortune, for many observers, she will always be personified by Vivien Leigh, who played her so memorably in the 1951 film. No less memorable was Marlon Brando as Stanley

Kowalski, and for some, Brando's voice will ever be that of Stanley.

When a story is so well known, and so closely tied to particular performers, resetting the tale as an opera can be a challenge. Would Blanche and Stanley sing, and if so, how should they sound? That was exactly the dilemma faced by composer/conductor/pianist André Previn (b. 1929) in completing his commission for the San Francisco Opera. *Streetcar*, which premiered at San Francisco September 19, 1998, was his first opera, but not his first classical work. A variety of chamber works and concertos – most notably, a concerto for violinist Anne-Sophie Mutter – had preceded it in his catalog. An opera, however, is an ambitious task indeed.

In place of Leigh and Brando, Previn had soprano Renee Fleming and baritone Rodney Gilfry. For their voices and those of the other cast members, he crafted music the rhythms and harmonies of which seek to capture their unsettled emotional states. Although the story is set in New Orleans and Previn has a strong background in jazz, the opera's score does not attempt to sound jazzy. Rather, it bears more relationship to mainstream operas of the mid-20th century, especially those of Benjamin Britten (1913 – 1976). Arias, such as Blanche's "I Want Magic" and "Sea Air," have grand melodies and nuanced orchestral support; ensembles seek to differentiate between the various characters involved by assigning them different styles of singing. The *verismo* composers of the past, focused as they were upon strong but believable emotions, would likely understand what Previn was doing and recommend that their audiences give it a try.

♩♩♩♩♩

Catán: *Il Postino (The Little Postman)*

Born in Mexico City, Daniel Catán (1949 – 2011) received most of his higher education in the US and England, but returned to his birthplace to serve as music administrator of the Palace of Fine Arts. That fact did not prevent his compositions from finding international attention. The two best known of his works were both commissioned and premiered by American opera companies, before going on to wider attention. The earlier of these was *Florencia en el Amazonas*, which premiered October 25, 1996, with the Houston Grand Opera. The later, and last of all Catán's completed works, was *Il Postino*, its premiere given by the Los Angeles Opera September 25, 2010.

The opera shares its story with the popular film of the same name, and both derive from the novel by Antonio Skármeta, *Ardiente paciencia*. Given a story of a young Italian postman developing a friendship with the aging Pablo Neruda, one might expect the postman to be written as a tenor and the poet as a baritone, to reflect their different levels of maturity. However, with the Los Angeles Opera having commissioned the work, Catán knew that he would have at his disposal the company's General Director, the unsurpassed tenor Placido Domingo (b. 1941). Domingo's age made him not suitable for the role of Mario the postman, but his voice, undiminished in power, was ideal for Neruda, giving the role all the gravitas and humanity it required. So both leading men are tenors with voices of different weight, and baritones appear only in supporting roles.

There are also sopranos for the wives of the two men. Catán's music deftly contrasts the two relationships, the mature couple sounding more settled, though no less loving, the younger couple brighter and more eager. In musical style, Catán's score is lyrical and flowing, not especially modern in flavor. If one were to imagine Puccini with an even broader palate of colors, one would draw near to what Catán achieves in *Il Postino*.

♪♪♪♪♪

Portman: *The Little Prince*

An Oscar winning composer, a long beloved philosophical fairy tale, and an opera company famed for its devotion to new works: with that happy alignment of stars, *The Little Prince* came to be. English composer Rachel Portman (b. 1960) won her Oscar in 1996 for the Gwyneth Paltrow film *Emma* and has also been nominated for other film scores. Given that both opera and film tend to think big, one might imagine that the two genres would be natural fits. However, few devoted film composers have found the time for opera, as has Portman.

Part of the problem is that both genres require such focused attention to ensure that all the parts complement one another that for many months at a time, all other projects tend to be left on the shelf. Film producers and opera producers alike dislike sitting on the back burner. Portman, however, managed to juggle her schedule so as to accommodate an opera, too, and *The Little Prince* had its world premiere at Houston Grand Opera May 31, 2003.

More Classical Insights

Antoine de Saint-Exupéry's novella of an unearthly young wanderer who relates his interplanetary adventures to an adult listener was reshaped into an operatic libretto by Nicholas Wright (b. 1940). In the process, some of the underlying philosophy fell by the wayside in favor of dramatic action, yet that fact does not make the piece a children's opera per se. Portman's *The Little Prince* appeals on many levels. Her chamber orchestra, particularly rich in woodwinds, is used in a gently melodic fashion appropriate to the mellow spirit of the tale. The vocal writing, if not intently virtuosic, has a matter-of-fact flow that also suits her subject.

Is it profound? Perhaps not, but profundity is often in the eye of the beholder, and if one wished to know if a 21st century film composer can successfully manage an art form that for 400 years has challenged even the greatest names in music history, the answer is affirmative. It is not a grand work, but neither is the original novella. So Portman seems to have captured the spirit of Saint-Exupéry's tale, which is just what an opera composer is supposed to do.

Chapter Nine: Stage and Screen

Long before movies came to be, there were plays, and both forms of entertainment may benefit from music. It may accompany specific action presented to the audience, or it may hint at things to come. These dark and determined notes by Ludwig van Beethoven (1770 – 1827) make clear that the stage work to follow, Goethe's *Egmont*, is no light piece of amusement. Rather, it is philosophical, political, and ultimately relates to man's highest dreams, which is exactly what Beethoven wants his listeners to understand. Such is music for stage and screen: a composer's attempt to reinforce what's happening in the dramatic story itself.

Live theater is often enhanced by music. Even though, visually speaking, the audience can readily distinguish between a love scene and a chase scene, and though, theoretically, a fight scene would be different yet, music still serves a valuable place as reinforcement and foundation. This is particularly true when the composer, in conversation with the playwright or director, decides to foreshadow upcoming events. A quiet walk in the garden accompanied by somber and tense music for cellos and trombones is a very different thing from a quiet walk in the garden accompanied by the warbling of flutes.

Such music for a stage production is called "incidental music," that is, that it is something added to the words and scenes on stage. One advantage of having great composers write incidental music is that its level of craftsmanship may match or even exceed that of the play itself, thus giving future audiences reason to remember that such-and-such a play ever existed. The draw becomes the music, more than the drama.

The same situation can apply to film music. For every great film for which a great musical score was composed, there are also not-so-great films raised to a higher standard by the music that was provided for them. Moreover, certain foreign films may never reach Western audiences, though their music may do so on its own. Even accompanied by the original film, the music can help audiences to imagine the color and character of that film, whatever the language of its dialog.

It is worth recalling that, though incidental music for plays is nearly always the work of a single composer, this may not be the case for film music. A composer may have been contracted to write the music for a particular film. However, so as to keep productions on schedule, he'll likely have assistants who tend to the editing and orchestrations, that is, preparing the music to fit perfectly with the lengths of the individual scenes and the resources available for the recording of the music. With live performance of incidental music, the conductor can adjust his tempos to the pace of action on the stage; in a film, those adjustments must be made before the final film can be assembled for distribution.

Some of the greatest film composers of all time are not to be found in this collection. This is not to deny their contributions, but rather to share the spotlight with a wider selection of composers. So Erich Korngold (1897 – 1957), Miklos Rózsa (1907 – 1995), and Bernard Herrmann (1911 – 1975) all appeared, along with various others, in my earlier collection of music articles, *Classical Music Insights*. The only film composer I have included in both collections is the one who has written more high profile film scores than any other: John Williams (b. 1932). However, with so many widely familiar film scores to his name, it was easy enough to select a different one for attention on this specific occasion.

♪♪♪♪

Purcell: *The Fairy Queen*

Henry Purcell (1659-1695) was the first important English composer and for nearly two centuries after his death, almost the only English composer any music aficionado would have been able to name. Indeed, there were other composers whose music earned impressive success in England. However, the majority were foreign born, and of the actual Englishmen, few made much of a mark. None had the impact of Purcell, who in his songs, choral works, keyboard pieces, and an abundance of theatrical music proved that the English could match the Italians, Germans, and French note for note.

Purcell would compose incidental music for over 40 plays, and if the plays themselves are long since forgotten, his music has survived. Additionally, he composed much sacred music, many secular songs and celebratory odes, one full opera (*Dido and Aeneas*), and a handful of "semi-operas." This latter category differs from full operas in that there is substantial use of spoken dialog, rather than having every word set to music. There is more than just incidental music to be inserted into a play, yet still not quite a full, through-composed opera. Nowadays, one might call such creations musical theater works. *The Fairy Queen* is one of these semi-operas.

The story comes from Shakespeare's *A Midsummer Night's Dream*, though here rather freely adapted. Purcell's version came to the stage in 1692 at London's Dorset Garden. For the production, Purcell composed an overture, entr'actes, songs, dances, and a few grand ceremonial scenes. As each of the pieces is more expansive than what one generally finds in sets of incidental music, Purcell composed fewer individual bits. Yet they showcase his flair for intricately entwined layers of music, making the most of the generally smaller instrumental ensembles that were popular in his day. Through Purcell's music for *The Fairy Queen*, one can gain a sense as to why the public and the royalty alike came to admire his craft.

♫♫♫♫

Beethoven: *Egmont*, op. 84

In 1788, one year prior to the French Revolution, the esteemed German writer Johann Wolfgang von Goethe (1749 – 1832) brought to the stage a hero of the past, a historical figure from a time that had strong parallels to Goethe's present day. His chosen hero was Count Egmont, a Flemish patriot of the mid-16th century, a time when the area now known as Belgium and the Netherlands lay under the rule of Spain's King Philip II. Though initially little interested in politics, Egmont's sympathies for Flemish dreams of freedom and his horror at the persecution of Flemish Protestants led him to espouse the cause of freedom. His continuing instigation of Flemish rebellion drew the anger of the king, leading to Egmont's imprisonment and execution. Yet even in death, Egmont inspired the Flemings to continue their fight for independence.

At this point in the tale, Ludwig van Beethoven (1770 – 1827) was but a young pianist and aspiring composer, living in his native Bonn and dreaming of finding an audience in Vienna. He had never seen the play *Egmont*, and certainly the playwright had not heard of the composer. However, the passage of years brought about an alteration of their relative positions. By 1809, Goethe still ruled the German literary world, but Beethoven had come to the top of musical realms, and a Viennese theatre producer asked him to compose incidental music to accompany a revival of *Egmont*. The staging would be in part a 20th anniversary tribute to the play, but it would also be a political statement, for, at the time, Vienna was under the occupation of Napoleon's armies. Against that background, any tale dealing with the oppression of a brave people by insidious outsiders was certain to play well with the Viennese. Delighted to be granted the honor of interpreting Goethe's text, Beethoven set to work at once, and produced ten musical numbers to accompany the play.

In addition to the well-known overture – the opening of which appears at the head of this chapter – there were also four entr'actes, two songs for the title character's lady love,

Clärchen, and three other numbers: music for her death scene, for Egmont's prison vision, and a final "victory symphony," implying the triumph of freedom despite its leader's own fate. With its new musical score, *Egmont* was staged in Vienna late in the spring of 1810. That the composer thought highly of the results is proven the fact that he bothered to send the music to Goethe himself. "You will shortly receive," he wrote, "the music for *Egmont*; that glorious *Egmont* which through you I have considered, felt and set to music with the same warm emotions as I experienced when I read it." Goethe had not attended the Viennese production. However, he was content with the composer's effort, remarking, "Beethoven has followed my intentions with admirable genius."

♪♪♪♪

Schubert: *Rosamunde* Overture

In the strictest sense, there is not and never was an overture by Franz Schubert (1797 – 1828) titled *Rosamunde*. There was, indeed, a play by that name, for which Schubert composed a variety of songs, choruses, entr'actes, and dances. However, he composed no overture, at least, not one unique to this production.

The year was 1823. Schubert, at the age of 26, was earning a poor living from writing songs, and eagerly accepted an invitation to provide incidental music for the production of a new play. With *Rosamunde*'s premiere barely six weeks away, Schubert began with the songs and ballet music, so stage rehearsals could begin. The overture was last on the schedule, but time ran out. Memoirs of the playwright, Helmina von Chézy (1783 – 1856), attest that 48 hours before opening night, there was still no overture in existence, so Schubert provided instead one from his earlier opera, *Alfonso and Estrella*. The production opened at Vienna's Theater-an-der-Wien December 20, 1823.

A subsequent performance featured a different pre-existing Schubert overture, *The Magic Harp*; this is the overture that is usually called *Rosamunde* today. Schubert might have eventually given *Rosamunde* an overture of its own, but the play, hampered by an improbable plot set in ancient Cypress, ran for only a few performances. When the curtain fell, Schubert's charming score retired from the stage. As had happened so frequently in his brief career, he had now another failure on his hands.

♪♪♪♪

Schumann: *Manfred* Overture, op. 115

Romantic composers found inspiration in diverse realms. Everything from politics to nature found its way into their music, though literature was the most frequent inspiration. Poems, plays and stories triggered the creation of uncounted compositions. Goethe and Schiller were perennial favorites, even beyond the borders of their native Germany, but English poets were also popular, particularly Shakespeare, and the dramatic and passionate Lord Byron (1788 – 1824) also stands high on the list. Many Byron protagonists, including Childe Harold, Don Juan, and Manfred, drew musical breath long after their literary creation.

Of those three protagonists, it was moody Manfred that caught the attention of Robert Schumann (1810 – 1856).

Manfred is a loner who so regrets his beloved's death that he seeks peace through spirits – not of the alcoholic kind, but of the magical kind. Ultimately, Manfred finds death to be more congenial than life. Schumann became so entranced by Byron's vision that he determined to make of it a musical/dramatic work. That *Manfred* is not, strictly speaking, a play did not trouble Schumann. His concept was that his music would be performed before and between readings of segments from Byron's work.

Schumann's incidental music for *Manfred* consisted of an introductory overture and several short interludes. They premiered together with a dramatic reading of the text in Leipzig June 13, 1852. Stern and wistful passages appear in turn, with turbulent emotions coming in waves. Manfred's moods of yearning and anguish are masterfully captured by Schumann, who knew personally about troubled soul-searching. In another year, he would attempt to take his own life, and spend the last years of his life in an asylum. With his own emotional fragility, Schumann may have been the best possible composer to see into the mind of Manfred.

♪♪♪♪

Delibes: *Le roi s'amuse (The King Enjoys Himself)*

Leo Delibes (1836 – 1891) was the son of a provincial French postal worker who would have directed the boy into civil service. However, Delibes Senior died when Leo was eleven, and left to his mother's inclinations, the boy ended up at the Paris Conservatoire for music studies. It was with theater music that young Delibes would make his reputation, composing over a dozen light operas, several ballets (most notably *Coppélia*), and a single opera, the exotic romance *Lakme*. He also devoted time to crafting incidental music for the dramatic theater, and it was that activity that brought him together with his nation's most respected playwright, Victor Hugo (1802 – 1885).

English-speaking theater goers mostly identify Hugo with *Les Miserables* and *The Hunchback of Notre Dame*, both of which have found life in music. However, the Hugo drama that came into Delibes' hands was *Le roi s'amuse*. In 1882, on the play's 50th anniversary, a revival was staged in Paris, and Delibes was asked to provide music for the occasion. Since Hugo's drama is set in a French court in the 17th century, Delibes sought to recapture the mood and style of that era, not of his own time. The set of dances that he created have little to do with his own time of rich French Romanticism. Rather, they exude the elegant balance of music by François Couperin and his contemporaries.

Those not familiar with the play under its French name may yet know the story. It came to the attention of the Italian master of opera, Giuseppe Verdi (1813 – 1901), who made of it his 1851 opera *Rigoletto*. This work is featured in my book *Operatic Insights*.

♪♪♪♪

Sullivan: Shakespearean scores

Few would be startled to learn that an English composer would find himself writing incidental music for Shakespeare's plays. Many of those plays specifically require the addition of songs, dances, and interludes, a fact that no Englishman could entirely ignore. However, the fact that Sir Arthur Sullivan (1842 – 1900), master of

More Classical Insights

comic operetta, had also turned his hand to more substantial theatrical work might be news. In fact, the first of Sullivan's compositions – his actual opus no. 1 – was written at the age of 19 for Shakespeare's *The Tempest*, and premiered in Leipzig's Gewandhaus April 6, 1861. The young Englishman was in Germany studying on a scholarship awarded in memory of Felix Mendelssohn, the late – but still adored – conductor of the Leipzig orchestra. Thus, it was the Germans who first heard any music, let alone Shakespearean music, by the quintessential English composer.

Four more sets of Shakespearean incidental music would follow that initial creation, all premiering in England, rather than Germany. Sullivan's music for *The Merchant of Venice* reached the public in Manchester April 5, 1862, scarcely a year after the premiere of *The Tempest*. It was followed by *The Merry Wives of Windsor* for London December 19, 1874, *Henry VIII* for Manchester August 29, 1877, and *Macbeth* for London December 29, 1888. The large gap of time between *Henry VIII* and *Macbeth* was filled by nine operettas with William S. Gilbert, including their super-hits *HMS Pinafore*, *The Pirates of Penzance*, and *The Mikado*. Sullivan was not a man to let time lie idle in his hands.

♪♪♪♪

Nielsen: *Aladdin*

The career of Carl Nielsen (1865 – 1931) is a rags-to-riches to story. He was born 7th of 12 children of a village housepainter on the Danish island of Funen. Music – specifically, the piano – provided an escape for the boy, who earned a scholarship to the Copenhagen Conservatory at age 18. Only after graduating from the Conservatory in 1886 did he give serious attention to composition. Nielsen developed a personal style that blended a bit of Wagner's bold use of the orchestra with a dash of Brahms' ideas of harmony and structure to form his own unique musical voice. By 1901, he was well enough regarded in his homeland to earn a state pension for the rest of his life, enabling him to devote his energy to composition, rather than teaching.

His *Aladdin*, dating from 1919, is a suite of incidental music intended to accompany performance of a play by the Danish writer Adam Oehlenschläger (1779-1850). The play was inspired by the tales of the Arabian Nights, and, in the early 20th century, was in the midst of a revival at the Copenhagen Royal Theatre. If one thinks of Aladdin only as slipping into a grotto to rub a lamp and conjure a genie, one misses the scope of his adventures. Nielsen, however, attended to the details, accompanying Aladdin in his wandering through the Middle East and beyond. So as to give even more color to his score, he included choral parts for the sinuous marketplace scene and the more vibrant African dance. All in all, his music proves that the Arabian Nights, which so famously inspired Rimsky-Korsakov's *Scheherazade*, was influential even in Scandinavia.

♪♪♪♪

Vaughan Williams: *Scott of the Antarctic*

Any epic film requires a stalwart central character and an adventure in which he or she can either triumph magnificently or perish tragically. If the adventure can be based on a true life story, so much the better: more immediacy and greater dramatic potential both for the screen and for the soundtrack. Few true life stories have more drama than that of English adventurer Robert Scott's 1912 attempt to be the first to reach the South Pole. Action, peril, and the impossible frustration of finding that Norwegian Roald Amundsen had barely beaten him to the prize: those elements alone would have been enough to make an exciting film. Add to them the fact that, on their return, Scott and his team got within a dozen miles of the sought-after supply depot before perishing in the cold, and it equaled a story that had everything except a grand film treatment.

In 1948, that single shortcoming was solved with film director Charles Frend's *Scott of the Antarctic*, staring Sir John Mills (father of actress Hayley Mills). The script was co-written by Ivor Montague and Mary Hayley Bell, who was Mills' wife. For the music, Frend recruited Ralph Vaughan Williams (1872 – 1958), then more associated with the concert hall than with cinema. However, Vaughan Williams was no stranger to the demands of film music, and was eager to tackle this tale of a thoroughly English adventurer.

As one would expect, the score contains spacious themes for those vast expanses of ice, and here Vaughan Williams most often turned to strings with sparkle added by woodwinds and glockenspiel. However, there is much else to the film: lively penguins, plaintive memories of home, and much physical exertion. Each aspect Vaughan Williams set out to capture in music, so that the soundtrack could reinforce the visual imagery.

So pleased was he with what he'd crafted for Frend that, after the film's release late in 1948, Vaughan Williams decided to make a full symphony from the film score. Rather than just pasting together the cinematic fragments end to end, he chose to take those evocative bits and create from them more extended compositional ideas, ambitious enough to hold up under lasting scrutiny. It would become his Symphony no. 7, sub-titled *Sinfonia Antartica*. It is not a misspelling; rather, he aimed for an Italianate version of the continent's name, so as to match the word "sinfonia." That which had begun as film music had taken on much broader expression when it premiered January 14, 1953.

♪♪♪♪

Stravinsky: *The Soldier's Tale*

Man against the Devil: it's a theme that for centuries has fascinated writers and their audiences. Medieval morality plays revolved around the concept, and folk tales, many of which are of even more ancient origin, are equally obsessed. Sometimes in such stories, man only bests the Devil through the intervention of heavenly powers; such is the case in Goethe's version of *Faust*. Yet other tales allow man to save himself through cleverness, and this approach may be the most popular, for who would not enjoy rooting for one who defeats a wily opponent by being even wilier? *The Soldier's Tale* of Igor Stravinsky (1882 – 1971) begins in this fashion; it is only when the soldier seeks one pleasure too many that his luck changes and his soul passes into the Devil's hands. "One happiness at a time," the text reads. "The road to twice-as-much leads to none."

More Classical Insights

It was 1917, and World War I had had a negative impact upon Stravinsky's financial resources. In need of an income-producing project, he created one with the help of his friend, the Swiss novelist C. F. Ramuz. They imagined a story that might be told with words by Ramuz and music by Stravinsky. The piece would not be an opera, for there would be no singers; rather, it would be more like an old morality play, in which actors, dancers, musicians, and a narrator performed together in one work.

For inspiration, they turned to a collection of Russian folk tales, and chose episodes from a variety of stories about a soldier who, while on leave from the army, has repeated encounters with the Devil in disguise. A side plot in the story concerns a princess who is offered as bride to anyone who can cure her illness. The soldier succeeds and marries her, hence the lyrical, romantic passages. It is when the soldier takes the princess home to meet his mother that the Devil captures the soldier's soul. Had the poor man simply settled for winning a princess, all would have been well.

The resulting work, *L'Histoire du soldat* (*The Soldier's Tale*), premiered in Lausanne, Switzerland, September 28, 1918, with sets and costumes by René Auberjonois, patriarch of the family of the modern actor bearing the same name. The performance went well, and Stravinsky hoped to take the work on tour, so as to maximize his income from the composition. Unfortunately, influenza intervened. The epidemic forced the closure of most European theatres, which was just as well, since the entire performing company, including Stravinsky, also caught the flu, and became too ill to have kept to their performance schedule. Only through later use of the score as a concert suite did Stravinsky get much financial benefit from the work.

As the story has a violin as recurring plot element – the soldier has the violin, the devil covets it – violin solos appear frequently in the work. The instrument can be seen as emblematic of the soldier's soul, which he first wins back from the Devil by beating him at cards, then loses it once more. Listen for the violin solo's bright and dark moods to guess in whose care the soul is at any given time.

♪♪♪♪

Prokofiev: *Lieutenant Kije*, op. 60

Military spoofs have long supplied diversion to audiences. In 1927, the Soviet author Yury Tynyanov published a short story titled *Lieutenant Kije*, the title character of which does not exist. Rather, Kije began as a typographical error in military orders, and when the aides are unwilling to admit that the tsar has misread their report, they concoct elaborate tales of the supposed lieutenant's life and adventures. When his imaginary existence proves inconvenient, the aides kill him off and bury him as a war hero.

In 1933, the Leningrad-based film director Alexander Feinzimmer decided to bring the tale to the silver screen and recruited Sergei Prokofiev (1891 – 1953) to write the music. Most of the years since the Russian Revolution late in 1917 the composer had spent in Paris and the US, and had only just returned home. This would be his first work written for his countrymen since the Revolution. It would also be Prokofiev's first film score, though he had already achieved international success with symphonies, concertos, ballets, and operas. A year after the film's debut, Prokofiev reworked the score as an orchestral suite, broadening the composition's audience.

His music for the film – and recaptured in the orchestral suite – offers obligatory brass fanfares for heroic scenes, including the imaginary hero's birth. There are also gentle romances, a boisterous wedding scene – sounding more like a drinking party than a solemn ceremony – and a brisk winter excursion in a troika, complete with sleigh bells adding sparkle to the scene. As for the music that accompanies Kije's burial, here is no funeral scene. After all, the military aides are delighted to have their problematic creation out of their hair, and with that idea in mind, Prokofiev chose high spirited moods for his music. One can imagine one of those aides declaring, "Kije is dead – let us all rejoice."

♫♫♫♫

Copland: *Music for Movies*

Long before John Williams (b. 1932) came along, Hollywood had a hunger for music. From silent screen adventures through the epics of the '40s, movies were made more effective and more memorable by the addition of well-crafted scores, whether incorporated into the film or played live in the theater. Of the legions of Hollywood film composers in the mid-20th century, many were European refugees fleeing Fascism in the 1930s. Yet home-grown talents also played a role. That most American of concert hall composers, Aaron Copland (1900 – 1990), composed music for eight films from 1939 through 1961. He was nominated several times for Academy Awards, and won once, for the 1948 film *The Heiress*.

Although some composers with international reputations equal to Copland's regarded film music as beneath them, Copland always insisted that it was the best means of reaching the largest audience, and the only means of reaching those movie-goers who don't attend concerts. As for those concert-goers who don't attend films, he had a simple solution: make concert suites from his film music, as Edvard Grieg (1843 – 1907) had done with his famed theater music for *Peer Gynt*. In either case, the composer is allowing diverse audiences to glance into a wondrous world that might otherwise have escaped them.

Music for Movies is a five-movement concert suite drawn from Copland's first three films. These are *The City*, a documentary screened at the 1939 World's Fair; *Of Mice and Men*, the John Steinbeck-inspired drama of the same year; and *Our Town*, composed in 1940 for a screen version of Thornton Wilder's classic play.

The suite begins with "New England Countryside," with music drawn from the opening scenes of *The City*. The second movement, called "Barley Wagons," is a pastoral scene from *Of Mice and Men*. For the third movement, "Sunday Traffic," the rural mood is exchanged for more hectic musical images borrowed from *The City*. The fourth movement, "Grover's Corners," borrows a gently flowing theme from *Our Town*. For its conclusion, *Music for Movies* returns to Steinbeck's realm for "Threshing Machines" from *Of Mice and Men*. *Music for Movies* premiered in New York on February 17, 1943.

More Classical Insights

♪♪♪♪

Bernstein: *On the Town*

It's a story of three sailors on leave in New York City during World World II, three vibrant young men seeking love, or its near imitation, before the clock strikes midnight and, like Cinderella, their days of freedom come to an end. It is a tale that caught the attention of Leonard Bernstein (1918 – 1990) more than once: for his ballet *Fancy Free* (premiering April 18, 1944) and his Broadway musical *On the Town* (premiering December 28, 1944). In this last year of World War II, it was a story guaranteed to win public affection.

The ballet could have been placed in Chapter Ten of this collection, the musical in Chapter Eight. However, as Bernstein's music for these sailors reached its widest audience when it came to Hollywood, *On the Town* is placed here with film music. That two of the three male leads were Gene Kelly and Frank Sinatra certainly ensured an audience; by comparison, their colleague Jules Munshin was little noticed. The film opened late in 1949, and won an Academy Award for best scoring of a musical.

Bernstein's name did not appear on the Oscar, for though the original music was his, other members of the technical crew had completed the final adjustments to the score so as to suit it to the demands of film. Such is the case with most movie scores: hardly ever are they a one-man job. However, when one hears the film's iconic song, beginning with the line, "New York, New York, a wonderful town," it is Bernstein's musical vision that rings out so vibrantly.

With all the accolades that would be coming his way in the next four decades, not being named as the Oscar winner was, in the long run of time, a small matter.

♪♪♪♪

Jarre: *Lawrence of Arabia*

It is one of the most spectacular of all film scores for one of the most spectacular of all films. The David Lean film *Lawrence of Arabia* (1962) featured music by French composer Maurice Jarre (1924 – 2009), and won a handful of Academy Awards, including one for Jarre. At the time, he was little known in the US; from this point onward, his name would stand at or near the top of any list of first-rate Hollywood composers.

Jarre had learned his craft at the Paris Conservatoire, which in earlier generations had produced Debussy, Ravel, and many of the other principal names of classical music. The fact that his studies began with percussion performance before branching into composition influenced the frequent prominence in his film music of percussion instruments, not just the usual suspects, but also an array of percussive tools providing great variety of colors.

This is especially clear in the opening minutes of his music for *Lawrence*. At first, the screen is occupied only with the simple word "Overture," a term with which many average film-goers would have been quite unfamiliar. In music for the stage, however, an overture is an instrumental introduction to that which follows, often featuring melodies – or at least fragments thereof – that will prove prominent in the main work.

That's exactly what Jarre does; his overture begins with violent, percussion-laden themes that will come to be associated with the quarreling Arab tribes before introducing a lush and flowing melody that becomes Lawrence's own theme. One hears it first in the strings. When it reappears elsewhere in the spacious film score, it is sometimes given to other sections of the orchestra, allowing Jarre to shade it according to his protagonist's moods and situations.

Also at his disposal is the ondes Martenot, an electronic instrument that predates the more modern synthesizer, but, like its successor, excels at conveying eerie, unsettling moods. The ondes Martenot (more details in the glossary) was a French invention, and though Jarre was not the first to bring it to Hollywood, he certainly gave to it a powerfully expressive role in this most epic of films.

At the beginning of the project, Jarre was to share musical responsibilities with two other composers, and admitted that he was deeply honored when he heard their names. Benjamin Britten (1913 – 1976) and Aram Khachaturian (1903 – 1978) were both acclaimed masters of the concert hall, having had little to do with music for cinema. That Jarre was being placed on a level equal to them was for him a great mark of respect. However, both Britten and Khachaturian had to pull out due to other obligations, and Jarre found himself taking on the entire film alone, producing well over an hour of music in all. Much of the power of the film came through Jarre's Olympian effort.

♪♪♪♪

Goldsmith: *Patton*

Born in Pasadena, California, Jerry Goldsmith (1929 – 2004) may have been pre-destined to find his way into film music. Amongst his music professors were Italian composer Mario Castelnuovo-Tedesco (1895 – 1968) and Hungarian Miklós Rózsa (1907 – 1995). The former of those also counted John Williams (b. 1932) amongst his students; the latter was himself a top-of-the-list film composer whose works included *Spellbound* and *Ben-Hur*, amongst much else. Goldsmith learned to handle musical expression for grand and dramatic scenes, but also to push the boundaries of expectation. If a surreal scene required surreal sounds, Goldsmith would ask his orchestra members to use their instruments in new and different ways, such as clicking keys rather than blowing through the instrument. Electronics were also a favorite Goldsmith tool, and with his list of films including several from the *Star Trek* series, as well as *Alien* and *Planet of the Apes*, unearthly effects were a valuable resource.

More down-to-earth in setting, if not in persona, was one of the most widely familiar of Goldsmith's films, *Patton* (1970); even those who were not around to see it when it was new likely have a visual image of a stern-faced George C. Scott standing imperiously against an immense flag image. The task of crafting music for a superstar military figure might have led some composers to create a host of brassy fanfares, but not Goldsmith. Indeed, bold brass is called upon to provide heroic color when it is needed, though often in fragmentary form, with poetically lyrical strings appearing in between those brass statements. For further contrast, Goldsmith sometimes paired piccolo and snare drum, as if to evoke fife-and-drum bands of Revolutionary War days, connecting the World War II general into a long history. Tense string harmonies and dissonant overtones serve for scenes of uncertain outcome. For all the unwavering self-confidence that the famed general chose to portray in public, Goldsmith's score makes clear that strained emotions were not far adrift, at least for those in Patton's circle. It is music that takes one directly to the side of the military hero.

♫♫♫♫

Williams: *Lincoln*

The compositions of John Williams (b. 1932) are among the most familiar in America, even for those listeners who do not know the composer's name. Who could not recognize the ominous two-note theme of the shark in the movie *Jaws*, or the five-note pattern used to communicate with the aliens in *Close Encounters of the Third Kind*, or the brisk and hearty marches heard with the opening titles of *Star Wars, Indiana Jones* and *Superman*? Other notable Williams film scores include *ET* and *Schindler's List* (both of which won Academy Awards), *Jurassic Park*, and *Saving Private Ryan*. He is already on board for the continuation of the *Star Wars* series that George Lucas is planning to re-launch in 2015. To date, Williams has scored well over 100 films, been nominated for Academy Awards nearly 50 times, and has been the dominant composer in Hollywood for the past three decades.

Having scored over two-dozen films for director Steven Spielberg, Williams was the director's first and only choice for 2012's *Lincoln*. In character, *Lincoln* is less overtly heroic than some of the films for which Williams has provided music. However, one must admit that there is heroism in Lincoln's unpopular stand for African-American rights – which serves as the focal point of the film – and further heroism in the historic people who join him in his campaign. At those times of heroism, the film music takes on bold moods. Lone trumpet calls prove effective for singling out brave individual decisions, and when the dialog is particularly crucial, as in Lincoln's speeches, Williams' music steps cooperatively into the wings. Civil War marches are evoked when necessary to mood and to on-screen imagery.

When the presidential couple spends an evening at the opera house (prior to that fateful night at Ford's Theater), Williams might have crafted his own operatic scene; instead he chose to include an excerpt from the opera *Faust* by French composer Charles Gounod (1818 – 1893). That opera had premiered in 1859, becoming immediately and wildly popular, the single most popular opera in the US for the last half of the century. At that time, opera was regarded as general musical entertainment, not something for wealthy society, so the Lincolns were highly likely to take in a performance. Both Williams and Spielberg were well aware of that historic fact, ensuring that film scenes and film music alike would reflect upon it. Whatever is happening on the screen, it is crucial that the music do something to reinforce those images.

♪♪♪♪

More Classical Insights

Barry: *Dances with Wolves*

Casual observers of Oscar winners may have spent some years supposing that film composer John Barry (1933 – 2011) was African by birth. Here, after all, was a man who took home Academy Awards for his film scores for *Born Free* (1966), *The Lion in Winter* (1968), and *Out of Africa* (1985). However, the second of those films dealt not with Africa, but rather with English history, dealing with the relationship between aging King Henry II (Peter O'Toole) and Eleanor of Aquitaine (Katharine Hepburn). Then there are the facts that Barry himself was born in Yorkshire in the north of England and that his list of film scores includes, amongst much else, eleven James Bond movies. Here was a man who could focus his musical vision upon a wide range of cinematic topics.

The fourth and last of Barry's Academy Awards was for the Kevin Costner film *Dances with Wolves* (1990). Here, the composer set his sights neither on the African veldt nor on the adventures of a master spy but rather upon the post-Civil War American high plains, where Costner's character, John Dunbar, finds himself amongst both nature and the Sioux. Barry's score is spacious and flowing, as if evoking waves of prairie grass. The theme he crafts for Dunbar is given to different instruments at different times: a lone trumpet, a wistful harmonica, or, more broadly, lush strings. Each resetting of that theme allows the composer to express some new side of the character's personality, generally reflecting what is presented on the screen.

Despite the frequent presence of Native American characters in the film, Barry's score is not overtly Native American in style; it is as if the music sets out to shade the scenes through Dunbar's eyes and ears, not through those of the natives who become his friends. Film music need not always be strictly literal. Like great opera, it can also serve an interpretive role.

♪♪♪♪

Glass: *The Hours*

Music for the cinema has been a continuing interest for Baltimore-born Philip Glass (b. 1937). His catalog includes dozens of film scores for all types of films. Prominent amongst these are the biographical epic *Kundun* (1997), the documentary *A Brief History of Time* (1992) and the philosophical/environmentalist piece *Koyaanisqatsi* (1982). Glass has also crafted new scores for classic films of the 1920s and '30s, and at the opposite extreme, turned his talents to high-profile Hollywood productions of recent years.

In this latter category is his music for *The Hours*, released late in 2002. The tale drew parallels between three women of three generations: a 21st century New Yorker (played by Meryl Streep), a 1950s housewife (Julianne Moore), and the author Virginia Woolf (Nicole Kidman). Each character in her own way is emotionally unsettled, a fact that Glass' music seeks to capture. Often moody, sometimes restless, the score tends toward long phrases flowing over gently repeated rhythmic fragments: a trademark of Glass' so-called "minimalist" style. Here, that style becomes less obsessively propulsive than is often the case, perhaps reflecting the fact that, to varying degrees, all three women come to feel that moving forward in their

More Classical Insights

lives is incredibly difficult. Glass' film score was nominated for both an Academy Award and a Grammy, and though it took neither prize, it has taken on a second life in transcriptions for solo piano. That fact proves that fine film music can endure even outside the context of the film for which it was written.

♪♪♪♪

Silvestri: *The Polar Express*

Alan Silvestri (b. 1950 in New York) began formal music studies as a guitarist at Boston's Berklee College of Music. From performing, Silvestri soon diverged into film scoring, and by 2008 had compiled a catalog of nearly 100 films. His works include the *Back to the Future* series, *Contact*, *Forrest Gump*, *The Abyss*, and more recently *Beowulf*. Though not yet an Oscar winner (at this writing in the summer of 2013), he has earned nominations as well as the favorable regard of his colleagues, who think highly of his finely-crafted scored. Consistently, he shows a deft hand with orchestral color, using the varied voices of the instruments for varied effects. Whatever is happening on the screen carries over brilliantly into Silvestri's scores.

Director Robert Zemickis' 2004 film *The Polar Express* was inspired by the 1985 children's book by Chris van Allsburg. Allsburg's tale of a boy whose belief in Santa Claus is so true as to earn him a magical train journey to the North Pole won the Caldecott medal for its inspired illustrations. Zemeckis and Silvestri faced the challenge of portraying those illustrations and the tale itself through their work. Silvestri's music brings one into the boy's adventure, conveying all the wonder of the journey, even evoking the motion of the steam engine that draws the train, as well as the dreamy sparkle of a child's view of Christmas. The song "Believe" was nominated for an Oscar and scored a Grammy Award for its recording. Even without the accompanying film, the music carries listeners along on the journey.

♪♪♪♪

Horner: *Titanic*

When one is born in Los Angeles, is of musical interests, and has a father who works in Hollywood, it may be inevitable that one will enter the world of film scores. Such is the case with James Horner (b. 1953). Although he spent some years in London, before long, he returned to southern California. For over three decades, Horner has been closely involved with the Hollywood community, scoring a great many important films, including *Apollo 13* and *Avatar*. However, he reached the highest mark – and earned a pair of Academy Awards – with *Titanic* in 1997.

Titanic's score blends strong, propulsive themes for the ship setting out, buoyant Celtic-like themes – complete with harps and penny-whistles – for steerage class passengers, and pounding brass and percussion for the ship in distress. The score's main theme is not the ship's, but rather that of the central female character, echoes of it occurring when she appears either on screen or in memory. That Celine Dion sang its vocal version may have helped the soundtrack to become the best-selling film soundtrack since John Williams' *Star Wars* in 1977.

More Classical Insights

The range of Horner's music for *Titanic* and its blend of dark energy and yearning romance are not far different in character from the work of some of the great composers of the past. Delve into Sergei Prokofiev's music for the 1938 film *Alexander Nevsky*, and one will find that Horner has taken inspiration from some of his most impressive predecessors.

♫♫♫♫

Zimmer: *Pirates of the Caribbean*

In the 1930s and '40s, the style of Hollywood film music was largely driven by European-born composers, fleeing politics and war at home to find a new life and work in southern California. Even now, long after those particular troubled times, European-born composers may find fertile fields for their musical ideas in American film, ensuring that film is an international industry.

One such figure is German-born Hans Zimmer (b. 1957). Starting from a background in pop and electronic music, he now blends those influences with a thorough understanding of orchestral approaches and has earned lasting critical and popular acclaim. Zimmer has worked with many of the top Hollywood stars and directors since his first big success with *Rain Man* (1988), and has remained at the forefront of film music all the years since that time.

Zimmer's highest profile work so far is for the *Pirates of the Caribbean* series in 2006, 2007, and 2011; a subsequent film is intended for release in 2015. The first film in the series (2003) did not feature Zimmer's music. Throughout the *Pirates* films that are Zimmer's, one finds a tendency for bold and driving themes to which one might set sea shanty-like lyrics. Zimmer also introduces more lyrical passages when the plot demands them, and given the occasional other-worldly images that one finds in the films, is able to indulge in his favorite electronic effects. So he has crafted deftly varied musical moods to reflect the on-screen action: heroic or romantic or surreal. Beethoven never had "on-screen" action to manage, but he, too, varied musical moods to taste; Zimmer is putting those established ideas to use in a new setting.

More Classical Insights

Chapter Ten:
Dance Inspirations

Russian composer Alexander Borodin (1833 – 1887) created this dance music for characters in his only opera, *Prince Igor*. Here, peasants lament the loss of their homeland and their freedom. However, when modern audiences hear it, they are unlikely to think of those colorful Polovtsians. For many listeners, it evokes images of "strangers in paradise," for those words came to be attached to it in later generations in the Broadway musical *Kismet*. Yet it began as dance music, and it is music intended for – or inspired by – dance that concerns us in this chapter.

Sometimes, dance-flavored music is composed for professional performance before an audience, with the music supporting dance that attempts to tell a story. In this chapter, there are several of these ballets, spanning about 200 years of creative expression.

Dancing might also serve as a component in other types of staged works, particularly operas. For many years, the Paris Opéra required that all operas include scenes to make use of the opera house's resident ballet company, and few composers would have been unwilling to comply, as such a decision would have shut those influential doors to their music. These dances might have been included in the chapter on opera. However, if the dance scene is even more frequently performed than the opera as a whole, I placed it here.

Dance music can sometimes be social in nature. Enough of this sitting in theater chairs to watch and listen: perhaps one might get up on one's feet and join personally in the dancing. In this case, the triple-meter pulse of the waltz becomes a particular favorite, though as we shall find, one need not be Viennese to take up waltzing.

Then there is the folk dance perspective. Folk dance may not be, in and of itself, classical music. However, that fact has not stopped composers from drawing upon its vibrant spirit to flavor their works, especially if they are borrowing that spirit from their own folk culture, in a practice known as "nationalism." Such approaches have proven especially popular with composers of Eastern European origin, so look for the flavors of those folk styles to appear even in the classical concert hall.

This chapter includes twenty different works. Amongst them are formal ballets, operatic excerpts, social dances, and dance-inspired concert works. As a whole, it is a broad sampling of how the dance might find its way into musical expression, whether or not there are actual dancers involved.

♫♫♫♫

Lanner: *Die Mozartisten,* op.196

The waltz was not an original invention of Viennese society. Rather, it evolved gradually, through many hands, from the Austrian folk dance known as the Ländler. By the early decades of the 1800s, the new dance – considered by some to be virtually scandalous, as couples embraced, rather than just chastely holding hands – had made its way into Viennese ballrooms, bringing with it some very popular dance bands. The personnel of one of those bands included two particular young men: the violist Johann Strauss Sr. (1804 – 1849) and the violinist Joseph Lanner (1801 – 1843). Before long, both men had set up business on their own, conducting rival dance bands, which for two decades were the most popular in all Vienna. Strauss Sr. may have won history's fame contest between the two, but in their time, Lanner was no less acclaimed and his waltzes are no less finely crafted.

Lanner composed well over 100 waltzes, as well as various dances of other types. Standing late in his catalog (he died of typhus just after his 42nd birthday) is *Die Mozartisten (The Mozartists)* of 1842. Its melodic material is drawn from two of the earlier master's operas, specifically *The Magic Flute* and *Don Giovanni*. Those who know either of those operas well may find themselves at a loss to think of any waltz to be found within them, and indeed, the waltz did not exist in Mozart's time. However, one can always shift the rhythm of an existing melody so that rather than stepping along steadily in a 2/4 meter, it instead prances in 3/4. This is exactly what Lanner does.

Lanner's work begins with the three opening chords of *The Magic Flute*, before proceeding to several of the tenor's themes: his plea for help and his rapturous aria to a portrait of a pretty young lady. None of this is structured as a waltz meter, as it was customary to open a waltz with a call to the dance floor in a moderate tempo. Quick recollections of the bird-catcher's flute calls lead off to *Don Giovanni*, and its famed duet "La ci darem la mano," here reshaped as a waltz. One also finds several more waltzified bits of *Don Giovanni*, notably "Das klinget so herrlich" and "Könnte jeder braver Mann," before the nimblest of all, the Champagne Aria arrives, also altered into ¾ time. Ultimately, Lanner moves back to *The Magic Flute*, recalling the three opening chords, and then the liveliest passages of that opera's overture. In all, it is clear he knew the opera well, and understood how to add a bit more lilt into Mozart's timeless melodies.

♪♪♪♪

Johann Strauss Jr.: *Roses from the South*, op. 388

In the world of Viennese waltzes, the Strauss family functioned as a royal dynasty. For much of the 19th century, some member of the Strauss family – sometimes, more than one at once – was at the helm of the most popular ballroom orchestras in the city, not only conducting, but also composing most of the music that would be performed.

The combined efforts of Johann Strauss Sr. and his sons, Johann Jr., Josef, and Eduard, led to the creation of roughly a thousand compositions, with waltzes most numerous on the list. Although all four men were prolific composers and active conductors, the younger Johann – eldest of the three brothers – proved to be the most influential of the clan. Johann Jr. (1825 – 1899) took a dance form that was still intended mostly for the ballroom and deftly raised it to concert-hall status, producing compositions almost symphonic in scope, making great demands on both his orchestra and himself. Concert tours took them as far afield as Russia, England, and the United States, but wherever they went, they brought Vienna with them.

A fine example of the artistry of Johann Jr. is his *Roses from the South* waltz, written in 1880. Here, he dispensed with the customary waltz introduction, generally achieved by slower, stately, and not particularly waltz-like music that invited listeners to find a place on the dance floor before the waltzing itself began. Instead, *Roses from the South* begins with an actual waltz theme, presented rather sotto voce, but there nonetheless. It is followed by a sequence of contrasting waltz melodies, some bright and buoyant, others sleepy and languid, spanning the better part of ten minutes before reaching a brilliant, percussion-tinged finale. Whether one is in the mood for swirling about the ballroom in 3/4 time or merely for listening and watching the action, it is a work that offers delights for all.

So popular did this particular waltz become that four decades later, when the very avant garde composer Arnold Schoenberg (1874 – 1951) wished to craft a chamber arrangement of some waltz music for an evening entertainment at the Society for Private Musical Performance, this is the waltz he chose. That arrangement, for piano, string quartet, and harmonium (a small parlor organ) has far more to do with Strauss than it does with Schoenberg. The latter composer's own works nearly always tended in a starkly modern direction, and here, he lets the original material stand unmolested. However, had Schoenberg not respected the source material, he would have looked elsewhere. It was a new generation, but *Roses from the South* still carried its appeal.

Betsy Schwarm

♪♪♪♪

Borodin: *Polovtsian Dances* from *Prince Igor*

Before he became a composer, Alexander Borodin (1833 – 1887) was a professor of chemistry. He came to music late, in part because before his generation, classical music in his native Russia was more often imported – especially from France – than created locally. Borodin's generation would change that situation, leading home-grown composers to begin to make themselves heard and to gain acceptance in concert halls throughout Europe and beyond.

Borodin's academic career was busy enough that he never found sufficient time to write down all the music in his mind. Even keeping a piano in his chemistry lab wasn't quite enough to get all his intended compositions down on paper. For 18 years, his opera of national spirit, *Prince Igor*, remained a work in progress, and progress was slow. It was still incomplete when he died, and it required the intervention of two of Borodin's music colleagues, Nicolai Rimsky-Korsakov (1844 – 1908) and Alexander Glazunov (1865 – 1936) – both of whom appear elsewhere in this collection – to bring it into performable condition. It premiered in 1890 at St. Petersburg's Mariinsky Theatre.

The beloved *Polovtsian Dances* from Act One of *Prince Igor* are amongst the sections that Borodin managed to complete himself. In this scene, the Prince's armies have been at war with the tribal Polovtsians, and have captured a group of Polovtsian women whom they are holding prisoner. The women sing of their longing for the homeland while the soldiers sing of the glory of their prince, setting up a marvelous musical contrast between the wistful and the warlike. The women's melody achieved particular fame when it later served as the theme for the song "Strangers in Paradise" in the Broadway musical *Kismet*. Although originally written for chorus and orchestra, Borodin's music is often performed only with instruments, the vocal parts being worked into the orchestration.

♪♪♪♪

Saint-Saëns: *Danse macabre*, op. 40

Dating from 1875, the *Danse macabre* by Camille Saint-Saëns (1835 – 1921) derives from a poem by Henri Cazalis (aka Jean Lahor), in which Death, armed with a violin, tempts the skeletons to come out of their graves at midnight to dance. They leap and run and jump, all to the pulse of his nimble playing, until dawn and a rooster's crow ends their night of revelry. Impressed by the poem's imagery, Saint-Saëns set about interpreting it in music, first as a song for singer and pianist, and then in orchestral form.

In the latter version, a busy xylophone stands in for the rattling bones, and an oboe offers the rooster's crow. It is bright, colorful, and intensely lively, with one restless waltz – one might suggest "diabolical" – theme after another. The piece so moved the virtuoso pianist/composer Franz Liszt (1811 – 1886) that he transcribed it for solo piano so as to be able to include it on his recitals. However, despite all the excitement of that keyboard version, its orchestral predecessor offers even more electric energy.

♪♪♪♪

Tchaikovsky: *Swan Lake*

The theatrical dance form known as ballet first apperaed in the 17th century, when French courtiers delighted in this dramatic mix of music and dance, and the greatest composers of that place and time, notably François Couperin (1668 – 1733), turned their talents to the field. The art form continued well into the 18th century, but by the 19th century, ballet's popularity had waned. Few important Romantic composers produced ballets, other than as scenes in their operas. Not until late in the century did a person of prominence, one of the most admired and respected composers of the day, chose to compose ballets, in large part because it was a field admired and supported by his nation's ruler. By bringing his reputation to a neglected field, Peter Tchaikovsky (1840 – 1893) restored ballet to its former prominence, and it has remained in the spotlight ever since.

One of the most famous of all ballets, *Swan Lake* was composed in the spring of 1876 at the request of Moscow's Bolshoi Ballet, which would give its premiere the following March. Tchaikovsky had just finished his Symphony no. 3 and Piano Concerto no. 1 the previous year. This would be his first foray into the ballet.

The year would be a turning point in his personal life as well, for in 1876 he acquired both a wife, Antonina, and a patron, Nadezhda von Meck. Of the two women, the latter was the far more positive influence and encouraged him in compositional endeavors. Antonina had largely bullied Tchaikovsky into marriage, claiming that if he refused her, she would take her own life. On the other hand, Madame von Meck provided years of financing and a ready ear for the composer's letters about life and music.

More Classical Insights

At this point, Tchaikovsky needed Madame von Meck's encouragement, for his music had not enjoyed much success. Moreover, at its first outing, *Swan Lake* was one of the disappointments. Its premiere was given with various cuts to Tchaikovsky's score, and the insertion of selections from other composers' works. The ballet director had declared that these changes were required so as to make the ballet easier for the dancers and the orchestra. Tchaikovsky's score he judged to be overly symphonic in its demands. One complaint against the work seems to have centered on lengthy passages of virtuoso dancing that had little relationship to the plot. *Swan Lake* ran in repertory for a half dozen seasons, and was revived after the composer's death as a memorial to his career.

As was usual with ballets of the time, *Swan Lake* includes not only grand ensemble waltzes, but also a variety of gentler pas de deux (duets) and a selection of dances in different national styles as music for a courtly gala. There is also a quantity of music for the swans. As the ballet's story has it, a group of girls is under magical enchantment and must spend much of their time in the form of swans. Tchaikovsky provides music for them both in their human forms and in their swan forms, taking care to differentiate one from the other. He must also differentiate one of the girls, the villainous Black Swan, whose music is cast as tense and shadowy of mood. The overall result is expansive enough and varied enough to seize the attention of the listener, regardless of what might be occurring within the choreography.

♪♪♪♪

Dvořák: *Prague Waltzes*

Talent does not always result in instantaneous fame. Far more frequently, composers spend years struggling for notice, and in some tragic cases, perish before achieving their goal.

At least Bohemian composer Antonín Dvořák (1841 – 1904) dodged that evil fate. There were years spent grasping at every job that came within reach, years in which his sweetheart's father withheld permission for their marriage, fearful that, with Dvořák, young Anna would starve. Then in the mid-1870s, for three out of four consecutive years, Dvořák took top prize in an Austrian government sponsored competition for young composers. With the victories came prize money, fame, and a publishing contract. Dvořák was on his way to international stardom.

Thanks to that new prominence, when a social club in Prague sought composers to write waltzes for its upcoming 30th anniversary ball, it added Dvořák to the list. He complied with the *Prague Waltzes*, which premiered December 28, 1879. A piano arrangement came to life later. At the time, the idea of symphonic waltzes was strongly associated with the Strauss family down the road in Vienna; A younger contemporary of Johann Strauss Jr. (1825 – 1899), Dvořák would have known his colleague's music. As the Viennese master would have done, Dvořák crafted not a single waltz melody, but a sequence of five contrasting ones, for richer variety, and all builds to a dramatic coda, quoting fragments of the preceding waltzes and bringing the set to a close with enthusiasm and high spirits.

♪♪♪♪

More Classical Insights

Richard Strauss: *Dance of the Seven Veils* from *Salome*

In November 1902 in Berlin, Richard Strauss (1864 – 1949) attended a German-language production of Oscar Wilde's play *Salome*. The friend with whom he attended asked if Strauss could make an opera of it, and Strauss supposedly replied "I am already busy composing it." For several years, the opera would remain a work-in-progress. First, Wilde's text – wordy and deeply philosophical in any language – had to be condensed and revised into singable form. Then other tasks, both as composer and as conductor on the international stage, forced their way into the foreground. Not until early summer of 1905 would the score be completed, and its premiere in Dresden would wait six months longer, until December 9, 1905.

Part of the delay was due to worries that the overtly sensual tale would enflame the censors; others problems arose when the soprano cast in the title role went on strike, declaring that a 'decent woman' should not be asked to do and sing such things. Indeed, though the story began in the Bible, it gained much erotic color in passing through Wilde's hands, as this depraved teenager seduces Herod, her step-father, demanding – and receiving – as payment the head of John the Baptist. Yet despite the furor, the opera attracted favorable attention from those whose views Strauss most valued: his professional colleagues. To those conservatives who attacked the opera to Strauss' face as a piece of trash, he responded only with a shrug and the wry observation that this 'trash' had paid for his villa in Garmisch – and a nice place it is, indeed.

Even once the conservative censors were silenced, *Salome* proved difficult to stage, as it requires a soprano who can sing like a grown woman – the part is musically demanding – but look like a teenager. Then there's the matter of dancing. Late in the opera, Salome dances the famed *Dance of the Seven Veils* for Herod, and even with costumers' magic, it is a rare soprano who can manage that striptease and still have enough breath to sing afterward. Yet the music of that scene is widely familiar, as it is often performed as an orchestral excerpt. Its swirling rhythms and driving beat steadily increase in intensity, rising to an exuberant frenzy. Even without the visual elements from the stage, it is music of passionate drama.

♪♪♪♪♪

Glazunov: *The Seasons*, op. 67

The stars seemed bright for Alexander Glazunov (1865 – 1936). Having studied with Nicolai Rimsky-Korsakov (1844 – 1908), he was only 16 when his Symphony no. 1 reached the public and not yet 20 when he made his conducting debut in Paris. Together with Rimsky, he helped to resurrect the music of a fallen comrade by completing scores left in fragments at the death of Alexander Borodin (1833 – 1887). In 1899, he joined the faculty of the St. Petersburg Conservatory. Sergei Prokofiev (1891 – 1953), Sergei Rachmaninoff (1873 – 1943), and Dmitri Shostakovich (1906 – 1975) – all of whom appear elsewhere in this collection – would be amongst his students. With his multi-faceted talents, Glazunov was perfectly placed to carry Russian music into a new age, and yet it was not to be, for a lasting problem with alcohol limited his productivity.

More Classical Insights

Of all Glazunov's compositions – over 100 published works – only a handful have retained an audience. Most notable amongst these is his ballet *The Seasons*, offering a wealth of melodic invention together with imaginative climatic portrayals. Dating from 1899, the ballet was composed at the request of the great choreographer Marius Petipa (1818 – 1910), who in earlier years had worked with Tchaikovsky on *Sleeping Beauty* and *The Nutcracker*.

Glazunov produced for him a short ballet – well less than an hour in length – with a simple story, generally a sequence of mythological scenes appropriate to the work's title. He begins with the icy storms of winter, before proceeding to the breezes, birds, and flowers of spring. Summer is occupied with lush fields and languorous warmth. For the final scene of autumn, Glazunov conjures up a boisterous bacchanal, which gradually draws to a close as the cold winds of winter return, brushing away the falling leaves and bringing visions of clear, starry skies. It is colorful, evocative, and memorable music that makes full use of the varied orchestral resources with which the composer had provided himself. It stands as proof that, despite his personal shortcomings, Glazunov was yet a master of orchestral effect.

♫♫♫♫

Ravel: *La Valse*

French composer Maurice Ravel (1875 – 1937) wrote *La Valse* in 1919 as a kind of homage to Vienna's past, a glory that seemed far distant in these post-war years. The composer himself provided a preface to the score that describes the scene as an Imperial court ball around 1855, with waltzing couples swirling beneath glimmering chandeliers and glimpsed through the mists of memory. The specified time frame is just when Johann Strauss Jr. (1825 – 1899) was dominating the waltz scene in Vienna, though Ravel opts for less structure than Strauss would have used. He also included a highly varied orchestra, with the usual suspects supplemented by piccolo, English horn, bass clarinet, contrabassoon, and myriad percussion, including the un-Viennese tambourine, castanets, tam-tam, and crotales.

One might suppose that a composition inspired by waltzing would be ideally suited to the ballet, and indeed, the work originated on a commission from Sergei Diaghilev (1872 – 1929), impresario of the Ballets Russes; seven years earlier, Diaghilev had commissioned Ravel's full-length ballet *Daphnis and Chloe*. Ravel labored over the new work for six months. At last, he presented the work to Diaghilev, who, to the composer's dismay, declared it to be undanceable. The ensuing argument caused a permanent rift in their friendship, and Ravel never again composed for the Russian company.

As for *La Valse*, a "poème choréographique" as the composer called it, Ravel reworked it as a piano duet in 1920, and premiered it in that form with a colleague; that same year, he also had the work staged as an orchestral showpiece, as it is usually heard today. Eight years later, nearly a decade after Diaghilev's rejection, *La Valse* finally came to the stage when Ida Rubenstein presented it as a ballet at the Paris Opera.

♪♪♪♪

More Classical Insights

Gliere: *The Red Poppy*

The early 20th century was a tumultuous time for Russian composers. Not only were the political waters in flux, there was additionally a musical revolution in progress. As in politics, where some clung to old ideas while others charged forward into a brave new world, so composers faced a choice between past and future. Those who bet on the future – Igor Stravinsky (1882 – 1971) and Sergei Prokofiev (1891 – 1953) amongst them – were likely to emigrate, as Soviet authorities were disinclined to approve of their radical efforts. Those who, musically speaking, preferred the past, might win approval, provided their style did not too closely resemble the old German or French schools of thought. Reinhold Gliere (1875 – 1956) managed to survive the tides of change even while remaining in his homeland.

Gliere's symphonic works and chamber works were persistently lyrical and often colorfully scored. When the Russian Revolution occurred in 1917, Gliere was already well-established and managed to weather the Soviet storm that drove some of his younger countrymen abroad. Particularly in dramatic works, he successfully fit his music to ideas that suited the tastes of the new establishment.

Such was the happy fate of Gliere's most famous work, *The Red Poppy* ballet, which premiered June 14, 1927, at the Bolshoi Theatre. Set in contemporary China, it concerns a Russian ship coming into a seaport where its captain intervenes to help abused Chinese workers. The Soviet government loved its focus upon the working classes, and the ballet became a popular success.

Its most famous scene, the vibrant Russian Sailor's Dance, occurs in Act One just after the ship's arrival. Incidentally, the flower of the title is used in the ballet as a symbol for freedom and love, for a local girl falls for the captain and gives her life to save him, thus allowing him to continue the fight for her people. As a whole, whatever one's politics, the ballet's highly varied charms offer something for nearly any listener.

♪♪♪♪

Falla: *The Three-Cornered Hat*

At the turn of the 20th century, Spanish composers were heavily influenced by musical developments in Paris. Many of them had studied at the Paris Conservatoire, and though they did not come home writing music exactly French in character, they certainly adopted the French idea of music freer in form than what the Germans were doing, yet less edgy than some of the Austrian and Russian approaches. They also came to a greater appreciation of their own culture's musical roots, often imitated by the French. Hearing what the French composers were making of Spanish rhythms and settings, some of the actual Spaniards decided to try their own hands with these materials.

The Three-Cornered Hat Ballet by Manuel de Falla (1876 – 1946) exemplifies this idea of musical nationalism in its choice of topic, its musical style, and its political subtext. The ballet's story is drawn from Alarcon's 1874 novel, *El Corregidor y la Molinera* (*The Magistrate and the Miller's Wife*), which itself is based on a Spanish folktale, concerning a local politician whose lustfulness exceeds his intelligence. His repeated attempts to seduce the miller's pretty young wife prove ludicrously unsuccessful, even when he brings a band of bodyguards to her door to arrest her husband on trumped-up charges. Ultimately, it is the Corregidor who is imprisoned – for foolishness, if for no other reason – while the townspeople rejoice at his humiliation.

The hat of the title is symbolic of the Corregidor's uniform. Here, it represents a long-standing Spanish delight at the outwitting of authorities by the common people. Notably, that dream is not restricted to the borders of Spain, which may account in part for the ballet's success when it premiered in Madrid in 1917, though the bright Spanish rhythms of the music must also be given some credit.

♪♪♪♪

Bartok: *Rumanian Dances*

Devoutly Hungarian, Béla Bartók (1881 – 1945) studied at the Budapest Academy of Music, first focusing upon piano and composition. Graduate studies followed in ethnomusicology, as he sought a deeper understanding of his nation's folk music. Realizing that folk music pays little attention to borders, Bartók expanded his studies throughout Eastern Europe, attempting to map out a survey of which rhythms and harmonies tended to be used in which areas. He recorded and studied many thousands of folk songs and folk dances, developing such a reputation in the field that in 1940 when New York City's Columbia University was seeking someone with expertise in Eastern European folk music, the job came to Bartók. Even beyond the borders of Hungary itself, there was no region of Eastern Europe the music of which he had not explored.

As to the *Rumanian Dances*, Bartók had known this music for years, and it was closer to his heart than many styles, as the region's shifting borders had moved his Hungarian birthplace of Nagyszentmiklós into the newly defined Rumania. In 1915, relatively early in his professional career, Bartók wrote a piano suite based on several Rumanian dances. Two years later, he arranged the score for orchestra. Here, one finds the varied moods of the original dances, alternately vibrant and melancholy, portrayed even more clearly through the instrumental changes that orchestral resources can provide. This form of the score premiered in Budapest in February, 1918 and was published four years later.

Although the work is structured as a sequence of seven dances, it is not a seven-movement suite. Rather, the different dances, of varying moods and tempos, follow almost without pause. Listen for syncopated rhythms, Gypsy-like pizzicato elements, and the close juxtaposition of poignancy and vibrancy, ultimately charging boldly into the final bars. Throughout, the emphasis is on strings and woodwinds with no prominent passages for brass, as Bartók was intent upon echoing the aura of the folk instruments, an area in which brass are virtually unknown.

♪♪♪♪

Kodaly: *Dances of Galanta*

Like Bartók, Zoltan Kodaly (1882 – 1967) was Hungarian born and studied at the Budapest Academy of Music. In fact, he and Bartók were classmates and worked together researching ethnomusicology. They traveled throughout Hungary and beyond, persuading peasants and villagers to sing or play into the bell-shaped horn of their Edison recording machine. Back in Budapest, the two men transcribed the songs and dances they had collected, and worked to catalogue and promote authentic folk music. Both Bartók and Kodaly used these melodies in their own compositions, particularly in stage works and orchestral pieces.

A fine example of this mix of classical concepts and folk traditions is Kodaly's *Dances of Galanta*, named for a town where the composer had lived from age three until age ten, when his father was employed as station master for the Hungarian state railways. At that time in western Hungary, though now in Slovakia, Galanta was no musical center in the artistic sense. It had no grand theaters or opera houses, yet it was famed for its gypsy orchestras, which were the first orchestras the boy had ever heard. From those highly skilled folk musicians, young Kodaly developed affection for strongly syncopated rhythms and abruptly changing tempos. He also absorbed the essence of the finest gypsy fiddlers who, for all their lack of formal training, were in their own field no less skilled than Paganini. In this work from the height of his career, the composer paid tribute to those beloved childhood sounds.

Dances of Galanta premiered in Budapest October 23, 1933, in a concert given for the 80th anniversary of the Budapest Philharmonic Society. The conductor was Kodaly's fellow Hungarian, composer Ernő (in its later German form, Ernst von) Dohnányi (1877 – 1960), grandfather of renowned conductor Christoph von Dohnányi (b. 1929).

♪♪♪♪♪

Stravinsky: *Petrushka*

In old Imperial Russia, the weeks before Lent were a time of celebration. The long winter was at last drawing to a close, and, although the sobriety of Lent was approaching, there was still time for fun. They called it "Maslenitsa," or "Butter Week," commemorating all the decadent dishes they planned to devour before Lenten fasts. It was essentially a Russian Mardi Gras, and, as in that event, the feasting was only one part of a grand jubilee. There were also street carnivals with ventriloquists and puppet shows, jugglers and dancing bears, elaborate costume balls and promenades and, for children and adults alike, marvelous slides built of ice and snow. All Russians would come out during Butter Week to see the sights and celebrate the season.

It is this festival world that Igor Stravinsky (1882 – 1971) evokes in his ballet *Petrushka*, one of several ballets on Russian subjects which he wrote for Ballets Russes of Sergei Diaghilev (1872 – 1929). The first of those was *The Firebird*, which premiered in Paris in 1910. The second, to be given the next year, was supposed to be *The Rite of Spring*, and, in fact, Stravinsky was on the verge of beginning that score when another musical idea forced its way into the spotlight: a ballet depicting a sorrowful but mischievous puppet, suddenly endowed with life. The puppet was a folk character found in the traditions of so many countries, known as Pierrot in France, Petrushka – Little Peter – in Russia. The dramatic possibilities of the scenario were clear to Stravinsky, and soon, to Diaghilev as well. With designer Alexander Benois, Stravinsky completed the scenario, and, soon, the score. The premiere took place on June 13, 1911, in Paris, with Vaclav Nijinsky (1890 – 1950) dancing the title role.

More Classical Insights

Due at least in part to Nijinsky's talents, the ballet was quite successful, but, years later, Stravinsky decided to revise the score. This occurred in the 1940s, after he had become an American citizen and had acquired a new publisher. Many of Stravinsky's earlier compositions, including this one, were not covered by US copyright laws, and would not be unless they were republished, so he set about revising old works. This new version, dating from 1947, uses a smaller orchestra and has somewhat simpler time signatures.

The action is set in St. Petersburg's Admiralty Square during one of the Carnival Fairs. Amidst a bustling, rollicking crowd, street entertainers are dancing and playing when a showman arrives with his puppets. They are Petrushka, a Ballerina and a Blackamoor, and they spring to life and dance amongst the revelers. When the performance ends, the showman unceremoniously tosses the hapless puppets back into their rooms, where Petrushka lies lamenting his fate, sighing with love for the Ballerina. However, she rejects his attentions, instead choosing to waltz with the Blackamoor. The jealous Petrushka interrupts, and a fight ensues. The Blackamoor chases Petrushka out into the crowded streets, and there the Blackamoor slays his rival. The frightened crowd disperses. The showman collects his puppets, and, as the ballet concludes, one hears the mocking laugh of Petrushka's ghost, a motif that Stravinsky called "Petrushka's insult to the public."

All the best ballets are filled with musical devices to dramatize and intensify the stage action. Stravinsky's score has many such details. There are echoes of organ-grinders in the opening scene, and a music box is clearly heard, thanks to the glockenspiel and celesta. The waltz of the

Ballerina and the Blackamoor takes place to melodies borrowed from the Viennese composer, Joseph Lanner (1801 – 1843), and Petrushka's furious entrance is heralded by angry trombones. Perhaps the most striking musical effect is at Petrushka's death, for when he is slain, a single tambourine is dropped to the floor.

Taken as a whole, the score of *Petrushka* clearly communicates the mechanical aspect of the puppets, contrasted to the human characters. With such a score, actual dancers are almost superfluous. One can envision the scene without seeing it at all.

♫♫♫♫

Prokofiev: *Cinderella*

Of the three great ballet scores by Russian-born composer Sergei Prokofiev (1891 – 1953), only one was a complete success. *Romeo and Juliet* languished for years before finally reaching the Soviet stage; *The Stone Flower* was not performed at all until nearly a year after Prokofiev's death. However, *Cinderella* was a brighter point in his career. It was commissioned in 1940 by the Kirov Ballet, which had recently given the belated Russian premiere of *Romeo*. Prokofiev set to work immediately and made good progress until World War II intervened.

When the Nazis invaded the Soviet Union in June, 1941, Soviet authorities decided to evacuate the best-known artists and composers from Moscow and St. Petersburg, which seemed much too close to the front lines. Thus, with his colleagues, Prokofiev spent the war years in the southern republics, mostly in the Caucasus Mountains. He continued composing, but *Cinderella* (known in Russia as *Zolushka*) became a temporary casualty of war. Rather than continuing with a gentle fairy tale, Prokofiev turned instead to bolder projects, notably the opera *War and Peace*. Two years passed before he returned to the waif who becomes a princess.

Completed in the summer of 1944, the ballet holds no taint of war; rather, its inspiration lies in the past, not only for its story, but also for its music. Prokofiev intentionally structured *Cinderella* in the manner of old ballets of the 1800s: a variety of ballroom-style dance scenes of varying tempos, perhaps a few national style dances to evoke folk roots, and a solo scene for each principal role. It was a work more reminiscent of Peter Tchaikovsky (1840 – 1893) than of Prokofiev's own contemporary, Igor Stravinsky (1882 – 1971), and audiences received it with delight.

Curiously, though the work had been intended originally for the Kirov Ballet Theater, its premiere November 21, 1945, was given instead by the Bolshoi Ballet, which, in the intervening years, had hired away from the Kirov ballerina Galina Ulanova and choreographer Leonid Laurovsky for whom Prokofiev had originally conceived the work. *Cinderella* was not seen at the Kirov until April of the following year, when it was staged in honor of the composer's 55th birthday.

♪♪♪♪♪

Milhaud: *La Creation du Monde* (Creation of the World)

Born in Aix-en-Provence, France, Darius Milhaud (1892 – 1974) first heard jazz in a club in London in 1920, but it was two years later in the US when he was able to immerse himself in it, hearing top bands such as Paul Whiteman's and visiting jazz clubs in Harlem. When he returned to France later that year, he brought with him a stack of jazz records purchased in a shop in Harlem, as well as a determination to evoke jazz effects in a chamber work.

Milhaud was in that frame of mind when he received a request to collaborate on a new ballet to a scenario by Blaise Cendrars telling an African creation tale: perfect for the African roots of jazz inflection. Sets and costumes would be by Fernand Léger, who drew upon design elements from African art; the choreography by Jean Bőrlin was less ethnic in nature, but still reflective of Milhaud's score, written for a chamber group of fewer than twenty that included a saxophone and piano for authentic jazz effects. The premiere was in October, 1923, at the Théâtre des Champs-Elysées. Initially, critics dismissed the piece as frivolous, but in another decade, Milhaud was amused to find those same critics, having warmed to jazz, declaring that it was his greatest work.

Even without the dancers, the instrumental parts follow the tale, which is thus worth summarizing. As the music opens, the three creation deities perform magic spells, and creatures begin to come to life: insects, birds, and mammals. Various deities join in a general dance. Then, the first man and first woman gradually emerge. With a kiss, humanity is launched on its journey.

Throughout the ballet – little more than a quarter hour in length – one finds bluesy moods and energetic ones appearing in turn, with much contrast of instrumental timbres. Many of the solo lines are for clarinet or trumpet, both of which were readily inclined to jazz styles. Moreover, Milhaud calls for a saxophone in this orchestra, further intensifying those echoes of Harlem. It isn't strictly jazz, as it's notated, not improvised, but Milhaud got the spirit right.

♫♫♫♫

Copland: *Billy the Kid*

Aaron Copland (1900 – 1990) was born in Brooklyn, not the Wild West. However, when it came to portraying that more exotic setting in music, few could manage it as well as Copland and none better. Part of his success was due to research into American folk songs, which are liberally quoted in the western-themed ballets *Rodeo* and *Billy the Kid*. Even beyond their American styles, they are ballet subjects that no composer from any other land would have been likely to choose.

Billy the Kid preceded *Rodeo* and was written for Lincoln Kirstein's Ballet Caravan, which premiered it October 6, 1938 in Chicago. The piece tells of the infamous Western outlaw, and such, is one of very few ballets in which toe shoes yield to cowboy boots.

Copland was himself no outlaw, either of the Wild West or of any other time. In fact, he was essentially conservative in his musical views, continuing to use old classic models for composition even when some of his friends and colleagues were seeking new ways to bend the rules. However, Copland and Billy had more in common that one would expect. Both men were born in New York City, the outlaw in 1851, the composer in 1900, though Copland did not know of that connection before completing the ballet. Also, both had family roots in Europe. Copland's were more recent, his parents having emigrated from Eastern Europe; Billy's family had come from Ireland several generations earlier. Historically speaking, the real Billy was brought down at the age of 21 by a sheriff. Copland made it to a few days after his 90th birthday.

Opening with the serenity of the open prairie, the action soon shifts to a lively frontier town, with horses galloping through the streets, boots clomping on wooden sidewalks, and a brief appearance by several Mexican cowboys, their syncopated rhythms standing in clear contrast to the forthright Western melodies that Copland also offers. Billy is here, as an innocent boy in the company of his mother. When a gunfight breaks out, one bullet goes astray, striking down Mama as the timpani rumble and a horrified Billy weeps. Revenge drives the youth into his life of crime.

The action skips forward in Billy's life, continuing with a prairie night, reflective and thoughtful with long flowing phrases, as he and his gang relax around the campfire. Then there is gunfire: the posse has cornered the outlaw. Captured alive, he is paraded through the streets to the piping of a jaunty piccolo. An escape attempt follows and fails; Billy is no more, his passing portrayed not with an outburst of brass and percussion but with gentle strings. Copland's ballet concludes with another prairie panorama – this time driven by brass instead of woodwinds – evoking the grandeur of wide-open spaces more vividly than any other Easterner ever managed to do.

♪♪♪♪

More Classical Insights

Khachaturian: *Gayne*

Son of an Armenian book-binder, Aram Khachaturian (1903 – 1978) was born in Tiflis (now Tblisi), in the rugged region where Armenia, Georgia, and Turkey come together. This distant corner of the Caucasus boasted a proud folk tradition that would eventually influence the native son's compositions. Although he earned undergraduate and post-graduate degrees from Moscow Conservatory, his own music remained colorfully nationalistic and redolent of Armenian rhythms. Khachaturian was no modernist, a fact that may have contributed to his success, since the Soviet government actively silenced composers who too closely embraced any new or radical idea. In his dramatic works such as the ballets *Gayne* and *Spartacus*, Khachaturian glorified the people, specifically peasants and slaves. Such philosophy fit well in the Soviet psyche, yet also won fans in the West.

Amongst his works rooted in his Armenian heritage is *Gayne*, rife with atmospheric and rhythmic character. With the German invasion of the western USSR in 1941, Khachaturian, like many of his colleagues, headed east in search of safer surroundings in which to work. He found sanctuary at a rural retreat near Perm, where the choreographer Nina Anisimova had also taken refuge. Knowing of an earlier Khachaturian ballet, called *Happiness*, she encouraged him to try again. The result, *Gayne*, premiered with the Kirov Ballet in December 1942.

Over a decade later, the composer decided to rework the score to a new plot; this later version came to the stage with the Bolshoi Ballet in May 1957. However, both plots are rooted in jealousy, crime, and ultimate redemption.

Moreover, the story is almost incidental, for *Gayne* is far more frequently performed as an orchestral suite than as a choreographed ballet. Its most famous number, the Sabre Dance, is of intensely vibrant character. Also notable is the equally fiery Lezghinka, though for the sake of variety, there are also reflective and melancholy scenes. Any selection of movements from *Gayne* proves Khachaturian's deft touch with orchestral color.

♪♪♪♪

Stucky: *DreamWaltzes*

Steven Stucky (b. 1949 in Kansas) composed his *DreamWaltzes* for the 1986 summer season of the Minnesota Orchestra. As the ensemble's theme for that summer season was Vienna, Stucky decided to base his new work on the idea of Viennese waltzes, as if refracted through a modern day dream. The structures and harmonies lean in a modern direction; the raw material derives from old Vienna, with classic waltzes appearing in fragmentary form. Stucky himself identifies these waltzes as the Brahms *Liebeslieder Waltz*, op. 52, no. 6, the Brahms Piano Waltz op. 39, no. 8, and the main waltz theme from Richard Strauss' *Der Rosenkavalier*.

This quarter-hour orchestral fantasy opens gently and mysteriously with wisps of melody that gradually build. A waltz pulse appears from time to time, but – like a dream – never endures; the composer admits that it is "always slipping away almost as soon as it has begun." Often surreal, haunting musical visions arise, shot through at times with bold accents. Ultimately, it fades away, much as a dream might fade.

More Classical Insights

DreamWaltzes is a glimpse of the classic Viennese waltz distilled through a haze of distance and a modern American perspective. It might be viewed as reminiscent not only of Vienna but also of Ravel's *La Valse*, which takes a similar journey from a French point of view. The work premiered July 17, 1986, with the Minnesota Orchestra under the direction of Leonard Slatkin.

♫♫♫♫

Feeney: *The Hunchback of Notre Dame*

New ballets appear relatively frequently in the world of dance. However, one most often finds that they are new choreography inspired by existing compositions which might not have been originally intended for dancing. New works composed specifically for the dance are less common. Even less common is for such a work to come from a composer who is a ballet specialist, but such is the case with England's Phillip Feeney (b. 1954). Although his catalog also includes non-dance works, by far the most numerous are ballets, thanks to long affiliations with the Northern Ballet Theatre of England and Ballet Central. Feeney's ballets have also reached North America, Australia, New Zealand, and Asia to great success, making Feeney the leading light amongst current composers of ballet.

Feeney's numerous full-length ballets – including *Cinderella, Dracula, The Hunchback of Notre Dame, Hamlet,* and *Peter Pan* – tend to be settings of familiar stories. This is both an advantage and a challenge. Familiar stories may more readily attract audiences.

However, the challenge lies in confronting expectations of how that story ought to be told. Particularly if a story had been given film treatment, with or without music, aspects of characterization and dramatic flow will inevitably be compared to those in the old familiar versions, and it is largely the composer who drives that characterization and flow. One needs a clear sense as to how to use music to color and drive a story while still producing danceable results. Feeney has mastered those goals.

Feeney's version of *The Hunchback of Notre Dame* was written in 1997 for the Northern Ballet Theatre and choreographer Michael Pink. It offers pseudo-Renaissance dances for street scenes, gypsy-like rhythms for Esmeralda, weightier, less nimble themes for Quasimodo, and broad, lyrical melodies for romantic scenes. When the story required focused attention on a particular character, Feeney provides somewhat lengthier scenes to allow for solo display by those dancers. His familiarity with how ballet works serves him – and, thereby, his dancers and the audience, too – exceptionally well.

Chapter Eleven: Choral Music

It is not the most famous "Hallelujah" in classical music; that honor belongs to one George Frideric Handel (1685 – 1759) composed for his *Messiah*. Here, instead, is music from the oratorio *Christ on the Mount of Olives* by Ludwig van Beethoven (1770 -1827), and though the four syllables of "hallelujah" fit it perfectly, that is not the word that Beethoven intended. Instead, he was setting the German phrase "Welten singen," that is, "Let the world sing." However, English speaking choirs have routinely sung it as "Hallelujah." As long as one sings it with reverence and enthusiasm, Beethoven likely would not have minded the change of language.

Both Handel and Beethoven, and countless other composers, have understood the power and beauty of music for large numbers of singers, with or without instrumental accompaniment. The technical term for "without instrumental accompaniment" is "a cappella," which can be used to describe some of the most elaborate classical works as well as something as humble as a barbershop quartet. This chapter includes several classical a cappella works drawn from various centuries, as well as a number with instrumental accompaniment.

Although some of the grandest and most familiar choral music is religious in nature, composers might also choose voices for secular expression, often with literary connections. One could write an instrumental piece inspired by Shakespeare, and many composers have done so. However, if the text is of high enough quality, it is perhaps well to let the text speak for itself, even if that text is not Biblical in nature. Both sacred and secular choral works are represented in this chapter.

The fact that England and Germany, as well as various other nations, have a long-standing tradition of amateur choral societies has led some composers to write for singers even if professional performance were not the intention. So sometimes, the individual vocal lines in a choral work are not seriously virtuosic. The challenge may lie more in making those individual lines all work together in a felicitous fashion. That is the composer's job, and also that of the conductor. However, as long as the singers pay attention to their individual parts, those parts have a fair chance of fitting in with the other musical layers.

For listeners, it works on either level. Our ears can focus on the component lines or the overall blend, and in either case, find satisfaction in the sound of voices raised to artistic expression. That is true for all the compositions represented in this chapter, though it ranges over 500 years of music. Josquin Desprez (c. 1440 – 1521) could have had no conception of the Virtual Choir projects developed for the internet by Eric Whitacre (b. 1971). Nonetheless, both men are writing for the human singing voice in combination with other human singing voices. Some musical ideas endure for generations.

♪♪♪♪

Josquin: *Ave Maria*

Long before recent pop stars came to be known only by their first names, there was Josquin. Properly speaking, he was Josquin Desprez (@1440 – 1521), but contemporary accounts of the man and his music reliably refer to him only by his first name, even in published versions of his works. Perhaps he was the only musical man of that name, or perhaps his genius was such that all other Josquins fell far in the shade. One way or the other, he was indubitably a genius, though apparently one with personality quirks that would make him stand out even today.

Josquin's original nationality remains less than certain, though some evidence suggests that he was born in what is now Belgium. What is certain is that, early in his career, he made his way to Italy where he found employment, first as a singer, then as a composer, at various royal courts. One cannot entirely say that he "served" at those courts, as Josquin remained entirely his own man. His reputation was that of a man who worked when he felt like it, and not when his employer commanded it; he also insisted upon salaries in excess of what anyone else in the area was receiving at the time. Such an attitude might have quickly led to unemployment. The fact that it did not stands as evidence of the quality of the music that he produced.

Josquin's surviving works – many hundreds by number – are uniformly for a cappella voices. Most of the best known are sacred works, but there are also a large number of secular songs, and sometimes he would blur the line between the two: borrowing a melody from a secular song to re-use in a sacred one. The sacred ones are the best known today, particularly a setting of the familiar prayer *Ave Maria*. He makes of it a motet, that is, an a cappella work of sacred nature distinct from any specific portion of the mass.

Working with four voice parts (soprano, alto, tenor, and bass), he begins by using the opening phrases of an ancient Gregorian chant, which he soon transmutes into entirely new melodies from his own imagination. Sometimes, the four voices are heard in smooth harmony; more often, each is occupied with its own music, overlapping with the various other voice parts in what is called "counterpoint." Attentive ears will note that what one voice part was doing moments earlier has likely reappeared in another voice part, while that first voice has moved on to something different. It was a musical trick that came to be especially identified with church music of the Italian Renaissance, and Josquin was doing it when the Renaissance was still in its infancy. One cannot fairly assert that Josquin invented the technique, but he certainly demonstrated its effectiveness.

♫♪♪♪♪

JS Bach: Cantata no. 80 – "Ein feste Burg", BWV 80
    (A Mighty Fortress)

In 1723, the prominent German city of Leipzig was seeking a new Kantor, that is, a composer/conductor/performer, all abilities in one man, to take charge of the community's Protestant sacred music needs. They were big shoes to fill, particularly because the position's previous occupant had been the now-retired Georg Philip Telemann (1681 – 1767), and city officials were determined to replace him with a name equally illustrious. The only problem was that the illustrious names in question were not interested. After much consideration, the job offer went a court musician in the employ of Duke Leopold of Anhalt-Cőthen. "Since the best is not available, he will have to do," they reportedly declared. Thus, much against the will of his future employers, the position of Kantor in Leipzig had fallen to Johann Sebastian Bach (1685 – 1750).

Much of Bach's time in Leipzig was devoted to composing cantatas: multi-movement sacred works for chorus and orchestra which served as the centerpiece of the worship service. How many cantatas he wrote for Leipzig may never be known. About 200 exist today, but church documents indicate that there may have been at least 400 initially, the remainder lost to time. Certainly, for much of his tenure in Leipzig, where he would remain until his death nearly three decades later, Bach was expected to produce a new cantata every week throughout the year, each using Biblical verses or newly written texts appropriate to that exact week in the church calendar, which limited when a cantata might be used again. The numbering the cantatas now bear came about well over a century later and bears no resemblance to the order in which pieces were originally composed.

One of the most beloved of his cantatas is number 80. Its first movement borrows the words and melody of the familiar Lutheran hymn "Ein feste Burg ist unser Gott" (A Mighty Fortress is Our God); later movements allow that main theme to reappear, in expanded and elaborated form, but often use new words by Bach's colleague Salomo Franck. Most of the work was composed around 1730, although here and there, Bach also borrowed bits and pieces from earlier compositions. The trumpets and timpani common in current performances of this cantata were not original to JS Bach himself, for the Leipzig church rarely opted for such demonstrative sounds. Rather, these effects of orchestration were added later by his eldest son, Wilhelm Friedemann (1710 – 1784), who was also a composer and apparently one not too timid to spruce up Dad's music better to fit changing tastes.

♫♫♫♫♫

Handel: Coronation Anthem "Zadok the Priest"

Though German-born (from Halle), George Frideric Handel 91685 – 1759) spent the vast majority of his career in England serving a sequence of monarchs as well as the English people, who thronged to performances of his operas and oratorios. He had first arrived in England in 1710 with the expressed wish of learning London's exciting musical developments for the benefit of his ostensible employer, the Elector of Hanover. However, visits back to Hanover were few and far between. Handel was simply having too much fun in London to wish to return to an unimportant community on the continent.

When England's Queen Anne died without immediate heirs, the throne passed to her German cousin, the Elector himself, and Handel no longer struggled with divided loyalties. He served the new king, George I, and later that monarch's son George II, with equal devotion. In fact, George II himself, preferring the work of his father's long-time favorite to that of native-born Englishmen, requested that Handel compose his coronation music.

Handel wrote four anthems for the October 11, 1727, coronation, which, according to tradition, took place in Westminster Abbey. Each anthem is a setting of a Biblical text appropriate to various moments within the ceremony. "Zadok the Priest," its text drawn from the first chapter of Kings I, served for the anointing of the new king. The music is a masterful progression of moods: from an opening sense of anticipation, through the commanding declaration "Zadok the Priest and Nathan the Prophet," building ultimately to the final cries of rejoicing. The anthem's power is such that it has been used for every English coronation since its composition.

♪♪♪♪

Pergolesi: *Stabat Mater*

Had his health been equal to his artistry, Giovanni Battista Pergolesi (1710 – 1736) might have been his generation's Rossini. Like his later countryman, Pergolesi mastered both comic opera and serious opera, and also made impressive contributions to the realm of sacred music. Yet it was not to be. Dying at age 26, apparently of tuberculosis, Pergolesi had much less than half the life span of the long-lived Gioacchino Rossini (1792 – 1868), and left tragically few genuine works.

The word "genuine" is significant, for in the decades after his passing, numerous compositions came to print under Pergolesi's name. Operatic, sacred, and even instrumental pieces were credited to him, and though some appear to have been his own work, others have been traced to other composers. In some cases, composers borrowed his name in order to sell their music more readily. In other cases, publishing houses made the decision on the same financial grounds. Interestingly, at the time of his death, Pergolesi was mostly a regional name whose comic operas were known only in Naples, and none beyond that region would have bothered to pretend their music was his. However, the popularity of those operas spread in later years, making the belated borrowing of his name profitable.

One work known to be his is this setting of the *Stabat Mater*, a sacred text relating to the Virgin Mary standing by the cross. Written in the last year of Pergolesi's life, it was intended for the religious community of St. Maria dei Sette Dolori in Naples, and scored for soprano and alto soloists with string ensemble and organ. The music is more gently poignant than anguished; Mary, it seems, rmourns her Son's death, but recognizes that he is going on to Heaven. Moreover, at Pergolesi's time in the late Baroque Era, strongly dramatic styles were not the norm in sacred music. Those were reserved for the opera house, and Pergolesi would have indulged his stronger musical moods with that field. If one is seeking a wistful side of sacred choral music, here is a fine option.

♪♪♪♪♪

Haydn: Mass no. 9 in C, *"Mass in Time of War"*

This mass is one of six written by Franz Joseph Haydn (1732 – 1809) in the waning years of his career. At this point in his life, the sixtyish composer was finally enjoying well-deserved rest after three decades of servitude with the noble Esterhazy family. His concert tours to London had been marvelously successful, and a quietly prosperous retirement seemed on the horizon, when the Esterhazys made one final request of their long-time employee. The reigning Esterhazy prince, Nicholas II, asked Haydn to compose one mass each year to celebrate the name-day of the ruling princess. Haydn agreed, producing six masses between 1796 and 1802. The so-called Mass no. 9 was first performed in Vienna on December 26, 1796.

The months leading up to that premiere had been a time of great uncertainty, not merely for Haydn himself, but also for Europe as a whole. Napoleon's armies were on the move, and the war which ultimately would see the French capture of Vienna had begun. Such a bellicose atmosphere was bound to affect Haydn's work, however closely he might cling to the standard mass form. Indeed, although the Latin text remains unaltered, the war still echoes through the orchestration. Trumpet-calls and drum-rolls abound, to such an extent that, despite Haydn's own chosen nickname for the piece (one of the rare cases where the nickname of a Haydn work was bestowed upon it by its creator), German-speakers called it the "Paukenmesse," or "Timpani Mass."

At times, it sounds almost as if two opposing armies were invading the church itself, even as the choir sings of the "lamb of God." In addition, even though most masses settle into serenity by the concluding "Dona nobis pacem" ("Give us peace"), Haydn chose to continue with his martial tone, as if he were not requesting peace, but rather demanding it at any price. It is unfortunate that the composer did not live to see the end of this war which seems to have troubled him so deeply. As Haydn lay dying in 1809, Napoleon was leading his armies in their occupation of Vienna.

Betsy Schwarm

♪♪♪♪♪

Mozart: *Vesperae solennes de confessore*
(Solemn Vespers of a Confessor)

Long before Wolfgang Amadeus Mozart (1756 – 1791) began his famously unfinished Requiem, he had composed – and completed – a great quantity of sacred music. Having spent his adolescent and young adult years on the musical staff of the Prince Archbishops of Salzburg, he was often called upon to provide liturgical music for one service or another. So Mozart composed nearly twenty masses, and a variety of Kyries, vesper settings, and the like.

Generally, these works tended to be relatively shorter than equivalent works by other composers. This is not due to a lack of inspiration on Mozart's part, but rather because the Vatican had declared that the musical component of a service should never dominate the spiritual portion. Prince Archbishop Colloredo, who came to the throne in 1772, was particularly insistent upon this requirement, so for him, Mozart composed straight-forward settings of specified texts. Being Mozart, he still managed to pack each sacred work with its fair share of unremitting beauty.

The *Solemn Vespers of a Confessor* dates from 1780, late in Mozart's time in Salzburg. In another year, he would be off for the bright lights of Vienna. Apparently intended for a saint's day ceremony, the work sets five psalms (bearing the numbering of 109-112 and 116 in the Latin Vulgate Bible), together with the Magnificat from Luke I, in which Mary rejoices upon hearing that she is to bear the Christ Child.

Despite the adjective in the work's title, there is little solemnity here; rather, the overall mood is one of jubilation expressed through the finest craftsmanship. From the serene soprano solo of the "Laudate Dominum" movement to the intricately operatic ensembles of the "Beatus vir" to the Bach-like fugal writing of the "Laudate pueri," the 24 year old composer shows himself to be master of his field in all its diverse expressions.

♫♫♫♫

Beethoven: *Christus am Ölberg*, op. 85
(*Christ on the Mount of Olives*)

In his entire career, Ludwig van Beethoven (1770 – 1827) wrote exactly one oratorio, and this is it. *Christ on the Mount of Olives* dates from early in 1803 and concerns Christ's last day of freedom before the Roman soldiers come to arrest Him prior to His crucifixion. At the time, Beethoven was first coming to terms with his failing hearing yet still retained some measure of that crucial sense. One may imagine that he found the strong choral moments of the score as moving as do modern audiences, and likely took pleasure in the solo passages as well.

The work's text was by Franz Xaver Huber, a poet of local reputation. Beethoven took only two weeks to set the words to music, virtually unprecedented speed for a composer who tended to rework his scores for years, seeking exactly the right effect. His haste was driven by the fact that a premiere date had already been set, and as the concert was being given as a benefit for the composer himself, he wanted to fill the program with impressive and, ideally, new works.

The concert was given April 5, 1803, at the Theater-an-der-Wien where his only opera, *Fidelio,* would premiere the following year. Also on the program were his Symphony no. 1, Symphony no. 2, and the Piano Concerto no. 3. Beethoven wrote the oratorio in such haste that his student Ferdinand Ries recalled the master sitting in bed the morning of the premiere finishing the trombone parts. The work's only rehearsal would be that day, and witnesses recalled that it did not go well. However, the oratorio proved to be the hit of the evening. Eight more years would pass before it came into print, delayed in part by the composer's determination to undertake revisions on the hastily completed score.

The most familiar selection from the oratorio, known as the Hallelujah from *Christ on the Mount of Olives*, serves as the finale of the entire work. In its original German version, it is not called "Hallelujah" and in fact does not even contain the word "hallelujah." However, for all the changed words, the music remains intact, as does the overall mood. The chorus is that of a gathering of angels which declares, "Let the world sing of thanks and honor to the great Son of God. Praise him, ye angel's choir, loudly in hymns of rejoicing."

Although different in detail, the English version captures the spirit of the original. Conveniently, the four syllables of the word "hallelujah" fit perfectly to the four syllables of Beethoven's phrase "Welten singen," (Let the world sing), which is repeated as many times in the original as the word "hallelujah" is repeated in the English version.

♪♪♪♪

Berlioz: *Requiem*, op. 5

Political intrigue and sacred music would not usually be found in company with one another. However, Hector Berlioz (1803 – 1869) was no usual composer. That the Frenchman was gifted most of his contemporaries would have admitted. That he was an iconoclast few would have denied, not even Berlioz himself. Immediately controversial for his ground-breaking *Symphonie fantastique* of 1830, he rarely met a protocol that he was not willing to flout. Then, contrary to even his own expectations, he received in 1836 a commission from the French Minister of Culture, whom the composer described in his autobiography as belonging "to that small section of our statesmen who are interested in music, and to the still more limited number who really have a feeling for it." That gentleman, Monsieur de Gasparin, requested of Berlioz a requiem and promised that the government would defray the costs of a premiere. So Berlioz set to work.

Unfortunately, Monsieur de Gasparin was on the verge of retirement. Others in the government objected to his choice of Berlioz for such a prominent commission. One expressed a preference for Beethoven, by that time nearly a decade in his grave. Others insisted that the only acceptable composer would be Luigi Cherubini (1760 – 1842), Italian-born, but long resident in Paris, and – unlike Beethoven – still available to accept the job. By fortunate happenstance, the sudden passing of a prominent military leader caused an immediate need for a requiem in his honor, and Berlioz was able to persuade his various opponents that his was the work to fill that need.

The ceremony – and the premiere of Berlioz' *Requiem* – took place December 5, 1837, six days before the composer's 34th birthday. Mid-concert, he had to step in for the officially appointed conductor, whom Berlioz suspected of setting out intentionally to ruin the premiere. With the composer at the helm, all held together, and, as Berlioz said of the event, "The success of the *Requiem* was complete, in spite of all the conspiracies." That the composer's promised financial compensation was long delayed even he admitted was almost beside the point. When the Requiem came to print, he dedicated it to Monsieur de Gasparin.

It is a grand work, spanning nearly an hour and a half, and requiring four brass ensembles, at times in opposition to one another, in addition to the standard orchestra and chorus. The music that Berlioz crafted for his performers is highly varied, often changing mood in a heartbeat. The Kyrie is sweetly sorrowful, the Dies irae alternately haunting and stormy. The Rex tremendae opens with shatteringly determined proclamations of the word "Rex" (King). The Lacrimosa is as changeable as the preceding movements, sometimes broad and flowing, at others punctuated by intense orchestral statements. With the concluding Offertorium, Berlioz seems to declare that the dead may indeed rest in peace, for here is music as serene and gentle as anything that has come before it.

Berlioz was not usually associated with idea of sacred music. However, given the opportunity to direct his vivid imagination in this new direction, he crafted one of the most startlingly original Requiems to come from the mind of any great composer.

More Classical Insights

♪♪♪♪

Mendelssohn: part songs

Many music lovers are familiar with the existence of the solo piano pieces called *Songs without Words* by Felix Mendelssohn (1809 – 1847). These were featured in Chapter Six. Here are some of his songs <u>with</u> words, and <u>without</u> a piano. Although Mendelssohn also composed songs for voice and piano, the part songs are for a cappella groups, and are known as "part songs" for the presence of various vocal parts: soprano, alto, tenor, and baritone.

Over the last dozen years of his all-too-brief life, Mendelssohn composed several dozen part songs. Often rich with natural imagery, the part songs offer moods ranging from bright and buoyant to wistful and poignant, depending upon the needs of the texts. The voice parts are always interestingly intertwined, without being so virtuosic as to stand beyond the talents of a local chorus. Mendelssohn could, and on other occasions, did write for professional singers, but here he clearly wanted to reach out to the masses and let them experience the delights of musical performance.

Some of these sets of part songs bear in their titles the statement that they are to be sung "Im Freien," that is, in the open air. It is a statement that suits the songs particularly well, as a great many of them set scenes of natural imagery: birds, moonlight, and the like. One likes to imagine that the singers, while raising their voices in praise of nature's wonders, would be standing in the midst of those exact wonders.

Betsy Schwarm

♪♪♪♪

Brahms: *Schicksalslied*, op. 54 (*Song of Fate*)

Study the catalog of works by Johannes Brahms (1833 – 1897) and one finds that vocal works – either small or large in scale – are more numerous than anything else. He was inspired in part by a number of talented singers amongst his circle of friends, as well as by several seasons in his 20s spent conducting choral groups. In Brahms' time, there was a strong movement in Germany promoting amateur choral singing, and some of his compositions were inspired by that trend.

The *Schicksalslied* (*Song of Fate*) was begun in 1869 immediately after another choral score, the *Alto Rhapsody*, and the two works carry consecutive opus numbers. However, the *Rhapsody*, in addition to chorus and orchestra, also includes a prominent part for alto soloist, whereas *Schicksalslied* has no soloist, only chorus with orchestra. Moreover, *Schicksalslied* spent longer on the drawing board, requiring two full years to reach completion, though throughout that time, it retained its low opus number. The delay was apparently grounded in the issue of balancing musical demands with demands of the text.

Schicksalslied is a setting of a poem by Friedrich Hőlderlin (1770 – 1843), beginning with musing upon the heavenly bliss of the gods, then, by way of contrast, turning to the miseries of humanity. Brahms was impressed by Hőlderlin's vision, and wished to give it musical expression, but found it artistically unsatisfying to begin in rapture but end in torment. He considered repeating the opening stanza, so as to bring the work full circle and close in a mood of optimism. However, he gradually became persuaded that such was not Hőlderlin's intention. In a search for compromise, Brahms closes out the choral portion in shadows as Hőlderlin dictated, then with a solid key change from c minor to C major and an echo of the orchestral opening, allows the orchestra to suggest that perhaps all is not lost. It is a masterful stroke, balancing music and text, and only one of the greatest composers would have thought of it. Here, his Symphony no. 1 not yet complete, Brahms proves his mastery which soon the world would acknowledge.

Schicksalslied premiered October 18, 1871, in Karlsruhe, where the orchestra's music director, Hermann Levi, was a good friend of Brahms, and inclined to give a hearing to Brahms' works. Not yet 40, the composer was finally becoming established as one of the very greatest of German-born composers. Before Brahms, that honor had been accorded to Beethoven; now, Brahms himself was proving worthy of comparison to his great predecessor.

♪♪♪♪

Vaughan Williams: *Serenade to Music*

England's greatest author and one of its greatest composers come together in this graciously soaring work, its text borrowed from Act Five of Shakespeare's *The Merchant of Venice*. In the scene, Lorenzo and Jessica are stargazing to the accompaniment of music, their love echoed by the glory of the night:

"How sweet the moonlight sleeps upon this bank! Here will we sit, and let the sounds of music creep in our ears... A man that hath no music in himself nor is not moved with concord of sweet sounds, is fit for treasons, stratagems and spoils."

What composer could resist such tribute to his chosen field? Not Ralph Vaughan Williams (1872 – 1958), who needed an appropriate text for a work to celebrate the career of the influential English conductor Sir Henry J. Wood. The *Serenade* premiered as part of a gala concert at Royal Albert Hall October 5, 1938. Three orchestras and three choral societies participated, as well as sixteen internationally known vocal soloists. Each of these singers received his or her own solo, perfectly tailored to the person's voice, and Vaughan Williams noted each soloist by initials at the appropriate moment in the score.

So a soprano with a lighter voice would be set against less assertive orchestral parts and given less resolute lines to express. By contrast, one with a bright and brilliant voice might be accompanied by trumpets, and both of those singers would be written in the most effective portions of their vocal ranges. Vaughan Williams took the same approach with the other vocal soloists – all sixteen of them – not only ensuring that each was placed in the best possible musical setting, but also that this tribute to a beloved conductor could come off exactly as desired.

As for the instrumental parts, these are sometimes gentle and serene, reflective of the moonlit night that surrounds Lorenzo and Jessica. At other times, the music takes on a stronger, more celebratory tone. In both the gentler and the stronger passages – though most obviously in the stronger ones, especially with trumpets and horns – there appears a repeated fragment of melody that one might swear was intended to evoke the work's title: "se-re-nade--- ser'nade to music." Those are not the words being sung when that fragment appears. In fact, those words appear nowhere in Shakespeare's text. However, imaginative minds observe that the syllables fit perfectly, and Vaughan Williams might have noticed it as well.

The piece was rapturously received by the audience, particularly by Sergei Rachmaninoff (1873 – 1943), who had played his own Piano Concerto no. 2 earlier in the evening. The great Russian composer/pianist, observed to be listening intently with tears in his eyes, claimed that he had never before heard a work so moving. Most of a century has passed since that performance, but many a listener still agrees with Rachmaninoff.

♫♫♫♫

Rachmaninoff: *The Bells*, op. 35

Unlike some prominent writers – Shakespeare, Goethe, and Whitman come to mind – Edgar Allen Poe (1809 – 1849) has not inspired much music. The dark intensity and surreal imagery of his works are undeniable, but do not often lend themselves to musical expression. After all, one could hardly sing or dance to "The Pit and the Pendulum," and though one could make an orchestral tone poem of it, the wash of sheer terror might be too much for repeated listening.

However, Poe's poem "The Bells" has far more potential. Not only are bells in and of themselves musical, but the poet's verses concern themselves specifically with four different types of bells, envisioned as emblematic of a man's life. First come carefree bells of youth, then wedding bells in the prime of life. These are succeeded by brassy alarm bells signifying trials and tribulations, then lastly the deep tolling of funeral bells. It is a vision of life, represented by sound, and handily falls into a four-movement symphony-like structure. Hand it to a gifted composer, and the possibilities are intriguing.

In this case, the 'gifted composer' is Sergei Rachmaninoff (1873 – 1943), who received an anonymous suggestion from an admirer. Neither the admirer nor the composer knew Poe's original English lines. It was a Russian setting by Konstantin Balmont (1867 – 1942) that came to hand. Not a straight translation, Balmont's version is rather shorter than the original, and in places sets aside Poe's own imagery in favor of new lines of Balmont's. Yet the overall concept survives. So Poe scholars ought not be too detail oriented with this work: take it more as a tribute than as a literal re-statement.

Rachmaninoff's piece, scored for orchestra and chorus, with soprano, tenor, and baritone soloists, was first heard in St. Petersburg late in 1913, then earned its formal premiere February 8, 1914, in Moscow, with the composer conducting. The piece was enthusiastically received. *The Bells* offers a half-hour or so of Rachmaninoff's most skillful balancing of parts with coloration that shifts with the flow of the text. Even a listener with no knowledge of Russian could follow the progress of scenes.

Listen for the evocative moods of the various bells: first sleigh bells, then wedding bells, then alarm bells, and lastly funeral bells. The musical moods largely speak for themselves, even as, in the closing bars, the tapestry of sound slowly fades into night.

♪♪♪♪

Stravinsky: *Symphony of Psalms*

Russian composers of the 20th century did not often write sacred music; the Soviet government would have frowned upon such endeavors. However, Igor Stravinsky (1882 – 1971) had lived abroad – mostly in France and Switzerland – since the Russian Revolution, and by 1930 cared not at all what Stalin might have wished. Moreover, the grand *Symphony of Psalms* was composed at the request of Stravinsky's countryman, conductor Serge Koussevitzky (1874 – 1951), who as conductor of the Boston Symphony was commissioning symphonies from all his favorite composers in honor of the orchestra's 50th anniversary.

Koussevitzky had not requested a sacred work, nor even something including chorus, but he got both. As Stravinsky recalled in his 1936 autobiography, "I had a free hand alike as to the form of the work and as to the means of execution I might think necessary." Having determined to use Bach-like intricacies of layered melodies, known in the business as counterpoint, Stravinsky decided that varied performing forces would better set off the melodic complexities. Furthermore, with Bach's counterpoint in mind, Bach's sacred cantatas were not far behind, and so a symphony for orchestra and chorus became the *Symphony of Psalms*.

The work premiered December 13, 1930, not in Boston, but in Brussels where Stravinsky was engaged at the time in a concert tour. The Boston premiere came soon thereafter on December 19. Serge Koussevitzky conducted.

Although he had decided to use some Bach-inspired compositional techniques, Stravinsky did not then produce a score that actually sounds like Bach. The harmonies and rhythms alike are more modern, as would have to be the case for a progressive such as Stravinsky. Also, the orchestra is Stravinsky's own conception, neither Baroque nor even Romantic. He gives it a darker color by leaving out some of the higher voiced instruments, specifically violins, violas, and clarinets, and he includes in the ensemble not just one piano, but two. Even the chorus is varied according to Stravinsky's own tastes. Rather than the standard SATB (soprano, alto, tenor, bass) plan, he replaced the sopranos with trebles: boy sopranos. The work is now often performed with female sopranos, but the composer planned it with trebles in mind.

The Psalms are sung in Latin, and each movement draws its text from a different Psalm. Which exact Psalms they are varies somewhat from one version of the Bible to another. In the Latin Vulgate that Stravinsky used, they are Psalms 38, 39, and 150. The English Bible has them as 29, 40, and 150. By either numbering, the varied moods of the texts let Stravinsky bring diverse colors to his music: entirely his intention upon having determined upon a blend of voices and orchestra.

♪♪♪♪

More Classical Insights

Poulenc: *Quatre motets pour le temps de Noël*
(Four Motets for Christmas Time)

In the early decades of the 20th century, Parisian composers generally cared more for theater music and solo piano pieces than for sacred musical expression. Francis Poulenc (1899 – 1963) participated actively in that trend, becoming known for his buoyant, somewhat sardonic scores. However, a tragic event in 1935 forever changed his choice of genres. In that year, a dear friend of the composer died in an automobile accident. Poulenc's devastating sorrow led him to a religious crisis, in which he, never a church-goer, rediscovered his father's devout Catholicism. For the first time, he visited a religious shrine that had been revered by his father, and he began work on the first of many sacred compositions.

In the early 1950s, Poulenc produced four motets: short a cappella sacred works of a type most popular in the Renaissance. Each is related to Christmas. The first of these, *O magnum mysterium,* is gently prayerful of mood, with occasional assertive outbursts. The second, *Quem vidistis pastores,* is a humble vision of gathering shepherds. The third, *Videntes stellam,* has those same shepherds gazing in awe at the Star of Bethlehem, with music that neatly evokes their breathless wonder. The last of the four, *Hodie Christus natus est,* is the only one of lively spirit. As Poulenc imagined it, the fact that "Christ is born today" is reason for dancing in joy.

Poulenc did not originally intend to create a coherent set of four Christmas motets. However, once he'd finished all four, he decided that they belonged with one another. Published together in 1952, the motets serve as evidence that even a secularly oriented composer/pianist once noted primarily for his dry wit could, when moved, set aside that humor in favor of creating music expressing profound religious devotion.

♪♪♪♪

Randall Thompson: *Frostiana*

A Harvard graduate and later faculty member at that institution for nearly 20 years, Randall Thompson (1899 – 1984) – not to be confused with another American composer of the same generation, Virgil Thomson (1896 – 1989) – is usually remembered for his lovely hymns, which have enjoyed great popularity with choral directors. However, his catalogue of compositions also includes larger scale choral pieces, many of patriotic inspiration. His *Testament of Freedom* is a setting of texts by Thomas Jefferson (1743 – 1826) written for the 200th anniversary of that statesman's birth. His *Ode to the Virginian Voyage* offers a similar tribute to the first European settlers in what became the state of Virginia.

Another work of more recent inspiration turns from politics and pioneers to poetry. In *Frostiana*, Thompson sets seven poems of Robert Frost (1874 – 1963), including the familiar and beloved "Stopping by Woods on a Snowy Evening" and "The Road Not Taken." Frost's words are austere yet evocative; Thompson's music is equal to its inspiration. Although neither man was a statesman, this union of their efforts is the essence of a particular side of the American spirit. *Frostiana* premiered in Amherst October 18, 1959.

More Classical Insights

♪♪♪♪♪

Britten: *War Requiem*, op. 66

The *War Requiem* of English composer Benjamin Britten (1913 – 1976) is no celebration of martial exploits. Rather, the composer – a determined pacifist who spent much of World War II in self-imposed exile in the US – imagined a lament of loss, combining the ancient text of the standard Requiem with the poetic musings of Wilfred Owen (1893 – 1918), who died while serving in the British military in France in World War I one week before Armistice Day.

The work was written for the re-consecration in 1962 of the Coventry Cathedral, destroyed 20 years earlier by German bombs. Britten was not himself a native of Coventry, being instead from Lowestoft near the North Sea. Yet he valued his nation's heritage and well understood the nature of the loss, both of the cathedral itself and of millions of lives in the course of the war. He dedicated the score to four friends who had died in the war. To make his viewpoint even more clear, Britten added to the title page a few lines of Owens', as follows: "My subject is War, and the pity of War. The poetry is in the pity... all a poet can do today is warn." The *War Requiem* premiered May 30, 1962, in Coventry.

On a simple level, the War Requiem is scored for the usual orchestra, an SATB chorus (soprano, alto, tenor, bass), and vocal soloists. However, there is nothing either simple or usual about it. The orchestra itself is unusually expansive, including, for example, six horns rather than four, and enough percussion to require five players. Furthermore, there are, in fact, two distinct orchestras: the full one of generous scoring and a chamber orchestra of only twelve players. Britten uses the full orchestra for the verses of the standard Requiem text and the chamber orchestra for the Owen verses. Similarly divided are the soloists: tenor and baritone soloists for the Owen, soprano soloists and chorus for the Requiem. Additionally, there is a boys' choir with organ accompaniment which the composer insisted should sound as though from afar. Only rarely are all these diverse forces combined at once.

Attentive listeners will observe that Britten took great care with the selection and placement of the Owen poems, matching them to parts of the Requiem with which they seem in sympathy. Thus, as the Dies Irae evokes the trumpets of Judgment Day ("Tuba mirum"), so Owen calls forth echoing bugles. As the Agnus Dei speaks of souls at rest, so Owen invokes those lost to war. As the Libera me calls for deliverance from eternal death ("Morte aeterna"), so Owen imagines escape from "some profound dull tunnel." Thus, from very different viewpoints, similar imagery emerges, bringing out the timelessness of the message and the appropriateness of Britten's plan.

One additional powerful tool at the composer's disposal is his adept touch for setting texts to music. At this point in his career (he was nearing 50), he had already composed nearly a dozen operas, a quantity of choral works, and dozens of song settings. With such experience, and the fact that his life partner, Peter Pears (1910 – 1986), was England's most highly regarded tenor (he was one of the soloists at the War Requiem's premiere), Britten was well able to bring out the essence of words in his composition.

More Classical Insights

♪♪♪♪♪

Argento: *Walden Pond*

Thanks to Henry Thoreau (1817 – 1862), Walden Pond is likely the most famous small body of water in North America. In the mid-1840s, the New England based philosopher spent two years living on the bands of Walden Pond, and soon after, published *Walden*, a collection of thoughtful essays on what he learned from the experience. The book stands at the heart of so-called Transcendentalism and has been widely read by persons from all walks of life. Pulitzer and Grammy Award winning American composer Dominic Argento (b. 1927) selected some of his favorite extracts from *Walden*, and in 1996 set them to music for the Dale Warland Singers.

The result is neither a cappella nor does it use full orchestral accompaniment. Rather, the voices are joined by exactly three cellos and one harp, a combination that the composer says seemed ideally suited for the watery scenes at hand. Thoreau's words, even as adapted by Argento, are prose, not poetry per se. However, set to music, the words quickly take on poetic spirit in the broader sense. One imagines that Thoreau, so sensitive to the beauty of nature, would have appreciated how Argento's setting conveys the natural reverence the author had in mind.

The first movement is serene and haunting, its long, languid vocal lines aptly reinforced by the instrumental ensemble. With the second movement, the scene is of Thoreau and a neighbor fishing, with their natural surroundings and the activity captured in the shape of the music. Liveliest of the five movements is the central one, with melodic lines that seem to rise like a gaze lifting itself to the treetops. In the fourth movement, the text becomes more conventionally poetic, with simple declarative statements – "Sky Water;" "Lake of Light," and more – boldly proclaimed by the chorus. For the finale, Argento opts for hymn-like moods, as he sets lines speaking of how Walden had changed to the eye but not to the memory. In all, it is music that vividly captures the inner poetry of Thoreau's words and ideas, proving that effective choral music need not be specifically liturgical, when there is also the church of nature at hand.

♪♪♪♪

Rutter: *When Icicles Hang*

English composer John Rutter (b. 1945) is often identified with Christmas carols, and indeed, he has written and arranged a large number of them. Long associated with the Cambridge Singers, he has produced much choral music for their use; however, his music is not all for singers, nor is it all for Christmas. His catalog also includes instrumental works – amongst them, a two-piano concerto on themes from Beatles songs – and even the choral works are not all specifically for Christmas.

Rutter's *When Icicles Hang* was written for the English choral conductor Russell Burgess, who requested a work that would fit into a seasonal program scheduled for December, but not restricted to Christmas music. The result, which premiered in London in 1973, offers six contrasting movements for SATB choir with chamber orchestra of strings, woodwinds, horns, and light percussion; one may also encounter the work with the orchestral parts reduced to a single piano.

Each movement offers not only thoughts about the winter season in cold climates, but also an impressive variety of musical moods. The opening movement, "Icicles," launches the suite with gentle mystery. It is followed by the light and dance-like "Winter Nights," then the even brighter and more festive "Good Ale." Quieter moods return with the fourth movement, "Blow, blow, thou winter wind," its delicate, wistful aura further mellowed with the fifth movement, the drowsy and reflective "Winter wakeneth all my care." That fifth movement does contain some more assertive passages, which seem to anticipate the buoyant spirit of the sixth and last movement, "Hay, ay."

In all, the suite is a tapestry of feelings that one might associate with the shortest days – and longest nights – of the year. All are brought vividly to musical life through Rutter's solid sense of what can be done with voices and instruments.

♪♪♪♪

MacMillan: *Strathclyde Motets*

Few contemporary composers trouble themselves to compose sacred music evocative of Renaissance styles. However, Scottish-born James MacMillan (b. 1959) is himself Catholic and found one of his first professional posts as conductor of Glasgow's St. Columba Church Choir.

Betsy Schwarm

Since those early years, compositional assignments and the public attention that comes with them have kept him too busy to serve at the church regularly for worship services. However, he conducts there when possible and composes liturgical music for the church's use as well. Other churches and choirs, too, have discovered the rich balance of MacMillan's vocal writing.

The *Strathclyde Motets*, over a dozen in number, were composed over a period of several years, mostly in the first decade of the 21st century. Their collective name derives from the Strathclyde University Choir which has often appeared at St. Columba's. "Motet" is an old term dating back to the Renaissance and denoting an a cappella work with richly layered melodies and harmonies, setting texts for use in worship services. Josquin Desprez (@1440 – 1521) composed motets; so does MacMillan, nearly six centuries later.

His Strathclyde works have a rapt poetry about them, not just in the sacred texts, but also in the musical textures. Vocal parts are written with richly chromatic harmonies and long liquid lines, giving the listener plenty of time to absorb the serene glow of the music. Often, he gives to one part of the choir lines of greater motion, and juxtaposes that with long, lung-testing notes in the other parts, so that the harmonies seem to shift with each new note of the more nimble vocal line. Here is not music for sacred revels, but rather music ideally suited to a prayerful reverie. It would be a hard heart, indeed, that refused to be touched by the beauty of MacMillan's motets.

♪♪♪♪

More Classical Insights

Whitacre: *Cloudburst*

Eric Whitacre (b. 1971 in Reno, Nevada) developed an interest in choral music through singing in his college choir, and before long was composing a great quantity of vocal works, often a cappella. His works have attracted favorable attention on five continents, and Whitacre is much in demand for appearances as conductor and choral clinician in choral festivals.

Late in 2009, Whitacre had the idea of reaching out to amateur choral singers around the world. He launched his Virtual Choir project, offering to distribute digitally copies of the music for his *Lux Aurumque* and then accept amateur video recordings of persons singing their chosen voice part. From these submissions, he compiled his Virtual Choir, assembled all the selected videos together into a patchwork of visual images and let these various singers – virtually all unknown to one another – blend in harmony. The resulting recording, posted on YouTube in March of 2010, received over one million viewers in only two months, and is still available for viewing. Three more Digital Choir projects have followed, the most recent of these in the summer of 2013.

Although the majority of Whitacre's choral works are a cappella, *Cloudburst*, published in 1995, is an exception. Indeed, for two-thirds of its length, the voices are unaccompanied, but then piano and percussion (mostly bells, chimes, and thundersheet) join in, as well as clapping and finger-snaps for the singers. The idea is to capture the mood of a sudden and intense thunderstorm, not dissimilar to one that Whitacre says he witnessed in the desert while at work on the piece.

The text, sung in Spanish, is adapted from a poem by Octavio Paz (1914 – 1998). Haunting, sustained lines, rich harmonies, driving energy, and even a few spoken lines all have their place in this evocative work. At times, Whitacre sets each of the vocal parts in motion with musical lines different from the others; then, he brings them back together in harmony. One also finds Whitacre briefly spotlighting a single voice part – for example, perhaps the baritones – singing alone before the other voice parts rejoin the action, allowing the harmonic colors to vary subtly with each addition. It gives the impression of a kaleidoscope turning and a new crystal adding its color to the mix with each rotation of the kaleidoscope's body.

In all, Whitacre calls it "a celebration of the unleashed kinetic energy in all things." At first, one might not think of vocal music as having kinetic motion. However, raindrops pelting the earth with increasing frequency and intensity surely do, and Whitacre has brilliantly used his musical textures to convey that image. Listen as the clouds gradually build, the storm bursts forth, and then smoothly recedes. As Beethoven had evoked a thunderstorm in his Symphony no. 6 (see Chapter Two), so Whitacre also manages it with more limited performing forces. A good idea, well executed, never grows old.

More Classical Insights

Chapter Twelve: Coda

This bold and propulsive theme, rising on waves of sound, was intended to call forth the heroic side of Scotland, perhaps an army of Highlanders striding proudly across the Scottish moors. The composer Felix Mendelssohn (1809 – 1847) was not himself a Scotsman, but, impressed by their history, was inspired to write a symphony colored with their spirit. Although some pages of that work seem to evoke Scottish mists, it ends with this triumphant theme in glorious sunshine.

Mendelssohn's "Scottish" Symphony appeared in Chapter Two. However, it serves as a fitting introduction to the conclusion of this collection of essays on music. The theme above is the last major theme of that symphony, and this chapter introduces the last major theme of the book, so as to bring it to a close. That's what a "coda" is in music: the concluding material that brings things tidily to a close.

Back in Chapter Six in an article about Mendelssohn's *Songs without Words*, I included a quotation from a letter the composer wrote to his friend Marc-André Souchay, on October 15, 1842, relating to words and music. Here is a different excerpt from that same letter:

"There is so much chatter about music, but so little is said. I absolutely believe that words do not serve for such a purpose and if I found they did serve, I would finally have nothing more to do with music."

Despite Mendelssohn's thought about the insufficiency of using words to convey ideas about music, I am here publishing my third book about classical music, another 100,000 words on the subject. Why do so?

To share with others what hundreds of millions of people find so exciting and fulfilling about this music, to convey the enthusiasm we feel for it. Convey that excitement, fulfillment, and enthusiasm well enough and the reader – or the listener, as I have devoted many hundreds of hours to speaking with live audiences – may be motivated to give that piece of music, or this other one, a try. Summarizing distinctive musical and historical features in words can give a willing listener something specific to seek in the act of listening, and increase the likelihood of that person finding a door by which to enter that world.

In my years as a classical radio announcer/producer, I found that what I most enjoyed – other than spending every working day with the finest music on earth – was telling stories about the composers and how they went about doing what they did. Recently, I heard an interview with filmmaker Ron Howard, speaking about his 2013 film *Rush*, inspired by the true-life stories of the superstar Formula One racing drivers James Hunt and Niki Lauda. Of the film, Howard observed that he wanted to explore "the way they went about the business of being great." That's what I hope to do in these various essays about

More Classical Insights

composers: examine how these highly talented artists achieved their greatness and how the rest of us can benefit from understanding that greatness, even if we are unlikely to achieve it ourselves.

So, wanting to share those stories with others, even when not actively on the radio, and wanting to be sure that those stories would be readily available to interested persons, I set about writing books. What stories inspired me? Hundreds of them stand between these covers, some hinted at in the questions on the back cover:

- Did Brahms really write a lullaby? Yes, and details were in Chapter Seven.

- Why were the Polovtsians dancing? In melancholy recollection of their lost freedom. Details were in Chapter Ten.

- Why didn't Schubert finish his "Unfinished" Symphony? He moved on to other projects, then died young, before he ever got back to it. Details were in Chapter Two.

- Are there any important women composers? Bunches of them, some of whom were detailed in Chapters Two, Four, Five, Six, Seven, and Eight.

- What did jazz clarinetist Benny Goodman have to do with classical music? Plenty, with his repertoire including everything from Mozart to Bartók to Bernstein; details were in Chapters Four and Five.

These stories and many more helped me to develop a fascination for classical music, and to want to share those tales with others. I would love for more people to begin to see great music as I see it: as a fascinating pleasure.

Writing and speaking about great music is like writing a travel guide or giving a talk about a particular destination. Space and time would never permit giving as full a sense of the place as would a lifetime of living there. However, if those words help a listener to make a start on understanding why others find this particular destination worthwhile and, ideally, stimulate a wish to experience that destination personally, then the words have appreciable value. So with all due respect to Mendelssohn – who, I must admit, is one of my very favorite composers – writing about music is not to give others a reason to "have nothing more to do with music," but rather to share reasons why they <u>should</u> have more to do with music.

In one way, Mendelssohn's remarks are correct: words are only words and the music itself remains the principal point. Few would wish to read a cookbook about an interesting cuisine without ever sampling that cuisine. So it is with music. For a full appreciation, one must sample it, and for all the delights of recorded music, live music is a measurably more powerful experience. Watch how the performers interact with one another. If there is only a single performer, notice how the whole body is involved in producing those sounds. Let the music envelop you and sink in. Perhaps the perspectives in these articles will help you to let that music in, and come to know it better once it's there. Certainly, that was my intention.

More Classical Insights

If live performances are not immediately available, recordings are a reasonable compromise. I am studiously not recommending any specific recordings, as tastes vary. Besides, exciting new options appear regularly, so any list would become instantly outdated.

One fine resource for recordings old and new is the superb Naxos Music Library, available online by subscription. Containing well over a million tracks of classical works, it is invaluable to both serious and casual listeners. Although the great majority of works featured in this book are ones I came to know through live performances, many of them I listened to anew on Naxos as I was editing the individual articles. However reliable one's musical memory, anyone can use a refresher. Besides, it's fun. So consider taking out a Naxos subscription; whatever you're looking for in music is likely there.

Here's a point with which Mendelssohn would not take issue: that classical music is one of the great creations of mankind. In great music, composers express their hopes and dreams and perspectives on the world around them. Those hopes, dreams, and perspectives change over time and place, as different influences and goals play a role. So not only doesn't JS Bach (1685 – 1750) sound like Leonard Bernstein (1918 – 1990), he doesn't even sound much like Antonio Vivaldi (1678 – 1741). Although Bach and Vivaldi were practicing their art at the same time, their musical styles are far different from one another. Therein lies one of the principal delights of great music: new ideas and experiences await around every corner.

Classical music has something to offer to anyone who invests the effort to listen attentively. Please investigate some of the music featured here, especially those works you've never heard before. Somewhere here is a work that is exactly the right thing for the mood you're in at this moment. It may be written by Wolfgang Amadeus Mozart (1756 – 1791) or Nico Muhly (b. 1981). It may be something in between, but whatever it is, it awaits discovery. I hope that this travel guide to classical music can help you to begin – or continue – that exploration.

Appendices

I. Glossary

- **A cappella** – voices without instruments; original meaning was "in the style of the chapel," as in the Renaissance, church music was performed in this fashion
- **Adagio** – a rather slow tempo; from the Italian word for "slowly"
- **Allegro** – a brisk tempo; from the Italian word for "cheerful"
- **Allegro ma non troppo** – literally, "fast, but not too fast"
- **Andante** – a moderately slow tempo; from the Italian word for "current" (as in a stream)
- **Arpeggio** – playing the several notes of a chord sequentially, rather than simultaneously
- **Art song** – a short musical setting of a poem, generally for one singer and one pianist, though some art songs may add more accompanying instruments; synonym of "lieder"
- **Avant garde** – the radical, progressive, cutting-edge of music, a term especially in use since the beginning of the 20th century

- **Baroque Era** – a time in European history, 1600–1750, in which the royal courts were supremely powerful and music tended to be highly detailed
- **Basso continuo** (or "continuo") – the accompanying foundation of a Baroque Era work, generally played by harpsichord and one other low-pitched instrument

- **Cadenza** – a totally solo portion of a concerto in which the orchestra waits while the soloist plays on; in the 1700s and 1800s, the soloist was expected to improvise

- **Cantata** – a multi-movement composition for chorus and orchestra usually intended for liturgical use in the Protestant Church; especially identified with JS Bach
- **Castrato** – a surgically created male soprano or alto; the practice fell out of favor by the late 18th century and even before then, was mostly practiced in Italy
- **Chaconne** – a compositional form in which a repetitive bass line underlies an array of varying melodies, emphasizing relationships between those themes; especially popular in the Baroque Era
- **Chamber music** – music for small groups of players (duets, trios, quartets, etc.) playing "one to a part," so that each player makes a unique contribution to the composition
- **Classical Era** – a time from 1750-1820 or so, when the royal courts were declining in influence and composers were increasingly composing for general audiences; music tending to be simpler in structure than formerly
- **Character piece** – a solo piano piece, perhaps somewhat free-form in nature, that is meant to convey an image or a mood to the listener
- **Chromatic** – a harmonic practice in which notes are often only very small intervals between one another; imagine a scale (or chord drawn from that scale) in which both the black and the white keys on a piano are used in large number
- **Coda** - the final minutes or moments of a composition (or of one of its constituent movements) that serve to bring it to a close
- **Coloratura** – a very high singing voice, either male or female, nimble enough to be able to sing many different pitches quickly; usually applied to sopranos
- **Commission** – a request to a composer that he/she write a composition in return for payment, usually requesting a particular type of music for a particular occasion

More Classical Insights

- **Concert overture** – a one-movement piece of program music
- **Concerto** – a multi-movement instrumental composition in which one or more soloists are contrasted with a full orchestra
- **Concerto grosso** – a largely Baroque Era genre, similar to a concerto, but with more soloists and possibly more movements
- **Continuo** (or "basso continuo")– the accompanying foundation of a Baroque Era work, generally played by harpsichord and one other low-pitched instrument
- **Contralto** – a particularly low women's singing voice; sometimes just "alto"
- **Counterpoint** – techniques for combining diverse melodies for simultaneous performance; especially important in music of the Renaissance and Baroque Era
- **Countertenor** - a naturally very high male singing voice, often into the female soprano range; quite rare

- **Dotted rhythms** – a manner of alternating long and short notes – perhaps a quarter note and an eighth note – so as to produce a sort of skipping pattern
- **Dynamics** – how loud or soft the music is played

- **Etude** – a short solo piece, often for piano, intended as a learning experience and usually designed to focus upon a particular performing technique

- **Fingerboard** – the portion of a string instrument in which strings stretch out along a long neck; it is here that the player uses fingers to select specific notes
- **Form** – the structure or blueprint of a composition, determining in what order its main components occur
- **Fugue** – a compositional form in which several simultaneous and equally prominent melodies are combined into a single tapestry of sound; especially

associated with the Baroque Era, though not unknown in later years

- **Gamelan** – a traditional music style from Indonesia characterized largely by xylophone-like instruments, plucked strings, and wooden flutes; after the Paris World Exhibition of 1889, gamelan sounds develop a following in Western Europe
- **Grand opera** – an operatic style that develops early in the 19th century, focusing upon melodramatic stories (often, though not always, tragic), large casts, and flamboyant singing
- **Ground bass** – a Baroque practice of using a repetitive low rhythmic figure that underlies all manner of other melodies

- **Harmony** – combinations of simultaneous notes, often as accompaniment to a melody; the three-dimensional aspect of music
- **Harpsichord** – a keyboard instrument popular in the Baroque Era and before the piano; keys are laid out the same as a piano, but the mechanism inside the instrument plucks the strings, rather than striking them with a hammer, leading to a more delicate soun
- **Impressionism** – a movement of the late 1800s/early 1900s emphasizing softer, subtler edges and structures in music; related to the artistic movement of the same name
- **Improvisation** – spontaneous creation of music, even in front of a live audience; although much identified with jazz, it was a skill much admired in earlier days, and both Mozart and Beethoven were known for their improvisatory abilities
- **Incidental music** – a set of short pieces to accompany performance of a play

More Classical Insights

- **Jazz** – American popular music style originating in the 1920s and emphasizing improvisation and syncopation; influential even in the classical world; especially associated with Gershwin and Ellington

- **Key** – the central set of notes upon which a composition is based, giving it a particular character; "major" keys generally sound bright and cheerful, "minor" keys dark and somber

- **Librettist** – the person who writes the text of an opera or operetta
- **Libretto** – the text of an opera or operetta
- **Lied** – a short musical setting of a poem, generally for one singer and one pianist, though some art songs may add more accompanying instruments; synonym of "art song;" the plural is "lieder"

- **Medieval Era** – roughly 450AD to roughly 1450AD; a time in history and music in which the Catholic Church was strongly influential in Europe
- **Meter** – the pattern of accented and unaccented beats in a composition. For example, $\underline{1}$-2-3, $\underline{1}$-2-3 (a waltz), as opposed to $\underline{1}$-2, $\underline{1}$-2, $\underline{1}$-2 (a march)
- **Minimalism** – a musical style of the late 20th century in which a hypnotically steady beat is prominent, with small, subtle changes to melodic fragments; especially identified with Philip Glass
- **Minuet** – originally a triple-meter (1-2-3, $\underline{1}$-2-3) ballroom dance of the 1700s; becomes a popular form for composition in the late 1700s
- **Motet** – an a cappella work of sacred nature distinct from any specific portion of the mass; especially popular in the Renaissance
- **Motif** – a fragment of a melody upon which larger musical structures may be built; one exceptionally

famous motif is represented in the first four notes of Beethoven's Symphony no. 5
- **Movement** – a self-contained chapter of a more extended composition

- **Nationalism** – expressing pride in one's nation or ethnic group through one's music; especially prevalent in the mid to late 1800s in Eastern Europe
- **Neo-Classical** – a movement in the early 1900s in which some ideas of the late 1700s were revived, though perhaps with more modern harmonies and a different selection of instruments
- **Neo-Romantic** – a movement in the early 20th century that sought to continue use of the grand melodic moods of late 19th century music

- **Ondes martenot** – an early 20th electronic instrument, invented in 1928 by Frenchman Maurice Martenot, it works with sound waves to vary the color of sounds; the word "ondes" literally means "waves"
- **One to a part** – each player makes a unique contribution to the composition, with no simultaneous duplication whatsoever
- **Opera** – a musical drama with singers and orchestra
- **Opera buffa** – a type of comic opera especially popular in the late 1700s and early 1800s
- **Opera seria** – a type of serious opera especially popular in the early 1700s
- **Operetta** – light opera with spoken dialog; a predecessor of modern musical theater
- **Oratorio** – a multi-movement composition for singers and orchestra, generally telling a Biblical story, though without sets or costumes, so not an opera; especially associated with Handel
- **Overture** – an instrumental introduction to a large-scale stage work, such as an opera; distinct from a "concert overture"

More Classical Insights

- **Parlor Songs** – short works for solo voice and piano, generally not too demanding in technique, and intended for amateur performers
- **Partita** – an instrumental composition often using dance rhythms in its various movements; particularly popular in the Baroque Era
- **Pas de deux** – literally "steps for two": a scene for two ballet dancers, usually a man and a woman
- **Pitch** – the highness or lowness of a sound
- **Pizzicato** – plucking of the strings on an instrument
- **Pointillism** – as in art, a style in which the substance of the creation is made up of many tiny dots – here, of sound; largely identified with Anton Webern
- **Polyphony** – the practice of having several simultaneous and equally important melodies; especially important in the Baroque Era, though not unknown in later times; various techniques of "counterpoint" are used to create it
- **Post-Romantic Era** – a time from 1890 to 1910 or so, in which music was moving away from the expectations of the Romantic Era, becoming even more free from any expectation
- **Program music** – instrumental music with a story to tell or a scene to paint; includes "tone poems," "symphonic poems," "concert overtures," and "program symphonies"
- **Prelude** – usually a short solo piece, rather abstract in form, and generally for piano solo

- **Renaissance Era** – after the Medieval Era but before the Baroque Era, therefore about 1600- 1750; increasing power of the royal courts and a greater tendency toward secular music
- **Romantic Era** – a time from 1820 to 1890 or so, in which music was moving away from the expectations of the Classical Era, generally (though not always)

becoming bigger, more dramatic, and more personal in its expression
- **Rondo** – a form for composition with several alternating and contrasting melodies

- **Scherzo** – a form for composition having a quick tempo, a forceful triple meter (<u>1</u>-2-3, <u>1</u>-2-3) and usually two distinct melodies; one heard at the beginning and again at the end, the other in the middle
- **Score** – all the notes of a composition, with all its many parts, on the printed page
- **Serialism** – the practice of using every note within an octave with exactly equal frequency; especially associated with the Second Viennese School
- **Sonata** – a chamber work for one or two players, generally including a piano
- **Song Cycle** – a set of related art songs, perhaps all by the same poet or all on the same literary theme
- **Staccato** – short and separated notes, whether sung or played on instruments
- **Sturm und Drang** – an artistic movement just before and after 1800 that led to stronger, more dramatic compositions; especially associated with Beethoven; German for "storm and stress"
- **Suite** – an instrumental composition (either orchestra or solo keyboard) in several short movements, often portraying different portions of a story, or (especially during the Baroque Era) perhaps based upon ballroom dance rhythms; a "suite" may also be a selection of movements from a larger work, such as "the suite from *Swan Lake*"
- **Symphonic poem** – a one-movement piece of program music, using instruments (not voices or dancers) to tell a story or paint a scene; roughly interchangeable with "tone poem"

More Classical Insights

- **Symphony** – a multi-movement instrumental composition distinct from a concerto in that a symphony has no featured soloist

- **Tempo** – how fast or slow the music is played
- **Timbre** – the general quality or color of a sound, whether vocal or instrumental
- **Tone poem** – a one-movement piece of program music, using instruments (not voices or dancers) to tell a story or paint a scene; roughly interchangeable with "symphonic poem"
- **Transcendentalism** – a philosophical movement of the early to mid-19th century that suggested the goodness of nature and the evil of organized society and the limitations it places on an individual; especially associated with Henry Thoreau and Ralph Waldo Emerson
- **Transcription** – the process of rewriting a musical work for different performers than were originally intended
- **Treble** – a boy soprano
- **Tremolo** – alternating quickly between two repeated tones, especially tones that are at a very close interval to one another
- **Trouser role** – a masculine operatic role written to be sung by a female singer, generally a mezzo-soprano
- **Twelve-tone** – a 20th century avant garde idea in which all 12 notes of the octave (including both white and black keys on the piano) are treated with exactly equal emphasis

- **Variations** – taking a basic melody and steadily changing it (perhaps its rhythm or its key) so as to create different views of that original melody
- **Verismo** – a late 19th century/early 20th century operatic style emphasizing realism

Betsy Schwarm

II. Composer Pronunciation Guide

Obvious names (such as John Adams) are not included. Although pronunciations are provided for all the last names given below, pronunciations are only given for first names that might prove problematic. The exception here is Ralph Vaughan Williams, for whom the first name is actually more unusual in pronunciation than the last. Accented syllables are written in CAPITAL letters.

This list includes two foreign sounds that are often difficult for English speakers:

- German "ch" The German "ch" (as in Johann Sebastian Bach, Richard Wagner, and Richard Strauss) is pronounced like the "h" in "hue".

- French "G". The French "G" (as in Georges Bizet) has a sort of buzzing "zh" sound.

Argento, Dominic	ar-GENT-oh	
Bach, Johann Sebastian	BAHCH	YO-han se-BAS-tian
(German CH as above)		
Bartók, Bela	BAR-tock	BAY-lah
Beethoven, Ludwig van	BAY-tow-ven	LOOD-vig van
Bellini, Vincenzo	bell-EE-nee	vin-CHEN-zo
Berlioz, Hector	BEAR-lee-ohz	
Bernstein, Leonard	BURN-styne	(Not "BURN-steeeen")
Bizet, Georges	bee-ZAY	Zhorzh
Brahms, Johannes	BR-AH-MS	yo-HAN-es
Bruch, Max	BREWCH	(German CH as in Bach)
Castelnuovo-Tedesco, Mario	CAS-tel-new-OH-vo ted-ES-ko	
Catán, Daniel	ka-TAHN	
Chaminade, Cecile	shah-me-NAHD	say-SEAL
Chausson, Ernest	shaow-SON	
Chopin, Frederic	SHOW-pan	
Copland, Aaron	COPE-land	(rhymes with "hope-land")
Couperin, François	coop-er-AN	fran-SWAH

364

More Classical Insights

Debussy, Claude   day-byu-SEE
Delibes, Leo   duh-LEEB   LAY-oh
D'Indy Vincent   dahn-DEE   VIN-sahn
Donizetti, Gaetano   DO-nih-ZET-tee   gay-TAH-no
Dukas, Paul   doo-KAH
Dvořák, Antonín   duh-VOR-zhak   AHN-tow-neen
   (The Czechs would roll that r.)
Enesco, Georges   ee-NES-ko   Zhorzh
Franck, Cesar   FRAHNK   SAY-zar
Gershwin, George   GURSH-win
Glazunov, Alexander GLAH-zoo-nawv
Gliere, Reinhold   glee-AIR   RYEN-hold
Golijov, Oswaldo   GO-lee-awv
Górecki, Henryk   gor-ET-ski   HEN-rik
Gottschalk, Louis   GOT-shalk
Grofé, Ferde   grow-FAY   FAIR-day
Handel, George Frideric HAN-dull
Haydn, Joseph   HY-din   (Not HAY-din)
Hindemith, Paul   HIN-day-mit
Ibert, Jacques   eee-BARE
Jarre, Maurice   ZHARAY
Joachim, Joseph   YO-ah-cheem   (German CH as in Bach)
Khachaturian, Aram   CATCH-a-TUR-ee-an   ah-RAM
Köchel, Ludwig   KUR-schel   LOOD-vig
   (The r sound barely there.)
Kodaly, Zoltan   koh-DIE-ee   ZOL-than
Korngold, Erich   CORN-gold   erich
   (German CH as in Bach)
Liszt, Franz   list
Mahler, Gustav   MAH-ler
Marais, Marin   mah-RAY   mah-RAN
Marsalis, Wynton   mar-SAL-is
Massenet, Jules   mass-uh-NAY   ZHUUL
Mendelssohn, Felix   MEN-del-son
Menotti, Gian-Carlo men-OT-ee   JOHN CAR-lo
Messiaen, Olivier   messy-AHN   oh-LIV-ee-ay
Milhaud, Darius   mee-YOH   DAR-ee-us
Mozart, Wolfgang Amadeus
         MOAT-zart   VULF-gahng   ah-mah-DAY-iss
Muhly, Nico   MEW-lee
Pergolesi, Giovanni PAIR-go-LAY-see

Poulenc, Francis	poo-LAHNK	frahn-CEES
Prokofiev, Sergei	pro-KOH-fee-ev	SAIR-gay
Puccini, Giacomo	poo-CHEE-nee	JAH-ko-mo
Purcell, Henry	PURR-sell	
Rautavaara, Einojuhani	RAOW-tah-VAR-ah	EI-no-you-HAH-nee

(RAOW rhyming with 'ow'.)

Ravel, Maurice	rah-VELL	
Respighi, Ottorino	res-PEE-ghee	auto-REE-no
Rimsky-Korsakov, Nicolai	RIM-ski KOR-sa-kov	
Rózsa, Miklós	ROW-zha	MEE-clowzh
Schoenberg, Arnold	SHOON-bairg	
Schubert, Franz	SHOO-bairt	
Schumann, Clara Wieck	SHOO-mahn	KLAIR-ah VEEK
Schumann, Robert	SHOO-mahn	
Shostakovich, Dmitri	SHOS-ta-KO-vitch	
Sibelius, Jean	sih-BAY-lee-us	ZHAHN
Strauss, Richard	SHTR-OW-ss	REE-chart

(German CH as in Bach)

Stravinsky, Igor	stra-VIN-skee	EE-gor
Tchaikovsky, Peter	chy-KOV-skee	
Tailleferre, Germaine	tie-FAIR	zher-MANE
Takemitsu, Toru	TAH-kay-MIT-zu	TO-roo
Tárrega, Francisco	TAH-ray-gah	
Telemann, Georg Philipp	TELL-ah-mahn	GAY-org
Turina, Joaquin	tur-EEN-ah	WAH-keen
Ullmann, Victor	OOL-man	
Vaughan Williams, Ralph		RAFE

(rhyming with "safe")

Verdi, Giuseppe	VAIR-dee	juh-SEP-ee
Vivaldi, Antonio	vih-VALL-dee	
Wagner, Richard	VAHG-ner	REE-chart

(German CH as in Bach)

Webern, Anton	VAY-bairn	
Weill, Kurt	VILE	koort
Ysaÿe, Eugene	ee-SIGH you-ZHAYN	
Zwilich, Ellen Taaffe	ZWILL-ik	

More Classical Insights

III. Source List

Note: Some information about recent and current composers and their works I obtained from interviews with the composers themselves and with respected interpreters of their works, either for my radio programs or in live interviews with audiences prior to concerts. These include John Adams, John Rutter, Lori Laitman, Kevin Puts, Gabriela Lena Frank, conductor JoAnn Falletta, conductor Andrew Litton, and the Takács Quartet (this last ensemble for their perspective as Hungarians on the music of Bartók – I spoke with the original members of the Quartet, before membership changes brought non-Hungarians to the ensemble.).

Further note: The German language sources I read in the original German, and translated myself when translations of quotations were needed.

Last note: Many current composers make a point of maintaining their own websites – or their publishers do – in which they comment upon their own lives and music; if the composer himself/herself is supervising the site, it can be considered authoritative. These include Michael Daughtery, Jay Greenberg, Jake Heggie, Karl Jenkins, Nico Muhly, Steven Stucky, Michael Torke, Eric Whitacre, John Williams, and Elllen Taaffe Zwilich.

- Adami, Giuseppe: editor. *Letters of Giacomo Puccini*. Vienna House: New York. 1973.

- Adams, John. *Hallelujah Junction: Composing an American Life*. Farrar, Straus and Giroux: New York. 2008

- Altmann, Dr. Wilhelm. *Richard Wagners Briefe*. Breitkopf und Härtel. 1905.

- Bailey, Kathryn, editor. *Webern Studies*. Cambridge University Press: Cambridge. 1996.

- Behague, Gerard. *Heitor Villa-Lobos: The Search for Brazil's Musical Soul*. Institute of Latin American Studies, University of Texas, Austin. 1994.

- Buckland, Sidney, editor and translator. *Francis Poulenc – Echo and Source – Selected Correspondence 1915 – 1963*. Victor Gollancz Ltd.: London. 1991.

- Burney, Charles. *A General History of Music*. Dover Publications: New York. 1957. First published 1789.

- Carr, Jonathan. *Mahler: A Biography*. Overlook Press: Woodstock and New York. 1997.

- Davies, Laurence. *César Franck and His Circle*. Barrie and Jenkins: London. 1970.

- Deutsch, Otto Erich. *Schubert: Erinnerungen von seine Freunden*. Breitkopf und Härtel: Leipzig. 1958.

- Dvořák, Otakar. *Antonín Dvořák, My Father*. Written 1961; published 1993 by Czech Historical Research Center of Spillville, Iowa. Edited by Paul J. Polansky, translated by Miroslav Němec.

- Eaglefield-Hull, A., editor. *Beethoven's Letters*. Letters translated by JS Shedlock. Dover: New York. 1972.

- Ellington, Edward Kennedy "Duke". *Music is My Mistress*. Da Capo Press. 1976.

- Glover, Jane. *Mozart's Women: His Family, His Friends, His Music*. Harper Collins: New York. 2006.

-
- Gottlieb, Jack. *Working with Bernstein*. Amadeus Press: Milwaukee. 2010

- *Gramophone Magazine*. Various editors over many years. London. In print since 1923, and a fine source of first-hand composer information, including interviews both with current and with now long-departed composers.

- Hanslick, Eduard. *Musikkritiken*. Philipp Reclam: Stuttgart. 1972.

- *Harvard Magazine*, July 2001 (information regarding alumnus Randall Thompson).

- Hildesheimer, Wolfgang. *Mozart*. Suhrkampf Verlag: Frankfurt am Main. 1977.

- Hilmes, Oliver. *Cosima Wagner: The Lady of Bayreuth*. Translation by Stewart Spencer. Yale University Press: New Haven and London. 2010.

- Honolka, Kurt. Translated by Anne Wyburd. *Dvořák*. Haus Publishing Limited: London. 2004

- Jarman, Douglas. *Kurt Weill: An Illustrated Biography*. Orbis Publishing: London. 1982

- Kennedy, Michael. *Master Musician: Britten*. Dent: London 1981.

- Kennedy, Michael. *Richard Strauss: Man, Musician, Enigma*. Cambridge University Press: Cambridge and New York. 1999.

- MacDonald, Malcolm. *Varèse: Astronomer in Sound*. Kahn and Averill: London. 2003

- Mahler, Alma. *Gustav Mahler: Erinnerungen und Briefe*. Verlag Allert de Lange: Amsterdam. 1940.

- Massie, Susanne. *Land of the Firebird: The Beauty of Old Russia*. Simon and Schuster: New York. 1980.

- Mendelssohn Bartholdy, Paul und Dr. Carl. *Briefe aus den Jahren 1830 bis 1847* von Felix Mendelssohn Bartholdy. Zusammengestellt von Dr. Julius Rieß. Leipzig. Dr. Hermann Mendelssohn 1863.

- Mersmann, Hans: editor. *Letters of Wolfgang Amadeus Mozart*. Dover: New York. 1972.

- Morgenstern, Sam. *Composers on Music: An Anthology of Composers' Writings from Palestrina to Copland*. Pantheon Books: New York. 1956.

- Mozart, Wolfgang Amadeus. *Briefe*. Philipp Reclam: Stuttgart. 1987.

- Musgrove, Michael. *A Brahms Reader*. Yale University Press: New Haven and London. 2000.

- Neumann, Werner: editor. *Bach Dokumente: Herausgegeben vom Bach-Arkiv Leipzig*. Bärenreiter: Kassel – Basel – Paris – London – New York. 1963.

- New York Philharmonic digital archives. http://archives.newyorkphil.org

- *New York Times* microfilm archives: various reviews of premieres of major works.

- Newman, Ernest: translator. *Memoirs of Hector Berlioz from 1803 to 1865*. Dover Publications: New York. 1932.

- Nichols, Roger: translator and editor. *Debussy Letters*. Faber and Faber: London and Boston. 1987.

- Orlova, Alexandra. *Tchaikovsky: A Self-Portrait*. Oxford University Press: London. 1990.

- Pleasants, Henry: translator and editor. *Hanslick's Music Criticisms*. Dover Publications: New York. 1950.

- Pleasants, Henry: translator and editor. *Schumann on Music: A Selection from the Writings*. Dover Publications: New York. 1965.

More Classical Insights

- Pollock, Howard. *George Gershwin: His Life and Work*. University of California Press: 2006.

- Price, Curtis Alexander. *Henry Purcell and the London Stage*. Cambridge University Press: Cambridge. 1984

- Prokofiev, Sergei. *Prokofiev by Prokofiev: A Composer's Memoir*. Doubleday and Company: New York. 1979.

- Rimsky-Korsakov, Nikolai. *My Musical Life*. Translated by Judah A. Joffe. Vienna House: New York. 1972.

- Ross, Alex. *The Rest is Noise: Listening to the Twentieth Century*. Picador: New York. 2007.

- Sadie, Stanley, editor. *Grove's Dictionary of Music and Musicians*. MacMillan Publishers: London. 1980. 2001.

- Schindler, Anton Felix. *Beethoven as I Knew Him*. Translated by Constance S. Jolly. Dover Publications: New York. 1996.

- Schonberg, Harold C. *The Great Pianists: From Mozart to the Present*. Simon and Schuster: New York. 1987.

- Schumann, Robert. *Schriften über Musik und Musiker*. Philipp Reclam: Stuttgart. 2010.

- Secrest, Meryl. *Leonard Bernstein: A Life*. Alfred A. Knopf: New York. 1994.

- Selden-Goth G. *Felix Mendelssohn: Letters*. Elek Publishers: London. 1946.

- Seroff, Victor Ilyich. *Dmitri Shostakovich: The Life and Background of a Soviet Composer*. Books for Libraries Press: Freeport and New York. 1970.

- Slonimsky, Nicolas. *Lexicon of Musical Invective: Critical Assaults on Composers since Beethoven's Time.* University of Washington Press: Seattle and London. 1953. 1994.

- Solomon, Maynard. *Beethoven.* Schirmer Books: New York. 1998.

- Solomon, Maynard. *Mozart: A Life.* Harper Collins: New York. 1995

- Spaething, Robert. *Mozart's Letters, Mozart's Life: Selected Letters Edited and Newly Translated.* Norton and Company: New York and London. 2000.

- Stendhal (Beyle, Marie Henri). *Life of Rossini.* Translation by Richard N. Coe. The Orion Press: New York. 1970.

- Strauss, Dr. Franz. *Richard Strauss Briefwechsel mit Hugo von Hofmannsthal.* Berlin. 1925.

- Stravinsky, Igor. *Igor Stravinsky: An Autobiography.* W.W. Norton and Company: New York and London. 1936.

- Tchaikovsky, Modest. *The Life and Letters of Peter Ilyich Tchaikovsky.* Translated by Rosa Newmarch. Vienna House: New York. 1973.

- Thomas, Nancy G. and Jaffe, Jane Vial, editors. *Kurt Oppens on Music: Notes and Essays for the Aspen Music Festival 1957 – 1995.* Science/Art Press: Aspen, Colorado. 2009.

- Vaughan Williams, Ursula. *R.V.W: A Biography of Ralph Vaughan Williams.* Oxford University Press: London. 1964.

More Classical Insights

IV. Works Featured in my Earlier Books

For those who may have wondered why a particular work or composer is not featured in this collection, the reason may well be that he/she/it is amongst the 400+ items in my earlier two collections. In case you are interested in seeking out information on one of those subjects, here are the works lists from those two books. The articles in *Operatic Insights* also include synopses and character lists with voice parts.

Classical Insights:
   Understanding and Enjoying Great Music

(published 2011)

Symphonies
   Haydn: Symphony no. 94 in G major, "Surprise"
   Mozart: Symphony no. 41 in C major, K. 551
   Beethoven: Symphony no. 5 in c minor, op. 67
   Beethoven: Symphony no. 9 in d minor, op. 125, "Choral"
   Schubert: Symphony no. 9 in C major, D. 944
   Berlioz: *Symphonie fantastique*, op. 14
   Mendelssohn: Symphony no. 4 in A major, op. 90, "Italian"
   Schumann: Symphony no. 1 in B-flat major, op. 38, "Spring"
   Bruckner: Symphony no. 4 in E-flat major, "Romantic"
   Brahms: Symphony no. 1 in c minor, op. 68
   Saint-Saëns: Symphony no. 3 in c minor, op. 78, "Organ"
   Tchaikovsky: Symphony no. 4 in f minor, op. 36
   Dvořák: Symphony no. 9 in e minor, op. 95, "New World"
   Mahler: Symphony no. 5
   Richard Strauss: *An Alpine Symphony*
   Nielsen: Symphony no. 4, "The Inextinguishable"
   Sibelius: Symphony no. 5 in E-flat major, op. 82
   Rachmaninoff: Symphony no. 2 in e minor, op. 27
   Hanson: Symphony no. 2, "Romantic"
   Chavez: *Sinfonia India*
   Copland: Symphony no. 3
   Shostakovich: Symphony no. 5 in d minor, op. 47
   Hovhaness: Symphony no. 50, "Mt. St. Helens"
   Bernstein: Symphony no. 2, "The Age of Anxiety"
   Glass: Symphony no. 7, "A Toltec Symphony"

Betsy Schwarm

Other Symphonic Works
Handel: *Water Music*
Handel: *Royal Fireworks Music*
Mendelssohn: *The Hebrides* Overture, op. 26
Liszt: *Les Préludes*
Wagner: *Siegfried Idyll*
Smetana: *The Moldau – Ma Vlast (My Fatherland)*
Brahms: *Academic Festival Overture*, op.80
Tchaikovsky: *Romeo and Juliet* Fantasy Overture
Mussorgsky: *Night on Bald Mountain*
Rimsky-Korsakov: *Scheherazade*, op. 35
Elgar: *Enigma Variations, op. 36*
Richard Strauss: *Don Juan, op. 20*
Sibelius: *Finlandia*
Debussy: *Prelude to the Afternoon of a Faun*
Vaughan Williams: *The Lark Ascending*
Holst: *The Planets*
Ives: *Three New England Sketches*
Respighi: *The Pines of Rome*
Villa Lobos: *Bachianas Brasileiras no. 2*
Revueltas: *Sensemaya*
Britten: *Young Person's Guide to the Orchestra*, op. 34
Ligeti: *Atmosphères*
Adams: *Short Ride in a Fast Machine*
Daughtery: *Route 66*
Higdon: *blue cathedral*

Concertos
Vivaldi: *The Four Seasons,* op. 8, no. 1-4
Bach: Brandenburg Concertos, BWV 1046 – 1051
Hummel: Trumpet Concerto in E-flat major
Mozart: Piano Concerto no. 21 in C major, K. 467
Mozart: Clarinet Concerto in A major, K. 622
Beethoven: Piano Concerto no. 5 in E-flat major, "Emperor"
Paganini: Violin Concerto no. 1 in D major, op. 6
Berlioz: *Harold in Italy* (Viola Concerto)
Mendelssohn: Violin Concerto in e minor, op. 64
Schumann: Piano Concerto in a minor, op. 54
Brahms: Violin Concerto in D major, op. 77
Bruch: Violin Concerto no. 1 in g minor, op. 26
Tchaikovsky: Piano Concerto no. 1 in b-flat minor, op. 23
Dvořák: Cello Concerto in b minor, op. 104

More Classical Insights

Elgar: Cello Concerto in e minor, op. 85
Richard Strauss: Horn Concerto no. 1
Richard Strauss: Oboe Concerto
Rachmaninoff: *Rhapsody on a Theme of Paganini*
Prokofiev: Piano Concerto no. 1 in D-flat major, op. 10
Hindemith: *Der Schwanendreher* (Viola Concerto)
Gershwin: *Rhapsody in Blue*
Rodrigo: *Concierto de Aranjuez*
Glass: Second Violin Concerto "Four Seasons"
Golijov: Azul (Cello Concerto)
Meyer: Triple Concerto for bass, banjo, and tabla

Chamber Music
Pachelbel: Canon in D major
Bach: Cello Suites, BWV 1007 – 1012
Haydn: String Quartet in C major, op. 76, no. 3, "Emperor"
Mozart: Serenade no. 13, K. 525, "A Little Night Music"
Beethoven: Piano Trio no. 7 in B-flat major, op. 97, "Archduke"
Schubert: Piano Quintet in A major, D. 667, "The Trout"
Mendelssohn: Octet in E-flat major for Strings, op. 20
Schumann: Piano Quartet in E-flat major, op. 47
Franck: Violin Sonata in A major
Brahms: Serenade no. 1 in D major, op. 11
Dvořák: String Quartet no. 12 in F major, op. 96, "American"
Schoenberg: Transfigured Night
Bartók: String Quartet no. 4
Clarke: Viola Sonata
Carter: String Quartet no. 2
Barber: Adagio for Strings
Messiaen: *Quartet for the End of Time*
Pärt: *Spiegel im Spiegel*
Williams: *Air and Simple Gifts*
Tower: *Island Prelude*

Keyboard Music
Bach: Toccata and Fugue in d minor, BWV 565
Bach: *The Well-Tempered Clavier*, BWV 846 – 893
Scarlatti: keyboard sonatas
Mozart: 12 Variations on "Ah, vous dirai-je, Maman," K. 265
Beethoven: Piano Sonata no. 8 in c minor, "Pathetique"
Beethoven: *Diabelli Variations*, op. 120
Chopin: Polish master of the piano

Liszt: Hungarian master of the piano
Clara Wieck Schumann: Four Fugitive Pieces, op. 15
Brahms: *Variations on a Theme of Haydn*, op. 56
Mussorgsky: *Pictures at an Exhibition*
Grieg: *Wedding Day at Troldhaugen*
Albeniz: *Asturias*
Debussy: *Suite Bergamasque*, including *Clair de lune*
Satie: *Trois Gymnopedies*
Vierne: symphonies for organ
Scriabin: Six Etudes
Cage: Sonatas and Interludes for Prepared Piano
Ginastera: Sonata no. 1, op. 22
Gabriela Montero: the art of improvisation

Art Songs and Lieder
Schubert: *Der Erlkönig*
Schubert: Ave Maria, D. 839, op. 52, no. 6
Schumann: *Dichterliebe, op. 48*
Brahms: *Liebesliederwalzer*
Tchaikovsky: *None but the Lonely Heart*
Dvořák: *Moravian Duets*
Chausson: *Poème de l'amour et de la mer*, op. 19
Mahler: *Des Knaben Wunderhorn*, op. 48
Wolf: *Spanischliederbuch*
Richard Strauss: *Four Last Songs*
Rachmaninoff: *Vocalise*
Vaughan Williams: *Songs of Travel*
Schoenberg: *Gurrelieder*
Canteloube: *Songs of the Auvergne*
Copland: *Old American Songs*
Barber: *Dover Beach*
Britten: Serenade, op. 31
Rorem: *Santa Fe Songs*
Lieberson: *Neruda Songs*
Larsen: *Sonnets from the Portuguese*

Opera and Operetta
Handel: *Julius Caesar*
Mozart: *The Marriage of Figaro*
Weber: *Der Freischütz*
Rossini: *The Barber of Seville*
Donizetti: *Lucia di Lammermoor*
Verdi: *La Traviata*

More Classical Insights

Wagner: *the Ring Cycle*
Gounod: *Faust*
Offenbach: *Orpheus in the Underworld*
Johann Strauss Jr.: *Die Fledermaus*
Bizet: *Carmen*
Massenet: *Werther*
Dvořák: *Rusalka*
Sullivan: *The Pirates of Penzance*
Richard Strauss: *Der Rosenkavalier*
Humperdinck: *Hansel and Gretel*
Puccini: *La Bohéme*
Berg: *Wozzeck*
Lehar: *The Merry Widow*
Gershwin: *Porgy and Bess*
Britten: *Billy Budd*
Floyd: *Susannah*
Adams: *Nixon in China*
Catán: *Florencia en el Amazonas*
Heggie: *Three Decembers*

Stage and Screen
Purcell: *Abdelazer* – incidental music
Mendelssohn: *A Midsummer Night's Dream*
Bizet: *L'Arlesienne*
Grieg: *Peer Gynt*
Prokofiev: *Alexander Nevsky*
Prokofiev: *Peter and the Wolf*
Virgil Thomson: *The Plow That Broke the Plains*
Korngold: *The Adventures of Robin Hood*
Copland: *The Red Pony*
Walton: *Henry V*
Kabalevsky: *The Comedians*
Rózsa: *Ben Hur*
Rota: *La Strada*
Herrmann: *Psycho*
Bernstein: *West Side Story*
Williams: *Star Wars*
Corigliano: *The Red Violin*
Shore: *Lord of the Rings*
Tan Dun: *Crouching Tiger, Hidden Dragon*

Music for Motion
Adam: *Giselle*

Johann Strauss Jr.: *On the Beautiful Blue Danube*
Delibes: *Coppélia*
Brahms: Hungarian Dances
Ponchielli: *Dance of the Hours*, from *La Gioconda*
Saint-Saëns: *Bacchanale*, from *Samson et Delilah*
Waldteufel: *The Skater's Waltz*
Tchaikovsky: *The Nutcracker*, op. 71
Tchaikovsky: *Marche Slav*, op. 31
Dvořák: *Slavonic Dances*, op. 46 and op. 72
Sousa: *The Stars and Stripes Forever*
Elgar: *Pomp and Circumstance March*, op. 39, no. 1
Ravel: *Bolero*
Stravinsky: *The Firebird*
Stravinsky: *The Rite of Spring*
Prokofiev: *Romeo and Juliet*
Copland: *Appalachian Spring*
Khachaturian: *Spartacus*
Ginastera: *Estancia*
Ellington: *The River*

Choral Music
Allegri: Miserere mei
Palestrina: *Pope Marcellus Mass*
Tallis: Spem in alium – motet
Bach: *St. Matthew Passion*, BWV 244
Handel: *Messiah* – oratorio
Haydn: *The Creation* – oratorio
Mozart: *Ave verum corpus*, K. 618
Mozart: Requiem in d minor, K. 626
Beethoven: Choral Fantasy in c minor, op. 80
Mendelssohn: *Elijah*
Verdi: Requiem
Brahms: A German Requiem, op. 45
Fauré: *Cantique de Jean Racine*
Orff: Carmina Burana
Randall Thompson: *Alleluia*
Finzi: *In Terra Pax*
Bernstein: Chicester Psalms
Tavener: *Song for Athene*
Rutter: carols (and a great deal more)
Whitacre: *Lux Aurumque*

More Classical Insights

Operatic Insights: Understanding and Enjoying Great Music for the Stage

(published 2012)

Opera Before Mozart
Monteverdi: *The Coronation of Poppea*
Purcell: *Dido and Aeneas*
Charpentier: *Médée*
Handel: *Giulio Cesare*
Vivaldi: *Orlando furioso*
Gluck: *Orfeo ed Euridice*

Opera 1780 – 1829
Mozart: *Abduction from the Seraglio*
Mozart: *The Marriage of Figaro*
Mozart: *Don Giovanni*
Mozart: *Cosi fan tutte*
Mozart: *The Magic Flute*
Rossini: *The Italian Girl in Algiers*
Beethoven: *Fidelio*
Rossini: *The Barber of Seville*
Rossini: *Cenerentola*
Weber: *Der Freischütz*

Opera 1830 – 1855
Bellini: *La Sonnambula*
Bellini: *Norma*
Donizetti: *Lucia di Lammermoor*
Donizetti: *The Daughter of the Regiment*
Verdi: *Nabucco*
Wagner: *The Flying Dutchman*
Donizetti: *Don Pasquale*
Wagner: *Tannhaüser*
Flotow: *Martha*
Wagner: *Lohengrin*
Verdi: *Rigoletto*
Verdi: *Il Trovatore*
Verdi: *La Traviata*

Opera 1856 – 1876
Offenbach: *Orpheus in the Underworld*
Gounod: *Faust*
Bizet: *The Pearl Fishers*
Wagner: *Tristan und Isolde*
Smetana: *The Bartered Bride*
Verdi: *Don Carlo*
Gounod: *Romeo et Juliette*
Wagner: *Die Meistersinger von Nürnberg*
Verdi: *Aida*
Mussorgsky: *Boris Godunov*
J. Strauss Jr.: *Die Fledermaus*
Bizet: *Carmen*
Wagner: *Die Walküre*

Opera 1877 – 1900
Saint-Saëns: *Samson et Dalila*
Sullivan: *The Pirates of Penzance*
Tchaikovsky: *Eugene Onegin*
Offenbach: *The Tales of Hoffmann*
Massenet: *Manon*
Verdi: *Otello*
Mascagni: *Cavallaria Rusticana*
Mascagni: *L'Amico Fritz*
Massenet: *Werther*
Leoncavallo: *I Pagliacci*
Verdi: *Falstaff*
Humperdinck: *Hansel und Gretel*
Puccini: *La Bohéme*
Giordano: *Andrea Chénier*
Puccini: *Tosca*

Opera 1901-1926
Dvořák: *Rusalka*
Debussy: *Pelléas et Melisande*
Puccini: *Madama Butterfly*
R. Strauss: *Salome*
R. Strauss: *Der Rosenkavalier*
Puccini: *Gianni Schicchi*
Korngold: *Die tote Stadt*
Vives: *Doña Francisquita*

More Classical Insights

Janáček: *The Cunning Little Vixen*
Romberg: *The Student Prince*
Berg: *Wozzeck*
Puccini: *Turandot*

Opera since Puccini
Weill: *The Three-Penny Opera*
Gershwin: *Porgy and Bess*
R. Strauss: *Capriccio*
Britten: *Peter Grimes*
Stravinsky: *The Rake's Progress*
Britten: *Billy Budd*
Menotti: *Amahl and the Night Visitors*
Floyd: *Susannah*
Moore: *The Ballad of Baby Doe*
Bernstein: *Candide*
Poulenc: *Dialogues of the Carmelites*
Prokofiev: *War and Peace*
Barber: *Vanessa*
Britten: *A Midsummer Night's Dream*
Ward: *The Crucible*

Recent and Current Operas
Glass: *Satyagraha*
Adams: *Nixon in China*
Catán: *Florencia en el Amazonas*
Adamo: *Little Women*
Harbison: *The Great Gatsby*
Saariaho: *L'Amour de loin*
Heggie: *Dead Man Walking*
Golijov: *Ainadamar*
Adés: *The Tempest*
Adams: *Dr. Atomic*
Rorem: *Our Town*
Tan Dun: *The First Emperor*
Heggie: *Moby Dick*
Laitman: *The Scarlet Letter*

Betsy Schwarm

V. Acknowledgements

Thanks to my family: Rick, Colin, Conor, and even Ferdi and Clara, for letting me talk about music, identify classical bits that go by on the television, and spend hours at the computer. The furry kids love that I am a writer, as it keeps me around the house a lot and they have company – even if that "company" is busy writing.

VI. Author Biographical Notes

With degrees in history and humanities, Betsy Schwarm has worked in classical music in various capacities since 1984, including:

- Classical radio announcer/producer, especially at KVOD, "The Classical Voice of Denver"
- Music department faculty at Metropolitan State University of Denver
- Pre-performance speaker for the Colorado Symphony, Opera Colorado, the Newman Center for the Performing Arts, the Colorado Music Festival, the Bravo Vail Valley Festival, and other organizations
- Program annotator for the Colorado Symphony, Opera Colorado, Cleveland Orchestra, the Huntsville Symphony, the Philharmonic Society of Orange County, the Phoenix Symphony, and other organizations
- Recording engineer for the Central City Opera
- Freelance reporter with National Public Radio

This book represents not quite ten percent of Ms. Schwarm's catalog of concert program notes for classical works. To see the full list, please visit her website: www.classicalmusicinsights.com.

More Classical Insights

Index

Abignale, Frank Jr.
  – 124-125
Adagio for Strings – 50, 214
Adams, John – 10,
  Hallelujah Junction
  –190-191
Afro-American Symphony
  – 46-47
Agee, James – 213-214
Aida – 144
Aladdin – 267-268
Albeniz, Isaac – 179
Alexander Nevsky – 284
Allsburg, Chris van – 283
An Alpine Symphony – 70
Also Sprach Zarathustra
  – 1, 70-72
Alto Rhapsody – 332
Amahl and the Night
  Visitors – 251
An American in Paris
  – 79, 83-84
Amèriques – 79-80
Andersen, Hans Christian
  – 203
Anisimova, Nina – 313
Anne, Queen of England
  – 322
Argento, Dominic – 10
  Walden Pond – 343-344
Ariadne auf Naxos
  – 245-246
Auberjonois, René – 271
Auer, Leopold – 105-106
Ave Maria – 319-320

Bach, Carl Philipp Emanuel
  – 57, 136
Bach, Johann Christian
  – 7
  Six Sonatas, op. 10
  – 136-137
Bach, Johann Christian
  Friedrich – 136
Bach, Johann Sebastian
  – 4, 7, 12, 54, 55, 57,
  94, 123, 136, 149,
  157, 167, 183, 186,
  188, 240, 327, 354
  Cantata #80 "Feste Burg"
  – 320-322, 327
  Chaconne – 129, 133-134
  Clavier-Übung – 169
  Double Concerto in d
  – 94-96
  Goldberg Variations
  – 168-169
  Partitas and Sonatas – 132
Bach, Wilhelm Friedemann
  – 136, 168, 322
Balfe, Michael – 7, 236
  The Bohemian Girl
  – 230-231, 236
Ballets Russe – 300
Balmont, Konstantin – 336
Barber, Samuel – 10
  Adagio for Strings – 50,
  214
  Violin Concerto – 120-121
  Knoxville: Summer of
  1913 – 213-214
  Symphony no. 1 – 49-50
The Barber of Seville – 231
Les barricades misterieuses
  – 167
Barry, John – 10
  Bond films – 282
  Born Free – 281
  Dances with Wolves
  – 281-282
  The Lion in Winter – 281
  Out of Africa – 281, 305

Bartók, Béla – 5, 9, 164, 352
Concerto for Orchestra
– 111-112
Contrasts – 152-153
Rumanian Dances
– 303-304
Baumel, Herbert – 120
Beach, Amy Cheney – 8
"Dark is the Night" – 41
Gaelic Symphony – 40-41
Becket, Samuel – 160
Beethoven, Ludwig van
– 2, 4, 6, 7, 11, 13,
17, 24, 38, 48, 50,
119, 130, 166, 172,
173, 179, 200, 258,
286, 329
Ah, Perfido – 23
Choral Fantasia – 23
*Christ on the Mount
of Olives* – 317,
327-328
Piano Concerto no. 4 – 23
Triple Concerto in C
– 97-99
Egmont – 258, 261-263
Fidelio – 61
Leonore Overture no. 3
– 60-62, 64
Mass in C – 23
String Quartets,
"Razumovsky"
– 140-142
Cello Sonata in A – 23
Piano Sonata no. 14 in c#,
"Moonlight"
– 171-172
Symphony no. 3 "Eroica"
– 20-22
Symphony no. 5 – 12, 23 ,
142, 173
Symphony no. 6
"Pastorale"
– 22-24, 81, 142,
348
Symphony no. 9 "Choral"
– 48

Piano Trios, op. 70 - 23
Belasco, David
Bell, Mary Hayley – 269
Bellini, Vincenzo – 7,
I Capuleti e i Montecchi
– 226-229
Norma – 227
La Sonnambula - 227
The Bells – 335-337
Benois, Alexander – 306
Berlioz, Hector – 7, 65
Benvenuto Cellini – 63
Harold in Italy – 27
Les Nuits d'ete – 197-198
Requiem – 329-330
Roman Carnival Overture
– 60-61
Romeo and Juliet, op. 16
– 26-27
Symphonie fantastique
– 198, 329
Les Troyens – 62, 229-230
Bernstein, Leonard
– 10, 46, 352, 354
Fancy Free – 275
On the Town – 275
Prelude, Fugue and Riffs
– 121-122
Billy the Kid – 311-312
Bizet, Georges – 180
Black, Brown and Beige
– 83-84
Boccaccio – 190
The Bohemian Girl
– 230-231, 236
Bolcom, William – 10
Cabaret Songs – 216-217
Bond films – 281
Börlin, Jean – 310
Born Free – 281
Borodin, Alexander – 7, 287,
298
Polovtsian Dances – 287,
292-293
Botticelli, Sandro – 76-77

More Classical Insights

Brahms, Johannes
   – 5, 7, 30, 44, 48,
   110, 121, 134, 199,
   268, 314, 352
Alto Rhapsody – 332
Double Concerto in a
   – 102-103
Lullaby – 192, 200-201
Schicksalslied – 332-333
Five Songs, op. 49
   – 200-201
Symphony no. 1 – 333
Symphony no. 4 – 31-32
Horn Trio, op. 40
   – 145 -146
Brando, Marlon – 253
A Brief History of Time
   – 282
Brigadoon – 249
Briselli, Iso – 120-121
Britten, Benjamin – 10, 110,
   254, 277
War Requiem – 341-342
Winter Words – 215-216
Brodsky, Adolph – 105-106
Brouwer, Leo – 10,
El Decameron Negro
   – 190
Bruch, Max – 8
Kol Nidrei – 104
Violin Concerto in g – 105
Scottish Fantasia
   – 104-105
Burghauser, Hugo – 108-109
Butterworth, George – 9
A Shropshire Lad – 211
Byron, Lord – 264-265

Cabaret Songs – 216-217
Cain, Henri – 241
Calm Sea and Prosperous
   Voyage – 63-64
Cantata no. 80 "Feste Burg"
Capriccio espagnole – 68

Capriccio italien – 66
I Capuleti e i Montecchi
   – 226-229
Carneval, op. 9 – 175-176
Carnival of the Animals
   – 64-65
Carnival Overture – 67-68
Caruso, Enrico – 243
Castelnuovo-Tedesco, Mario
   – 9, 278
Guitar Concerto no. 1
   – 114-115
Catán, Daniel – 10
Florencia en el Amazonas
   – 255
Il Postino – 254-255
Cavafy, Constantine – 219
Cazalis, Hneri – 293
Cellini, Benvenuto – 63
Cendrars, Blaise – 310
Cendrillon (Cinderella)
   (Massenet)
   – 241 – 242
Chaconne – 129, 133-134
Chadwick, George – 46
Chaminade, Cecile – 8,
Etudes de concert
   – 180-181
Chanson perpétuelle
   – 204-206
Charles, Prince of England
   87
Chausson, Ernest – 8
Chanson perpétuelle
   – 204-206
Chézy, Helmina von – 197,
   263
Chopin, Frederic – 7, 178,
   179, 183, 186
Piano Concerto no. 1 in e
   – 100-101
Christ on the Mount
   of Olives – 317,
   327-328
Cinderella (Prokofiev) –
   308-309
Clavier-Übung – 169

La Clemenza di Tito
– 222-224
Close Encounters of the Third Kind – 279
Cloudburst – 347-348
Colloredo, Prince-Archbishop of Salzburg – 326
Concertos:
   Clarinet (Mozart) – 137
   Double (JS Bach) – 94-96
   Double (Brahms)
   – 102-103
   Duett-Concertino (Strauss)
   – 108-109
   Escapades (Williams)
   – 124-125
   Flute (Ibert) – 113-114
   Guitar (Castelnuovo-Tedesco) – 114-115
   English Horn (Donizetti)
   – 99-100
   Orchestra (Bartók)
   – 111-112
   Piano no. 1 (Chopin)
   – 100-101
   Piano (Gershwin) – 117 118
   Piano (Grieg) – 91, 107-108
   Piano no. 1 (Shostakovich)
   – 118-119
   Piano no. 2 (Rachmaninoff)
   – 335
   Piano no. 17 (Mozart)
   – 96-97
   Piano – left hand (Ravel)
   – 109-110
   Prelude, Fugue & Riffs (Bernstein)
   – 121-122
   Triple (Beethoven) – 97-99
   Trombone (Zwilich)
   – 125-127
   Veni veni Emanuel (MacMillan)
   – 127-128

   Violin (Barber) – 120-121
   Violin (Korngold)
   – 115-117
   Violin (Rautavaara)
   – 122-123
   Violin (Tchaikovsky)
   – 105-106
   Four Violins (Vivaldi)
   – 93-94
Concertpiece for four horns
   – 102
Contrasts – 152-153
Coolidge, Elizabeth Sprague
   – 77
Copland, Aaron – 9
   Billy the Kid – 311-312
   The Heiress – 273
   Music from Movies
   – 273-274
   Rodeo – 311
   12 Songs of Emily Dickinson
   – 212-213
   The Tender Land
   – 249-250
Coppélia – 265
Corelli, Arcangelo – 6
   Trio Sonatas, op. 1, 3 & 4
   –130-131

Costner, Kevin – 281
Couperin, François – 6, 75, 151, 266, 294
   Pieces de clavecin, Book 2
   – 167-168
The Creation (Handel) – 325
La Creation du monde (Milhaud)
   – 309-311
Cros, Charles – 205

Dance of the Seven Veils
   – 297-298

More Classical Insights

Dances of Galanta – 304-305
Dances with Wolves
    – 281-282
Danse macabre – 293
Dante – 35
Daphnis and Chloe – 300
Daugherty, Michael – 10
    Jackie O – 50
    Metropolis Symphony
        – 50-51
    Motor City Triptych – 50
    Niagara Falls – 50
    Route 66 – 50
El Decameron Negro – 190
Debussy, Claude – 8, 43, 72,
    77, 158, 276
    Prelude to the Afternoon
        of a Faun – 183
    Preludes – 183
    Sonata flute/viola/harp
        – 150-152
Deprez, Josquin –
    see Josquin Desprez
Delibes, Leo – 8
    Coppélia – 265
    Lakme – 265
    Le roi s'amuse – 265-266
deMille, Agnes
Deutsch, Otto – 12, 173
Diaghilev, Sergei – 300, 306
DiCaprio, Leonard – 124-125
Dickinson, Emily – 212-213,
    217-218
Dido and Aeneas – 261
Dion, Celine – 284
Dohnanyi, Christoph von
    – 305
Dohnanyi, Ernst von – 305
Domingo, Placido – 255
Don Giovanni – 39
Donizetti, Gaetano – 7, 227
    The Elixir of Love – 99
    English Horn Concertino
        – 99-100
    Lucia di Lammermoor
        – 99
Downes, Olin – 248

Dreams and Prayers of
    Isaac the Blind
    – 161-162
DreamWaltzes – 314-315
Duett-Concertino – 108-109
Dukas, Paul – 8, 58
    The Sorcerer's Apprentice
        – 58, 72-73
Dvořák, Antonín – 8, 38-39
    Carnival Overture – 67-68
    Gypsy Melodies – 201-202
    In Nature's Realm – 67
    Othello – 67
    Piano Trio "Dumky"
        – 147-149
    Stabat Mater – 33
    Symphony no. 8 – 34-35
    Symphony no. 9 – 35
    Prague Waltzes – 296

Edward VII of England
    – 70, 204
Egmont – 258, 261-263
Elgar, Sir Edward – 8,
    Enigma Variations – 69
    In the South – 69-70
    Pomp and Circumstance
        – 69
The Elixir of Love – 99
Eliot, TS - 193
Elizabeth II of England – 87
Ellington, Edward "Duke" –
    9, 86, 191
    Black, Brown, and Beige
        – 85
Enesco, Georges – 9
    Rumanian Rhapsodies
        – 78
Enigma Variations – 69
Esterhazy, Prince Nikolaus
    – 16, 134, 135,
    324-325
ET – 279
Etudes de Concert – 180-181
Eugene Onegin – 237

The Fairy Queen – 260-262
Falla, Manuel de – 9
7 Popular Spanish Songs – 210
The Three-Cornered Hat – 302-303
La Fanciulla del West – 242-244
Fancy Free – 275
Fantasia on a Theme of Thomas Tallis – 42, 74-75
Far Away Songs –218-219
Feeney, Philip – 10
The Hunchback of Notre Dame – 315-316
Feinzimmer, Alexander – 272
Finian's Rainbow – 249
The Firebird – 306
Die Fledermaus – 236-137
Fleming, Renee – 254
Florencia en el Amazonas – 255
Flynn, Errol – 115
Franck, Cesar – 7, 205
 Symphony in d – 30-31, 84
Frank, Gabriela Lena – 11
 Leyendas – An Andean Walkabout – 163-164
Frank, Salomo – 321
Frend, Charles – 269
Frobenius, Leon – 190
Frost, Robert – 212, 340
Frostiana – 340

Gautier, Théophile – 197-198
Gayne – 313-314
George I and George II of England – 322
Gershwin, George – 9, 79, 83, 86

An American in Paris – 79, 83-84
 Piano Concerto in F – 117-118
 Rhapsody in Blue – 83, 117
Gilbert, William S. – 239-240, 167
Gilfry, Rodney – 254
Glass, Philip – 10, 217
 A Brief History of Time – 282
 The Hours – 160, 282-283
 Koyaanisqatsi – 160, 282
 Kundun – 282
 Mishima – 160
 String Quartet no. 2, "Company" – 160
 The Thin Blue Line – 160
Glazunov, Alexander – 8, 292
 The Seasons – 298-299
Glennie, Evelyn – 127
Gliere, Reinhold – 9
 The Red Poppy – 301-302
Goethe, Johann von – 63, 73, 199, 258, 261-263, 264, 270, 335
Goldberg, Johann Gottlieb – 168 -169
Goldberg Variations – 168-169
Goldsmith, Jerry – 10, 115
 Patton – 278-279
Golijov, Osvaldo – 10,
 Dreams and Prayers of Isaac the Blind – 161-162
Good Friday Spell – 232-233
Goodman, Benny – 122, 151-152, 352
Górecki, Henryk – 10,
 Symphony no. 3 – 50-52
Gottschalk, Louis – 7
 The Union – 178-179
Gounod, Charles – 280
Goyescas – 184-185

Granados, Enrique – 8, 179
  Goyescas – 184-185
Grand Canyon Suite – 82-83
Greenberg, Jay – 2, 11,
  Symphony no. 5 – 53-55
Grieg, Edvard – 8, 274
  Piano Concerto in a – 91,
    107-108
  Heart's Melodies, op. 5
    – 202-203
  Peer Gynt – 274
Grimm Brothers – 241
Grisi, Giuditta – 228
Grofé, Ferde – 9,
  Grand Canyon Suite
    – 82-83
Guicciardi, Giulietta – 171
The Gypsy Baron – 235-236
Gypsy Melodies –201-202

Haffner, Elisabeth and
  Siegmund – 139
Hallelujah Junction
  – 190-191
Hammerstein, Oscar II
  – 250
Hampton, Lionel – 125
Handel, George Frideric
  – 7, 60, 317, 324
  Messiah – 317, 324, 325
  Zadok the Priest –
    322-323
Hansel und Gretel – 241
Hanslick, Eduard – 31, 106
Happiness – 314
Hapsburg, Archduke Rudolf
  von – 98-99
Hardy, Thomas – 215-216
Harold in Italy – 27
Hausman, Robert – 103
Haydn, Franz Joseph – 7, 20,
  119, 157
  The Creation – 325
  Mass in Time of War
    – 324-325

  String Quartet "Lark"
    – 134-135
  The Seasons – 324-325
  Seven Last Words of
    Christ – 210
  Symphony no. 101 in D,
    "Clock" – 16-17
  Heart's Melodies – 202-203
Heifetz, Jascha – 116
Heine, Heinrich – 199
The Heiress – 273
Hepburn, Katharine – 281
Herman, Woody – 122
Herrmann, Bernard – 260
Hindemith, Paul – 9
  Sonatas – 154-155
Der Hirt auf den Felsen
  – 196-197
HMS Pinafore – 239, 267
Hofmannsthal, Hugo von
  – 245-246
Holderlin, Friedrich – 332
Homer, Louise – 214
Honegger, Arthur – 9, 153
  Pastorale d'ete – 81-82
Horner, James – 10
  Apollo 13 – 284
  Avatar – 284
  Titanic – 284
The Hours – 160, 282-183
Houseman, AE – 211
Howard, Ron – 351
Huber, Franz Xaver – 327
Hughes, Langston – 248
Hugo, Victor – 266
Humperdinck, Englebert
  – 241
  The Hunchback of
    Notre Dame
      – 315-316
Hunt, James – 351
Hüttenbrenner, Anselm – 25

Ibert, Jacques – 9
　Flute Concerto – 113-114
Indiana Jones – 279
d'Indy, Vincent – 8
　*Symphony on a French
　Mountain Air*
　– 36-37
In Nature's Realm – 67
Isbin, Sharon – 190

Janissary Bands – 170
Jarre, Maurice – 10
　Lawrence of Arabia
　– 276-277
Javelin – 88-89
Jaws – 279
Jazz Suites – 86-87
Jenkins, Karl – 10
　Palladio – 87-88
Joachim, Joseph – 103
Jókai, Maurus – 236
Josquin Desprez – 6, 318
　Ave Maria – 319-320
Jurassic Park – 279

Kelly, Gene – 84, 275
Keyserling, Count – 168
Khachaturian, Aram – 9, 277
　Gayne – 313-314
　Happiness – 314
　Spartacus – 313
Kidman, Nicole – 282
Kismet – 287
Klingsor, Tristan – 209
Knoxville: Summer of 1913
　– 213-214
Kodaly, Zoltan – 9
　Dances of Galanta
　– 304-305
Köchel, Ludwig – 12
Kol Nidrei – 104
Korngold, Erich – 9, 110, 260
　Violin Concerto 115-116
Kotek, Josif – 105

Koussevitsky, Serge – 46, 214, 337
Koyaanisqatsi – 159
Kubrick, Stanley – 1, 71
Kundun – 282

Lady Macbeth of Mtsensk
　– 158
Laitman, Lori – 10
　Four Dickinson Songs –
　217-218
Lakme – 265
Lanner, Joseph – 7, 308
　Die Mozartisten
　– 288-290
Lauda, Niki – 3551
Lawrence of Arabia
　– 276-277
Lean David – 276
Léger, Fernand – 310
Leigh, Vivien – 253
Leonora Overture no. 3 –
　60-62
Leopold II of Austria – 222
Lewis, Jerry Lee – 166
*Leyendas – An Andean
　Walkabout*
　– 163-164
*Lieder eines fahrenden
　Gesellen* – 206-207
Lincoln – 279-280
The Lion in Winter – 281
Liszt, Franz – 7, 107-108, 175, 183, 293
　Piano Sonata in b
　– 177-178
Lobkowitz, Prince Franz von
　– 21, 99
Louis XIV & Louis XV of
　France – 132, 151
Lt. Kije – 272-273
Lucas, George – 279
Lucia di Lammermoor – 99
Lullaby (Brahms) – 192, 200-201, 352
Lux aurumque – 347

More Classical Insights

M*A*S*H – 137
Macbeth – 234-235
MacDowell, Edward – 8
   Woodland Sketches
      –181-182
MacMillan, James – 10
   Strathclyde Motets
      – 346
   Veni veni emanuel
      – 127-128
Madama Butterfly – 243
Maffei, Andrea – 235
Mahler, Gustav – 8, 48
   Lieder eines fahrenden
      Gesellen – 206-207
   Symphony no. 1, "Titan"
      – 37-38, 207
Manfred – 264-265
Manon Lescaut – 243
Marais, Marin – 6, 151
   La Sonnerie du Ste.
      Genevieve du Mont
      du Paris – 132
Marsalis, Branford – 124
Marsalis, Wynton – 11
   Swing Symphony – 52-53
Mary Queen of Scots – 28
Mass in Time of War
      – 324-325
Massenet, Jules – 8, 205
   Cendrillon (Cinderella)
      – 241-242
   Thais – 242
Mazzola, Caterino – 223
Meck, Nadezhda von – 66
Melville, Herman – 159
Mendelssohn, Felix – 7, 102,
   179, 267, 350-354
   Calm Sea and Prosperous
      Voyage – 63-64
   Part songs – 331
   Songs without Words
      – 174-175
   Symphony no. 3, "Scottish"
      – 26-27
Menotti, Gian Carlo – 10

Amahl and the Night
      Visitors – 251
   The Saint of Bleecker
      Street – 251-253
Menuhin, Yehudi – 112
Messiaen, Olivier – 9, 158,
   165
   Turangalîla Symphony
      – 45-46
   Vingt Regards sur l'enfant
      Jésus – 188-189
Messiah
Metastasio, Pietro – 223
Metropolis Symphony
      – 52-53
The Mikado – 239-240, 267
Milder-Hauptmann, Anna
      – 196
Milhaud, Darius – 9, 153
   La Creation du monde
      – 309-311
Mills, Hayley – 269
Mills, Sir John – 269
Les Miserables – 221
Mishima – 160
Moliere – 245
Montegue, Ivor – 269
Moore, Julianne – 282
Morris, Joan – 216
Quatre motets pour le temps
      de Noël – 339-340
Moÿse, Marcel – 113
Mozart, Constanze
      – 17-18, 138, 224
Mozart, Leopold – 18-19
Mozart, Wolfgang Amadeus
      – 2, 4, 6, 7, 12, 13,
      15, 37, 54, 55, 56,
      108, 109, 118, 125,
      126, 130, 136, 144,
      154, 157, 165, 166,
      187, 220, 290, 355,
      352
   La Clemenza di Tito
      – 222-224
   Clarinet Concerto – 137

Piano Concerto no. 17 in G
  – 96-97
Don Giovanni – 37, 289
Eine kleine Nachtmusik
  – 139-140
The Magic Flute – 222,
  289
Clarinet Quintet in A –
  137-138, 152
Requiem – 222
Serenade in D, K. 250,
  "Haffner" – 139-140
Solemn Vespers of a
  Confessor
  – 326-327
Sonata in a, Alla Turca"
  – 165, 169-170
Sonata for Two Pianos,
  K. 448 – 96
Symphony no. 36, "Linz"
  – 17-19
Die Mozartisten – 288-290
Muhly, Nico – 11, 355
  Far Away Songs 218-219
Müller, Wilhelm – 194, 195
Munshin, Jules – 275
Music from Movies
  – 273-274
Mussorgsky, Modest – 76
Mutter, Anne Sophie – 254

Nabucco – 235
Napoleon – 20, 21, 59, 262,
  325
Nash, Ogden – 65
Naxos Music Library – 354
Neruda, Pablo – 255
Neupert, Edmund – 107
Newman, Maria – 11,
  Pennipotenti –162-163
Nielsen, Carl – 8,
  Aladdin – 267-268
Nietzsche, Friedrich – 71-72
Nijinsky, Vaclav – 307

Norma – 227
Les Nuits d'ete –197-198

O come, Emanuel – 75
Ode to the Virginian Voyage
  – 340
Oehlenschläger, Adam – 268
Offenbach, Jacques – 65
On the Town – 275
ondes Martenot – 48, 277
Othello (Dvořák) – 67
O'Toole, Peter – 281
Out of Africa – 281
Owen, Wilfred – 341-342

Paganini, Nicolo – 27, 121,
  305
Paisiello, Giovanni – 96
Palladio – 87-88
Paltrow, Gwyneth – 256
Parsifal – 232-233
Part Songs – 331
Partitas and Sonatas
  (JS Bach) – 133
Pastorale d'ete – 81-82
Patton – 278-279
Paul, Jean – 35
Pavlova, Anna – 63
Paz, Octavio – 347
Peanuts® – 174
Pears, Peter – 215-216, 342
Peer Gynt – 274
Pennipotenti – 162-163
Pergolesi, Giovanni – 7
  Stabat mater – 323-324
Perrault, Charles – 241
Petipa, Marius – 299
Petri, Endre – 152
Petrushka – 306-308

More Classical Insights

Piave, Francesco – 234-235
Pictures at an Exhibition
  – 76
Pieces de clavecin – 167-168
Pink, Michael – 316
Pirates of the Caribbean
  – 285-286
The Pirates of Penzance
  – 239, 167
Ployer, Barbara von – 96-97
The Polar Express – 283
Polovtsian Dances – 287,
  292-293, 352
*Pomp and Circumstance
  March* – 69
Poe, Edgar Allen – 73,
  335-336
Portman, Rachel – 10
The Little Prince
  – 256-257
Il Postino – 254-255
Poulenc, Francis – 9, 153
*Quatre motets pour le
  temps de Noël*
  – 339-340
Prague Waltzes – 296
Prelude, Fugue and Riffs
  – 121-122
Preludes:
  Preludes (Debussy) – 183
  Preludes (Rachmaninoff)
  – 185-186
  Preludes and Etudes
  (Villa Lobos)
  – 186-187
  Preludes and Fugues
  (Shostakovich)
  – 187-188
*Prelude to the Afternoon of a
  Faun* – 183
Previn, Andre – 10
A Streetcar Named Desire
  – 253-254
The Little Prince – 256-257
Prokofiev, Sergei – 9, 110,
  158, 284, 298, 301
  Alexander Nevsky – 284

Cinderella – 308-309
Lt. Kije – 272-273
Symphony no. 5 – 44-45
War and Peace – 309
Puccini, Giacomo – 8, 114,
  208, 248, 249, 252,
  255
La Bohéme – 243
La Fanciulla del West
  – 242-244
Madama Butterfly – 243
Manon Lescaut – 243
Tosca – 242
Turandot – 243
Purcell, Henry – 6
Dido and Aeneas – 261
The Fairy Queen
  – 260-261
Pushkin, Alexander – 237
Puts, Kevin – 11
River's Rush – 90

Quartets:
  Unnumbered (Tailleferre)
  – 153-154
  no. 2 "Company" (Glass)
  – 160
  no. 3 (Ullmann) – 156-157
  in e (Verdi) – 143-145
  Lark (Haydn) – 134-135
  Razumovsky (Beethoven)
  – 140-142
The Queen of Spades
  – 237-238
Clarinet Quintet in A
  – 137-138
Piano Quintet in g – 157-158
String Quintet in C – 142-143

Rachmaninoff, Sergei – 8,
    144, 298, 335
  The Bells – 335-337
  Piano Concerto no. 2 – 335
  Preludes – 185-186
Ramuz, CF – 271
Rautavaara, Einojuhani – 10
  Violin Concerto – 122-123
Ravel, Maurice – 8, 276. 315
  Piano Concerto for
    Left Hand
    – 109-110
  Daphnis and Chloe – 300
  Sheherazade – 208-209
  Le Tombeau de Couperin
    – 75-76, 111
  La Valse – 299-300, 315
Razumovsky, Count Andreas
    – 140-141
Recuerdos de la Alhambra
    – 179-180
The Red Poppy – 301-302
Reiner, Fritz – 111
Reinhardt, Max – 116,
    245-246
Requiem (Berlioz) – 329-330
Requiem (Britten) – 341-342
Requiem (Mozart) – 221, 326
Respighi, Ottorino – 9
  Trittico Botticelliana
    – 77
Rice, Elmer – 248
Richter, Johanna – 207
Ricordi Publishing – 243
Ries, Ferdinand – 21, 329
Rigoletto – 234
Rimsky-Korsakov, Nicolai
    – 8, 33, 209, 268,
    292, 298
  Capriccio espagnole – 68
  Russian Easter Overture
    – 68-69
  Scheherazade – 68, 268
  The Rite of Spring – 306
  River's Rush – 90
  Rodeo – 311
Rodgers, Richard – 250

Le roi s'amuse – 265-266
Roman Carnival Overture
    – 62-63
Romani, Felice – 227
Romeo and Juliet (Berlioz)
    – 26-27
Romeo and Juliet
    (Prokofiev) – 308
Rondo alla Turca – 165, 170
Rosamunde – 263-264
Der Rosenkavalier – 108,
    245
Roses of the South – 290-291
Rossini, Gioacchino – 7, 99,
    221, 226, 240, 247,
    323
  The Barber of Seville – 231
  William Tell – 225-226
Rózsa, Miklós – 260, 278
Rubenstein, Ida – 300
Rubinstein, Artur – 143
Rückert, Friedrich – 199
Rumanian Dances (Bartók)
    – 303-304
Rumanian Rhapsodies
    (Enesco) – 78
Russian Easter Overture
    – 68-69
Rutter, John – 10
  When Icicles Hang
    – 344-345

The Saint of Bleecker Street
    – 251-253
Saint-Saëns, Camille – 7, 36
  Carnival of the Animals
    – 64-65
  Danse Macabre – 293
  woodwind sonatas
    – 146-147
  Symphony no. 3 – 34
Salome – 297-298
Salomon, Johann Peter – 16
Sarasate, Pablo de – 105

More Classical Insights

Saving Private Ryan – 279
Scheherazade (Rimsky)
  – 68, 268
Schicksalslied – 332-333
Schiller, Friedrich von
  – 225, 264
Schindler, Anton – 98
Schindler's List – 279
Schmidt, Alexander – 119
Schoenberg, Arnold – 156, 292
Schubert, Franz – 7, 12, 14, 192, 206, 219, 352
  Wanderer Fantasy – 25, 172-173
  Der Hirt auf den Felsen – 196-197
  String Quintet in C – 142-143
  Rosamunde – 263-264
  Symphony no. 8 in b, "Unfinished" – 14, 24-26, 352
  Der Winterreise – 193-195
Schumann, Clara Wieck – 7, 103, 110, 175-176, 177
  Songs from Liebesfrühling – 199-200
Schumann, Robert – 7,
  Carneval, op. 9 – 175-176
  Concertpiece for 4 horns – 102
  Manfred – 264-265
  Songs from Liebesfrühling – 199-200
Schuppanzigh, Ignaz – 141
Scott, George C. – 278
Scott, Sir Walter – 104
Scott of the Antarctic – 268-270
Scottish Fantasia – 104-105
Scriabin, Alexander – 110
The Seasons – 298-299
The Secret of Susanna – 246-247

Segovia, Andras – 114, 179, 1867
Serenade in D, "Haffner" –139-140
Serenade to Music – 333-335
Seven Last Words of Christ – 210
Shakespeare, William
  – 26-27, 227, 234-235, 237, 261, 264, 266-267, 318, 333, 335
Sheherazade (Ravel)
  – 208-209
Shostakovich, Dmitri – 9, 298
  Piano Concerto no. 1 – 118-119
  Jazz Suites – 86
  Lady Macbeth of Mtsensk – 158
  Preludes and Fugues – 187-188
  Piano Quintet in g – 157-158
A Shropshire Lad – 211
Sibelius, Jan – 8, 48, 122-123
  Finlandia – 38
  Symphony no. 2 in D – 38-39
Silvestri, Alan – 10
  The Abyss – 283
  Back to the Future – 283
  Beowulf – 283
  Forrest Gump – 283
  The Polar Express – 283
Simrock – 33 , 202
Sinatra, Frank – 275
Sinfonia Antartica – 270
Sinfonia Sevillana – 43-44
Les Six – 153
Sixty Minutes – 54
Skármeta, Antonio – 255
Slatkin, Leonard – 315
Smithson, Harriet – 26
The Soldier's Tale – 270-272

395

Im Sommerwind – 80-81
Solemn Vespers of a
  Confessor
  – 326-327
Sonatas:
  Sonatas, op. 10 (JC Bach)
  – 136-137
  Flute, viola & harp
  (Debussy)
  – 150-151
  Piano in b (Liszt) – 177-178
  Piano "Alla turca" (Mozart)
  – 165, 169-170
  Piano "Moonlight"
  (Beethoven)
  – 171-172
  Trio sonatas (Corelli)
  – 130-131
  solo violin (Ysaÿe)
  – 149-150
  various (Hindemith)
  – 154-155
  woodwind (Saint-Saëns)
  – 146-147
Sondheim, Steven – 160
Songs:
  Cabaret (Bolcom)
  – 216-217
  Chanson perpétuelle
  (Chausson)
  – 204-206
  Dickinson Songs
  (Copland)
  – 212-213
  Dickinson Songs
  (Laitman)
  – 217-218
  Far Away Songs (Muhly)
  – 218-219
  Fahrenden Gesellen
  (Mahler) – 206-207
  Gypsy Melodies (Dvořák)
  – 201-202
  Heart's Memories (Grieg)
  – 202-203
  Der Hit auf den Felsen
  (Schubert)

  – 196-197
  Knoxville Summer of 1913
  (Barber) – 213-214
  Liebesfrühling
  (Schumann)
  – 199-200
  Lieder eines fahrenden
  Gesellen (Mahler)
  – 206-207
  Les Nuits d'été (Berlioz)
  – 197-198
  Sheherazade (Ravel)
  – 208-209
  Shropshire Lad
  (Butterworth) – 211
  Part Songs (Mendelssohn)
  Six Songs, op. 27 (Strauss)
  – 207-208
  Five Songs, op. 49
  (Brahms)
  – 200-201
  Spanish Songs (Falla)
  – 210
  Winter Words (Britten)
  – 215-216
  Der Winterreise
  (Schubert)
  – 193-195
  Songs my Mother Taught
  Me – 202
  Songs without Words
  – 174-175
  Swan Lake – 294-295
  La Sonnambula – 227
  La sonnerie du Ste.
    Genevieve du Mont
    du Paris – 132
  The Sorcerer's Apprentice
  – 72-73
Souchay, Marc-Andre
  – 174, 350
In the South – 69-70
Spartacus – 313
Spielberg, Steven – 124, 279-280
St. Exupéry, Antoine de
  – 256

More Classical Insights

Stabat Mater (Pergolesi)
– 323-324
Stadler, Anton – 137-138
Stalin, Joseph – 45
Star Wars – 279
Steber, Eleanor – 214
Steinbeck, John – 274
Still, William Grant – 9
 Afro-American Symphony
  – 46-47
Stokowski, Leopold – 77
Stolz, Teresa – 144
The Stone Flower – 308
Strathclyde Motets
  – 346
Strauss, Johann Jr. – 7, 288,
  296, 300
 Die Fledermaus – 236-237
 The Gypsy Baron
  – 236-237
 Roses of the South
  – 290-291
Strauss, Johann Sr. – 289,
  290
Strauss, Richard – 1, 8, 110,
  192, 199, 314
 An Alpine Symphony – 70
 Also sprach Zarathustra
  – 1, 70-72
 Ariadne auf Naxos
  – 245-246
 Duett-Concertino
  – 108-109
 Dance of the Seven Veils
  – 297-298
 Der Rosenkavalier – 245
 Six Songs, op. 27
  – 207-208
 Till Eulenspeigel – 208
Stravinsky, Igor – 5, 6, 9, 62,
  77, 123, 301, 309
 The Firebird – 306
 Petrushka – 306-308
 The Rite of Spring – 306
 The Soldier's Tale
  – 270-272
 Symphony of Psalms

– 337-338
Streep, Meryl – 282
Street Scene – 248-249
A Streetcar Named Desire
  – 253-254
Stucky, Steven – 10
 DreamWaltzes – 314-315
Sullivan, Sir Arthur – 8
 HMS Pinafore – 239, 267
 The Mikado – 239-240,
  267
 The Pirates of Penzance
  – 239, 267
 Shakespearean scores
  – 266-267
Superman – 279
Swan Lake – 294-295
Swing Symphony – 54-55
Symphonies:
 Afro-American Symphony
  (Still) – 46-47
 French Mountain Air
  (D'Indy) – 36-37
 Gaelic (Beach) – 40-41
 Metropolis (Daugherty)
  – 50-51
 No. 1 (Barber) – 49-50
 No. 1 "Titan" (Mahler)
  – 37-38, 207
 No. 1 (Brahms) – 333
 No. 2 (Sibelius) – 36-37
 No. 2 "London"
  (Vaughan Williams)
  – 42-43
 No. 3 "Eroica" (Beethoven)
  – 20-22
 No. 3 "Scottish"
  (Mendelssohn)
  – 28-29
 No. 3 (Gorecki) – 50-52
 No. 4 (Brahms) – 31-32
 No. 5 (Beethoven) – 12,
  142, 173
 No. 5 (Prokofiev) – 44-45
 No. 5 (Greenberg) – 53-55
 No. 6 "Pastorale"
  (Beethoven)

– 22-24, 142, 348
No. 6 "Pathetique"
(Tchaikovsky)
– 32-34, 106
No. 8 "Unfinished"
(Schubert) – 24-25
No. 8 (Dvořák) – 34-35
No. 9 (Dvořák) – 35
No. 36 "Linz" (Mozart)
– 17-19
No. 101 "Clock" (Haydn)
– 16-17
Romeo and Juliet (Berlioz)
– 26-27
Sinfonia Sevillana
(Turina) – 43-44
Swing Symphony
(Marsalis) 54-55
Symphony in d (Franck)
– 30-31, 84
Turangalîla Symphony
(Messiaen) – 47-47
Symphony of Psalms
(Stravinsky)
– 337-338
Symphonie fantastique
– 198
Szigeti, Joseph – 111,
149-150, 152-153

Tafelmusik – 59-60
Tailleferre, Germaine – 9
String Quartet – 153-154
Takemitsu, Toru – 10
Toward the Sea – 158-159
Tallis, Thomas – 74
Tárrega, Francisco – 8
Recuerdos de la Alhambra
– 179-180
Tchaikovsky, Modest
– 32-33, 237
Tchaikovsky, Peter – 8, 92,
121, 299, 309

Capriccio Italian – 66
Violin Concerto in D
– 105-106
Eugene Onegin – 237
The Queen of Spades
– 237-238
Swan Lake – 294-295
Symphony no. 6 ,
"Pathetique"
– 32-34, 106
Telemann, Georg Philipp – 7,
320
Tafelmusik – 59-60
The Tender Land – 249-250
Testament of Freedom – 340
Thais – 242
The Thin Blue Line – 160
Thompson, Randall – 9
Frostiana – 340
Ode to the Virginian
Voyage – 340
Testament of Freedom
– 340
Thomson, Virgil – 340
The Three-Cornered Hat
– 302-303
Thoreau, Henry – 343
Thun, Count Johann – 18-19
Till Eulenspiegel – 208
Titanic – 284
Le Tombeau de Couperin
– 75-76, 111
Torke, Michael – 11
Bright Blue Music – 88
Ecstatic Orange – 88
Javelin – 88-89
Tosca
Toscanini, Arturo – 243
Tost, Johann – 134
Tosti, Paulo – 8, 203-204
Toward the Sea – 158-159
On the Town – 275
Horn Trio in E-flat – 145-146
La Traviata – 12, 234
Treffz, Jetty – 236
Dumky Trio, op. 90
– 147-149

More Classical Insights

Trittico Botticelliano
   – 76-77
Les Troyens – 60, 229-230
Turandot – 243
Turangalîla Symphony
   – 47-48
Turina, Joaquin – 5, 9
   Sinfonia Sevillana – 43-44
Tynyanov, Yury – 272

UCLA – 115
Ullmann, Victor – 9
   String Quartet no. 3
   – 156-157
The Union – 178-179
Upshaw, Dawn – 51
Utitz, Dr. Emil – 156

La Valse – 299-300
Varèse, Edgard – 9
   Amériques – 79-80
Vaughan Williams, Ralph
   – 8, 48
   Fantasia on a theme of
   Thomas Tallis
   – 42, 74-75
   The Lark Ascending – 42
   Scott of the Antarctic
   – 268-270
   Serenade to Music
   – 333-335
   Sinfonia Antartica – 270
   Symphony no. 2, "London"
   – 42-43
Veni veni Emanuel
   – 127-128
Verdi, Giuseppe – 7, 12, 99,
   227, 231, 249, 252
   Aida – 144
   Macbeth – 234-235
   Nabucco – 235
   String Quartet – 143-145
   Rigoletto – 234
   La traviata – 12, 234
   Il trovatore – 231
Victoria of England – 29
Villa Lobos, Heitor – 9
   Preludes and Etudes
   – 186-187
Vingt Regards sur l'enfant
   Jésus – 188-189
Virtual Choir – 347
Vivaldi, Antonio – 6, 12, 85,
   92, 126, 354
   Four Violin Concerto
   – 93-94

Wagner, Richard – 7, 30, 50,
   108, 205, 246, 252,
   268
   Good Friday Spell
   – 234
   Parsifal – 232-233
   The Ring Cycle – 232
   Transformation Music
   – 234-5
   Die Walküre – 84
Walden Pond – 343-344
Wanderer Fantasy – 172-173
War and Peace – 309
War Requiem – 341-342
Webern, Anton – 5, 9
   Im Sommerwind – 80-81
Weill, Kurt – 9
   Street Scene – 248-249
Weinstein, Arnold – 216
When Icicles Hang
Whitacre, Eric – 11, 318
   Cloudburst – 347-348
   Lux aurumque – 347
   Virtual Choir – 347
Whiteman, Paul – 82-83,
   310
Whitman, Walt – 335
Wilde, Oscar – 297
William Tell – 215-216

Williams, John – 10, 115, 260, 273, 278, 284
   Close Encounters – 279
   Escapades – 124-125
   ET– 279
   Indiana Jones – 279
   Jaws – 279
   Jurassic Park – 279
   Lincoln – 279-280
   Saving Private Ryan – 279
   Schindler's List – 279
   Star Wars – 279
   Superman – 279
Williams, Tennessee – 253
Wilson, President Woodrow – 184
Der Winterreise – 193-195
Winter Words – 215-216
Wittgenstein, Paul – 109-110
Wolf-Ferrari, Ermanno – 9
   The Secret of Susanna – 246-247
Wood, Sir Henry – 334
Woolf, Virginia – 282
Wright, Nicholas – 256

Ysaÿe, Eugene – 8
   Solo sonatas – 149-150

Zadok the Priest – 322-323
Zemikis, Robert – 283
Zetlan, Jennifer – 219
Zimmer, Hans – 10
   Pirates of the Caribbean – 285-286
Zinman, David – 52, 53
Zwillich, Ellen Taaffe – 10
   Trombone Concerto – 125-127

More Classical Insights

www.ingramcontent.com/pod-product-compliance
Lightning Source LLC
Chambersburg PA
CBHW071656170426
43195CB00039B/2208